ROYAL TRAINS

ROYAL TRAINS

PATRICK KINGSTON
with additional material in chapters 9–11
by Geoffrey Kichenside

DAVID & CHARLES
Newton Abbot   London   North Pomfret (VT)

(half title page)
*LNWR compound 2-2-2-2
locomotive, No 2054* Queen
Empress, *was painted in a special
livery to honour the Queen's
Diamond Jubilee of 1897, in creamy
white and mauve, with elaborate
lining, brass boiler bands and white
tyres. With No 2053 painted scarlet
it was thought that successive engines
painted red from Euston to Crewe,
white from Crewe to Carlisle and
blue on the Caledonian in Scotland, it
would be more patriotic. It would
have been interesting to have heard
the Queen's comments on such an
unusual colour scheme for a railway
engine but it is probable that she
never even had sight of* Queen
Empress *as painted in this colour for
no record appears to have survived of
the engine working the royal train.*
(Courtesy National Railway Museum)

(opposite title page)
*The smoking compartment in King
Edward VII's LNWR 1902 saloon.*
(Courtesy National Railway Museum)

*To my Mother and three feline friends, Frisky, Timmy
and Rocket who, in dark moments of despair during
preparation of the manuscript, were a source of
encouragement to continue the task in hand.*

British Library Cataloguing in Publication Data

Kingston, Patrick
  Royal trains.
  1. Royal trains – Great Britain – History
  I. Title   II. Kichenside, Geoffrey
  385'.22   HE3018

  ISBN 0-7153-8594-1

Typeset by Typesetters (Birmingham) Ltd,
Smethwick, West Midlands
and printed in Great Britain
by Butler and Tanner Limited,
Frome and London
for David & Charles (Publishers) Limited
Brunel House   Newton Abbot   Devon

Published in the United States of America
by David & Charles Inc
North Pomfret   Vermont 05053   USA

CONTENTS

INTRODUCTION

Although some rail routes in Britain have long passed their 150th anniversaries it is only just over 140 years since Queen Victoria made her first journey by rail, five years after the first part of the London & Birmingham Railway had opened, and four after what might be termed her own local railway, the Great Western, the nearest to Windsor Castle, had started services between Paddington and Maidenhead with an intermediate stop – if not a station – at Slough, in 1838. Her then suitor, Prince Albert, had used the Great Western in 1839 and doubtless described to the young Queen the advantages of rail travel. Even then she was not the first reigning monarch to travel in an English train for the King of Prussia used the GWR some months before the Queen ventured forth by train in 1842.

From then on what might be termed the ritual of royal trains evolved, with stringent measures taken for the security of the royal journey, the formal farewells as the royal party boarded the train, the equally formal greetings at the end of the journey as the sovereign set foot on the red carpet, not to mention the organisation needed to ensure that royal eyes did not see anything dubious, like toilets, discreetly hidden behind hoardings or drapes. In the last century many of the safety measures now taken for granted did not exist, for trains in the early days of Victorian travel did not have power brakes through the train, there was often no communication between stations and signalboxes so that trains ran on the time interval system, and there was no interlocking between points and signals. Thus extreme measures were taken to ensure that nothing should befall the royal special. Queen Victoria once remarked that she hoped that the same careful attention should be given to trains carrying her subjects. Nobody felt it was their duty to explain to Her Majesty that if it was then the railways would almost shut down.

But if improvements in safety standards came gradually for all then improvements in the facilities on royal trains frequently came years ahead of their introduction in normal public service. Indeed, it seems that the royal saloons were often the prototype for many new developments, as for example the provision of toilets, flexible gangway connections between coaches, heating, lighting, refreshment facilities, sleeping accommodation, bathrooms, and, more recently, air conditioning.

This book looks at the many royal journeys, the trains and the individual coaches that have been formed in them, from the purpose-built principal saloons not only for the Sovereign, but also the Prince of Wales in the 1890s, to what might be described as the semi-royal coaches used in royal trains for the suite, attendants and railway officers who travelled with the train, but which sometimes had other special uses in between. The detail of the coaches varies from early GW broad gauge saloons and the highly

ornate heavily quilted London & North Western saloons of the 1860s to the plainly functional Mark III coaches of the present royal train. Furnishings follow tastes of the period covered by six reigns, the decorated oil lamps so beloved by Queen Victoria, to the writing desk, stationery and the telephone of the LNWR King's saloon as it ran in the 1930s and the modern style of today.

Some of the many royal journeys by the Sovereign, and other members of the Royal Family are surveyed in detail, particularly some of the complex visits and extended tours, and the arrangements that made them possible, not forgetting some memorable royal tours abroad involving rail travel. There is much of what today is called memorabilia – the notices, the special instructions, the train details, the seating plan of Queen Victoria's funeral train to mention just a selection – although it is a sad reflection of the times that for security reasons similar details of train operation for recent years cannot be included. There are anecdotes, some amusing, some serious, of the behind the scenes negotiations between the 'Palace' and the railway administrations on the organisation of royal journeys, some even acrimonious when the railway and the Palace staff could not agree.

Photographs of Queen Victoria entering or leaving trains are virtually non-existent due as much to the technical limitations of taking photographs then prevailing, and restricted lighting conditions of railway station platforms. Equally important was the Queen's wish for privacy until she had regained her composure after a journey. In this rare picture, Queen Victoria can just be discerned (before the age of telephoto lenses!) sitting in a horse drawn carriage leaving Sheffield Midland Railway station to open the new town hall on Friday afternoon, 21 May 1897. Part of the LNWR Queen's saloon can be seen in the right-hand background and in which the Queen later resumed her journey from Windsor to Ballater. (Courtesy Sheffield City Libraries)

7

Interior of the former Midland Railway royal saloon in LMS days as No 809 being prepared at Willesden carriage sidings to convey the Duke and Duchess of Gloucester from St Pancras to Kettering on 6 November 1935 for their honeymoon journey after their marriage.
(The Photo Source/Fox)

Illustrations have come from many sources; a few from earlier years may perhaps not have the crisp technical quality of modern photographs, but they have been included for their rarity value. Others may have been seen before at the time and are included here for completeness, but the great majority will be seen here for the first time by a general audience.

Naturally a royal visit will attract the media, hundreds of photographs will be taken and it will make the front pages or a principal item on television news. It is though a little difficult to understand the lack of enthusiasm by the media for anything rail, for the contrast when the present Queen travelled by Concorde which made banner headlines, and her first trip in one of the new Inter-City 125 High Speed Trains, which brought nothing more than 'the Queen arrived by train' was quite marked. This does though illustrate the fact that royal journeys are not always made in the royal train or even in a special coach added to an ordinary train. They might not even be on wheels, for one of the latest royal journeys in guided transport was on the Birmingham Airport Maglev system, the transport of the future, and a contrast indeed to the days of 100 and more years ago with royal train pilot engines, the disc and crossbar signal on the roof of the royal saloon to transmit instructions on the speed of the train, the plush, the candles and much else and what came in between.

Patrick Kingston
Royal Leamington Spa, Warwicks

8

1

THE ROYAL TRAIN RITUAL

The image of Queen Victoria is one of an awesome lady who resisted change, rarely known to smile in public and strongly disliked travelling at speed. But it was during the early years of the Queen's reign that some of the greatest changes took place, changes in which the coming of the railways was to prove to be a great liberator of people, in turn resulting in revolutionary changes to the economic and social life of an island people who were mostly rural in character. The railways were also to draw the monarchy and the people closer together in a way hitherto unknown. It is now almost impossible to attempt to comprehend the very real fears that ordinary people had about the building of railways to link towns, the penetration of small, previously isolated communities and the mixing, in large numbers, of people who spoke with different accents. Long journeys that took one, two or more days with horse power would now take only hours with steam power. And what of these *new fangled* steam machines that now, over a hundred years later, in a new age of terrifying electronic wizardry, where the very mention of computers spells fear and scepticism to the uninitiated, we affectionately cherish examples of steam engines that, all those years ago, were branded as fire eating monsters tearing through green and pleasant fields! Perhaps sufficient now to set the scene, as much has already been written, of the early days of railways. One can only speculate on what otherwise might have been had Queen Victoria not approved of railway travel.

In pre-railway days moving the Sovereign around the country with suite and Royal Household was a major, and thus rare, operation, for it entailed the provision of a large number of carriages, and horses, some for pulling the carriages and others for individual riders. Accompanying the Sovereign would be a mounted troop of guards, partly for ceremonial duties but also to provide security, for even in early nineteenth century Britain the Monarchy was not always held in high esteem – the Regency period had seen to that – and there was always the chance of an anarchist attempting to change the course of history. Indeed however settled the country has seemed to be the potential danger has always existed to a lesser or greater degree.

With the development of the railways, security on royal travels took on a different meaning, for the early railways, while having the technology to transport man – and the Sovereign – at higher speeds than ever before, did not have the matching technology to stop with any sense of urgency from those higher speeds, nor any means for knowing the precise location of trains out on the line. Until the 1860s and 1870s there was no real certainty either that the train would actually travel along the line shown by the signals at junctions since it was perfectly possible for the signals to show

The approach to Stratford-Upon-Avon Station, decorated by the Western Region Publicity Unit for the visit by King George VI, Queen Elizabeth and Princess Margaret, on 20 April, 1950. (British Rail/OPC Collection)

9

CAMBRIAN RAILWAYS.

For the use of the Company's Servants only.

SPECIAL NOTICE

OF

ROYAL TRAINS

TO CONVEY

THEIR ROYAL HIGHNESSES

The Prince & Princess of Wales

THURSDAY, JUNE 25th, to SATURDAY, JUNE 27th, 1896.

7

On arrival at Welshpool, the G.W. Engine must be promptly detached and run into the Neck.

The Cambrian Engine will stand on the Down Main Line near the Water Column, and follow the G.W. Engine into the Neck, and then set back to its Train. The G.W. Engine to remain in the Neck until the Royal Train has left.

Mr. Pryce will see to this being done expeditiously.

Enginemen must be careful not to blow off steam during the time the Royal Train stands at Welshpool.

No. 48 (12 15 p.m. ex Machynlleth) must be shunted clear into the Goods Yard 15 minutes before the Royal Train is due.

The 11 45 a.m. (No. 47) Goods ex Oswestry must run punctually to Moat Lane, and leave the latter station at 3 0 p.m., arriving at Machynlleth at 4 40 p.m.

No. 66.—If this train is 15 minutes late out of Moat Lane, it must shunt at Montgomery for the Royal Train to pass.

No. 47.—Run in altered times, arriving Machynlleth 4 45 pm. See separate Notice.

No. 72.—Not to leave Machynlleth until the Royal Train has arrived. See separate Notice.

The Royal Train must, as soon as possible after arrival, be marshalled ready for Friday as follows:—Engine, Van, Royal Saloon, First Class Saloon, Compo, Van. Mr. Harris to see that this is done before the train is put away in the North Neck where it will stand during the night.

Mr. Harris to arrange for a Porter to act as Watchman of the Royal Train during the time it stands at Machynlleth.

The station must be cleared of the public after the arrival of the 4 40 p.m. ex Aberystwyth.

The 6 30 p.m. Down (No. 71) to leave Machynlleth at 6 15 p.m., and only persons holding Train Tickets or Special Tickets of Admission to be admitted to the platform.

The Fourgon with the Royal luggage will leave London (Paddington) by 9 50 a.m. train on Thursday, 25th inst. Mr. Pryce, Welshpool, to see that it is duly sent forward from Welshpool. Mr. Harris, Machynlleth, to see that all arrangements are made for having the luggage unloaded **immediately** on arrival, having the required teams in readiness to make delivery **without delay.**

Cambrian Railways Notice, June 1896, extracts (Courtesy Ifor Higgon)

one instruction and the points which guided the trains to be in a conflicting position. That at least was the situation for ordinary trains. For the Sovereign such methods simply would not do. Thus was evolved a complex set of rules to be observed for trains carrying the Sovereign, and for other members of the Royal Family. The rules were expanded in the light of experience and some still apply today in so far as they are relevant, some of the precautions have been eased or abolished while others introduced.

One of the earliest parts of the developing ritual was that the royal train should have personal supervision at the highest level, being attended by the senior officials and directors of the company, while along the line stationmasters had to oversee personally that the train was properly signalled on the correct line and watch the train pass. To ensure that switches at points were correctly set they had to be clipped and locked for the right line; a pilot engine ran ahead of the royal train and points were not to be moved between the passage of the pilot engine until after the royal train had passed. This was based on the theory that if the pilot engine got through safely, then if nothing was altered the royal train would also pass safely. Only right at the end of the journey at a terminal station would the pilot engine be diverted off the main line to allow the royal train a clear run into an empty platform.

Once the block system had been established whereby the line was divided into sections for signalling purposes, with signalboxes equipped with electric telegraph instruments at the boundaries between sections – known as block sections – special arrangements were made for royal trains. Ordinary trains merely needed the section ahead to be clear to be allowed to proceed but for the royal train two sections ahead were kept clear, and two behind it as well so that a following train could not get too close. At stations and junctions, where signalboxes were sometimes close together, additional sections were cleared, and trains on branch lines were held back so that they could not approach junctions while the royal train was crossing on a conflicting track.

But it was not just the signalling and operation which called for special security arrangements if Queen Victoria's royal specials were not to come to grief. Stations through which the royal train passed or stopped were kept private which meant closing off platforms for a time until the Queen's train had cleared the area. Partly this was for privacy, partly for security and partly because of safety since it would have been dangerous to have large numbers of people on a station platform waving at their Sovereign as there might have been a surge forward as the train approached. Thus stations needed special policing, even where arrangements had been made in advance for the Queen to receive a declaration of loyalty from local civic representatives en route. Police and railway staff were also positioned at bridges and at intervals along the line.

However, in spite of her almost total pre-occupation with safety and her rigid dislike of speed – no train in which she travelled was permitted to exceed 40mph, reduced to 30mph after dark – Queen Victoria was always concerned for the welfare of the men on the engine footplate. From time to time, the Queen would ask if the driver and his fireman wished to rest or more likely could a relief crew be summoned to ensure that they did rest.

To an extent Queen Victoria herself instigated much of the ritual surrounding the running of her special trains because of her own personal likes and dislikes, and as she grew older the conservatism in keeping the things she liked rather than try anything new. In that she was no different from most of her older subjects. The refusal to pass through the flexible gangway between the twin LNWR day and night saloon coaches while the train was moving was one, which meant that a stop had to be made when Her Majesty was ready to retire for the night. Another was her insistence on taking meals on terra firma, even though the principle of railway dining cars had first been seen in 1879, 22 years before she died. Certainly her saloons from about the 1860s had been equipped with a small spirit stove and kettle for making hot drinks while on the move but meals were not taken on board. Perth was undoubtedly the principal place where the royal train made a halt for meals, usually breakfast going north to Balmoral after an overnight journey from Windsor or Gosport, or dinner coming south before the night journey. The Caledonian provided a royal suite of rooms in the station hotel which adjoined Perth station, including a retiring room and a dining room. Royal waiting rooms at stations were few and far between largely because the Queen did not use more than a handful of stations regularly, and of course it was not done to keep the Queen waiting. But at the 'royal' stations – Paddington, Windsor, Ballater and later Wolferton rooms were kept aside for royal use so that the Queen and the Royal Family could get ready for the journey or refresh themselves after a journey before the official welcome. Paddington's royal waiting room was particularly opulent with ornate panelling to the walls and exquisite furniture. Sometimes for a one-off visit rooms in an adjoining station hotel, or station offices, or the normal public waiting room would be specially prepared as a royal retiring room for the day.

All royal railway journeys have been surrounded by varying degrees of secrecy, considered necessary in maintaining privacy and, more importantly, security. It is against this background that the planning of such a journey takes place, though some of the operating precautions of earlier years have been relaxed. The running of a pilot engine in advance of a royal train, for example, ceased many years ago, although even in early BR days the train in front would be regarded as the royal train pilot with special supervision. Equally, though, the general security surrounding the planning and operation of royal journeys today, whether by rail, road, sea, or air, is very much tighter than say 50 years ago, and is precisely organised.

The complex arrangements concerned with a royal train journey are contained in a printed booklet occupying several pages. Its contents are not for the eyes of the general public or, indeed, any member of railway staff not involved in the train's operation. The cover of earlier 'notices', as they are known in railway jargon, have been endorsed 'Private – for the use of staff concerned only'. These notices contain information on the route, arrival and departure times together with passing times en-route at various stations and junctions. For security reasons this document may not always indicate by name which members of the Royal Family are travelling. Such information would be contained in a separate document circulated only to those officials who, in carrying out their duties, had need of such information. When the running of a pilot engine, 10 to 15 minutes in advance of a royal train was normal practice, the notice would give

instructions to signalmen along the route, not to allow shunting or movement of other trains on adjacent lines between the passing of the pilot engine and a royal train. In steam days, no other train was ever allowed to pass a royal train on water troughs, for very obvious reasons!

Indeed there was a substantial list or what were really common sense instructions on the precautions to be taken before a royal train passed. Where multiple track existed, goods and parcels trains which could be running on an adjoining line in the same direction as the royal special had to be stopped before they could be overtaken by the royal train, and moreover goods trains had to be examined to make sure that the loads were secure. Passenger trains could be allowed to proceed on a parallel line in the same direction but had to reduce speed so that they would not run neck and neck with the royal train. Horses, at one time used extensively in everyday railway service, pulling drays or for shunting at small yards, had to be kept well under control if they normally worked near the line on which the royal train was to pass. Platform barrows had to be checked to make sure they could not roll by vibration anywhere near the platform edge on the line to be used by the royal train, and staff were forbidden from taking barrows over the line on barrow crossings within 10 minutes of the special train being due.

Over the years various special telegraphic codes have been used as a form of secret identity for royal trains. During the 1939–45 war and for some years afterwards, two code words were 'Grove' and 'Deepdene'. A Grove special would generally be a full royal train conveying the Sovereign and identifiable by four headlamps or white discs on the front of the locomotive, arranged in a triangle, one at the base of the chimney, one each over each buffer and the other, in the centre, below the smokebox door. The Deepdene code could also be applied to a royal train not usually conveying the Sovereign but more generally used for ordinary trains to which had been attached one or more royal saloons. Just such an occasion occurred on 16 March 1951 when Royalty returned to London from attending the races at Cheltenham. An instruction in the notice read '4.48 pm Hereford to Paddington – to run under "Deepdene" instructions from Kingham to Paddington'. This meant that the Royal Party, for which two saloons had been allocated, was travelling, as it were, by ordinary passenger train. Earlier, the two royal saloons had arrived at Kingham attached to the front of the 5.45pm stopping train from Cheltenham (St James) via Bourton-on-the-Water which on that day also ran as a Deepdene special, before being coupled to the leading end of the express for Paddington. For a Deepdene special the normal express passenger train headlamp code was used, with one lamp above each buffer. The regulation tail lamp for a long number of years has been supplemented on royal trains by an extra lamp carried opposite to the one normally carried and this applied equally to both Grove and Deepdene trains. When British Railways introduced its four-digit train identification code, now no longer to be seen on the front of diesel and electric locomotives, the code for principal royal trains was 1X01 with 1X02 and 1X03 being used to denote other royal workings depending on priority. 1X00 indicated an empty royal train.

PREPARING FOR THE RED CARPET

The laying of the red carpet on a station platform is the culmination of much detailed planning for a royal train journey. From Queen Victoria's first train journey in 1842, the responsibility for conveying royalty has become a cherished railway tradition, although much of the colourful pageantry of earlier years has disappeared. Locomotives decorated with flags and other adornments had virtually been abandoned by the end of King George V's reign. Now on only very rare occasions, where a journey is part of a public celebration, such as the honeymoon special for the Prince and Princess of Wales from Waterloo in 1981, is any form of decoration to be found on locomotives. In addition to the decorated steam locomotives used for some of Queen Victoria's and King Edward VII's journeys it was not uncommon for the top layer of coal in the tender to be whitewashed. Some railway companies even insisted that the driver and fireman should wear white gloves which, no doubt, were kept in the engineman's tuck box

The crew of the LNWR royal train pose in front of Queen Victoria's personal saloon, at Ballater before the Queen's last journey south from Scotland to Windsor in November 1900. Those pictured represent the Victorian equivalent of today's Wolverton royal train crew and are, back row (left to right) Clarke, electrician; Lee Smith, lifter; F. Dudley, tinsmith; Smith, telegraph dept; W. Whitlock, trimmer; A Rock, electrician carriage dept. T. Hillyard, brake fitter; T. Jacks, finisher. Front Row (left to right) Clarke, telegraph dept; E. Thompson, gas fitter; D. Lampitt, painter; J. Coker, royal train foreman; T. Townsend, painter, H. Twitchen painter (Courtesy National Railway Museum)

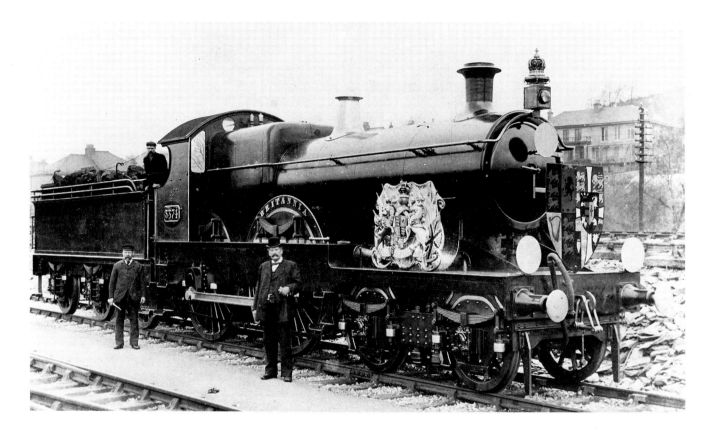

GWR Atbara class 4-4-0 No 3374 Britannia, specially renamed for working royal trains for King Edward VII and Queen Alexandra from Paddington to Kingswear and Plymouth to Paddington in March 1902 – the first non-stop runs ever achieved on these routes. It is pictured at Laira shed, Plymouth before the non-stop Plymouth – Paddington journey of 4 hours 24 minutes on 10 March. (L&GRP/ David & Charles)

during the journey and hastily retrieved, for appearances sake, as the train steamed into the red carpeted platform. It was also usual for drivers on the LBSCR to wear special uniform on such occasions, similar to the one worn by the GWR driver of the 1897 Diamond Jubilee royal train from Windsor to Paddington. The firemen, apparently, were not always so lucky in being given a special uniform and, except for the white gloves, had to shovel coal just the same, even on a royal train!

The meticulous planning and operation of a railway journey for royal passengers begins when the railway authorities receive a request for travel from the Royal Household, specifying the approximate required departure and arrival times together with the total number of persons travelling. A draft timetable is prepared and also a train plan showing the number of vehicles forming the train and the accommodation reserved for each member of the royal party and suite, which is submitted to Buckingham Palace for approval. Following Palace approval, the railway operating staff set about the task of embracing a multitude of detailed plans which, on the oppointed day, ensures that a locomotive, train crew and, of course, the vehicles of the royal train, have been prepared and ready for the journey to begin.

The train plan is a most important ingredient in planning a journey with the royal train, for it will show the total length of the complete formation as well as the length of each vehicle. From these measurements the distance from the front of the locomotive to the door of the saloon from which the royal party will alight can be calculated. This enables the precise point to be marked at which the driver must stop the train to bring the saloon doorway exactly in line with the red carpet. Usually it is done by stationing a man holding a yellow flag (years back it was a red flag), but sometimes a yellow marker post is used instead. The driver's instructions tell him that he must bring the train to a stand with the locomotive cab exactly opposite the man holding the flag or the marker post. Very infrequently the train overshoots the red carpet and the driver, perhaps through no direct fault of his own, gets the reddest face of all, not to mention those of the dignitaries and bowler-hatted railway officials. The embarrassment is usually relieved by a royal smile and a word or two signifying that a few extra steps to walk are of little hardship. As a boy, Prince Charles was always intrigued to know how the engine driver knew how to stop with the carriage door in line with the carpet. Then he was told about the man with the flag whom, afterwards, he was eager to spot.

Staff from the railway public relations department will have arranged for local dignitaries and press to be accommodated to greet and record the royal arrival or departure. At local level, railway officials will need to have established the precise area on the station platform where the red carpet is to be laid and to ensure that the carpet arrives from a headquarters store with adequate time for it to be put down and vacuum cleaned for royal shoes to tread upon it. Gone are the days when stations were transformed and hidden beneath a mass of bunting and flags. More modest decorations are now customary. Floral displays, usually provided by the municipal parks and gardens department line the red carpet between the station entrance and the position on the platform where it has been arranged for the train to stop, with the doorway of the royal saloon opposite the red carpet.

Sometimes, where only a small number of people are travelling, or if the journey is of a private nature, a reserved first class carriage, attached to an ordinary service train, will prove adequate. Such an arrangement eliminates the cost and necessity of a special train. Many believe the Royal Family enjoy free railway travel. Even in the days of private ownership although rolling stock was provided and maintained for royalty's exclusive use as now, the normal first class fare was charged for each member of the Royal Family plus the Household staff accompanying them, an arrangement which continues today. Additionally, the appropriate rate per mile is charged for the running of a special train, hence the desire to dispense with such a facility when not absolutely necessary. Royal finances are something

A Southern Region royal special conveying the King and Queen of Belgium on their State Visit from Gatwick Airport to Victoria on 14 May 1963. The royal party is travelling in the third carriage from the locomotive, one of Edwardian era built East Coast royal saloons; the remaining vehicles are Pullman Cars while the locomotive, bearing the special headboard with the flags of Belgium and England, is rebuilt Battle of Britain class 4-6-2 No 34088 213 Squadron. (John Scrace)

LONDON AND NORTH WESTERN RAILWAY.

ARRANGEMENT OF CARRIAGES

COMPOSING

HER MAJESTY'S TRAIN

FROM BALLATER TO WINDSOR,

ON WEDNESDAY, THE 16TH, AND THURSDAY, THE 17TH JUNE, 1897.

Engine.	Break.	For Men Servants.	For Pages and Upper Servants.	Dressers and Ladies' Maids.	Lady Ampthill. Hon. Mrs. Mallet. Hon. Ethel Cadogan. Miss Loch.	Princess Victoria of Battenberg. Mdlle. du Perrut.	Queen's Dressers. Her Majesty. Personal Servants.	Princess Christian.	Princess Leopold and Maurice of Battenberg and Attendants.	Lieut.-Col. Sir Fleetwood Edwards. Lieut. F. Ponsonby. Sir James Reid. Mr. Muther. Hon. A. Yorke.	Munshi Abdul Karim. Indian Attendants.	Directors.	Directors.	Queen's Fourgon.	Break.
	Van. No. 210.	Sleeping Carriage No. 870.	Day Saloon. No. 72.	Day Saloon. No. 73.	Double Saloon. No. 153.	Double Saloon. No. 62.	Royal Saloon.	Double Saloon. No. 132.	Double Saloon. No. 65.	Double Saloon. No. 131.	Double Saloon. No. 71.	Double Saloon. No. 180.	Lavatory Compo. No. 999.	Carriage Truck. No. 137.	Van. No. 272.

<----- 264 feet 8 inches -----> <----- 318 feet 4 inches ----->

LNWR royal train plan for Queen Victoria's return from Balmoral, before her Diamond Jubilee Celebrations in London, 1897. (Author's Collection)

of a taboo subject. However, it is known that in the Civil List – the money voted by Parliament each year to the Queen and certain members of her family to carry out official duties – expenditure for rail travel is part of the budget, with the exception of private journeys, such as those to Balmoral for holidays, which would be paid for from the Queen's personal income.

Catering arrangements are today the responsibility of British Rail through its subsidiary organisation, Travellers-Fare which is responsible for refreshments at most of the railway stations where such facilities still exist, and on Inter-City trains. Only experienced and generally senior Travellers-Fare staff are chosen for the prestigious honour to serve on the royal train. While the food is provided by British Rail, it is prepared in accordance with a menu suggested and approved by Buckingham Palace. Packets of sandwiches, offered for sustenance to ordinary railway travellers, are denied to royalty. If the length of journey is short, requiring little more than a light snack, delicately cut watercress sandwiches are often served along with the Queen's own special brand of tea.

Although present day royal train journeys might lack much of the colourful spectacle, particularly of King Edward VII's reign, some of the magical atmosphere remains. Stations, or at least those parts likely to be glimpsed by royal eyes, get a special clean-up and a lick of paint, adding sparkle to the occasion. The locomotive selected for the royal train will have received a very thorough mechanical check. It is quite likely that the exterior will also be repainted with buffer heads burnished. No locomotive is specially reserved for royal duty except on the Southern Region which, in recent years, has nominated one of its electro-diesels No 73142

16

King George V and Queen Mary arrive at Immingham for the formal opening of the Great Central Railway's Dock on 22 July, 1912. Sam Fay, General Manager who was later to be knighted in a ceremony in the Dock's No 2 transit shed, is the second figure from the left holding his top hat. The GNR-built King's saloon, No 395, is in the background. (George Dow Collection and Negative)

HM Queen Elizabeth II about to alight at Newton Abbot from ex-LMS saloon No 799 where she had arrived to visit the Royal Show on 2 July 1952. The royal train had left Paddington the previous evening hauled by King class locomotive No 6018 King Henry VI, and spent the night on a branch line 'somewhere near Exeter'. The Moretonhampstead branch was sometimes used to park the royal train overnight. (British Rail/OPC Collection)

President Ceausescu of Romania is greeted by the Queen on platform 2 at Victoria Station when he arrived on a State Visit, after travelling in the royal train from Gatwick, on 13 June, 1978. (Author)

Broadlands. In today's harsh economic climate few railway accountants would smile on keeping expensive locomotives on limited duties, particularly as it is now rare for such journeys to be made at short notice. It is usual for at least several days' notice to be given, allowing sufficient time for a locomotive to be chosen and suitably prepared. Whatever locomotive is used a mere glance will tell from its immaculate appearance that it has been prepared for a *very* special train!

Stand-by locomotives are still provided to cover the rare event of failure, but are rarely cleaned to the same standard as the one for which they might be called upon to replace. Although rare, there have been at least two occasions in the last two decades when a royal train locomotive has broken down. In January, 1961, the Queen was returning to Sandringham from London in one of the 12-wheel East Coast saloons attached to the 4.36pm Liverpool Street–King's Lynn Fenman express when the Brush Type 3 diesel, No D5667, hauling the train, came to a halt south of Audley End resulting from the failure of the main lubricating oil pump. A steam locomotive was sent from Cambridge to take the train on to King's Lynn, where the Queen was driven on to Sandringham. The breakdown caused the Queen and other passengers to be delayed for nearly an hour. A few days later during a conversation with the Headmaster and a senior pupil of King Edward VII School, King's Lynn, the Queen referred, lightheartedly, to the diesel breakdown, and said she was 'completely unworried' by the incident. She also expressed how sorry she was for the makers of the locomotive and for British Railways which was encountering troubles with its modernisation programme and appreciated the inconvenience caused to the other passengers on the train. However, one respected national newspaper gave the unfortunate incident headline coverage 'Queen in diesel train failure' and a bold sub-headline '56-minute wait for steam engine'.

Twenty years elapsed before the next royal locomotive failure occurred on the most appropriate of all days, Friday, 13 November 1981. Fortunately for British Rail, the circumstances of the incident were such that the press never learnt of the failure. This time the Queen was not delayed and might even have been unaware that the chosen locomotive for the royal train, class 47 diesel No 47449, could not be coaxed to start from an overnight stop. Hastily another locomotive of the same class, No 47434, was summoned to the rescue and when the double-headed cavalcade arrived at the red carpeted platform at Wellington, Shropshire, the only hint that unlucky Friday the thirteenth had made its contribution, was a murmur or two from one of the reception party's dignitaries, 'oh, BR forgot to clean the leading diesel engine'. The excitement of meeting Her Majesty extinguished further thought on the matter! There was also an occasion in the early 1960s when a diesel locomotive on a train ahead of the royal train on the main line out of Euston seemingly ran out of fuel – in fact it was inadvertently drawing fuel from the reserve tank, with the main tank full but it was not realised at the time. There were many red faces since the royal train alas was caught in the delay while following trains were switched to adjoining tracks to by-pass not only the failed train but also the royal train as well, which was well and truly trapped until the train ahead could be moved. It was just one of those unfortunate things, but it is rare indeed for anything to go wrong 'on the night'. The ritual has seen to that.

2

QUEEN VICTORIA
Reigned 1837–1901

Despite the undoubted benefits of the newly emerging railways, more than 15 years elapsed from the opening of the Stockton & Darlington Railway in 1825 until the first royal railway journey. Clearly though, with the isolated pioneering railways so far apart there was no compelling reason to use them and certainly King George IV would have cared little about a new railway in North East England. There had been horse drawn waggonways for many years and the new steam locomotive engines had yet to be proved. Perhaps there might have been a case for requesting a royal opening of the Liverpool & Manchester Railway in 1830 but doubtless the Duke of Wellington accompanied by Sir Robert Peel and pro-railway Member of Parliament William Huskisson, was a vastly more popular figure than King William IV, who in any case had only been on the Throne for just over two months. Huskisson's tragic fatal accident on opening day would not have helped the railway cause, but perhaps memories were short. Seven years elapsed before the next major railway opening, the first stage of the trunk route from Euston. By then the young 18 year old Princess Victoria had just succeeded to the Throne as Queen only a matter of weeks before, and the Victorian era had begun. Despite the development of railways in and around London it was to be five years after her accession before Queen Victoria made her first railway journey. Certainly it was not for her honeymoon as portrayed in the Herbert Wilcox film *Victoria the Great*, starring Anna Neagle and Anton Walbrook, made in 1937, in which Queen Victoria and her Consort Prince Albert are seen travelling to Windsor after their marriage in 1840 behind Liverpool & Manchester Railway locomotive *Lion*! In real life they travelled by road.

In June 1840 the GWR opened its station at Slough and hoped for royal patronage. It was not long in coming for Prince Albert soon found the railway acceptable for his frequent comings and goings between London and Windsor Castle. Little is known of these early flirtations with the new railway except that the Prince was favourably impressed. With enthusiastic encouragement from her open-minded Prince Consort, Queen Victoria was persuaded to try out a railway journey. After suitable arrangements had been made, Queen Victoria and Prince Albert drove by carriage from Windsor Castle to Slough station on the morning of Monday 13 June 1842. We can visualise something of the scene at Slough and, from contemporary reports, speculate on what this first British royal train looked like. The royal saloon is reported to have been brown in colour, as were the ordinary carriages, with large windows at each end for viewing the line. There were three compartments, the centre one being used by the Royal occupants. For the accompanying members of the Queen's Household, who are known to have dreaded the prospect of the railway journey, other ordinary carriages were prepared and marshalled in the royal special. The Great Western's Engineer, Isambard K. Brunel, and his Superintendent of Locomotives, Daniel Gooch, were on the footplate of the 2-2-2 tender engine *Phlegethon*, barely a month old and not quite fully run-in. In advance of their arrival, at Slough, the Queen's Master of the Horse had already imspected the station building, engine and train, expressing some misgivings on the prospect of the journey ahead to London. Reassured by Brunel, Gooch and other leading railway dignitaries that all would be well, the apprehensive gentleman is supposed to have communicated his satisfaction to the Queen and Prince, who also were keen to look over the train before stepping aboard.

At 12 noon the journey began, with the Queen's coachman riding on the engine, since nobody could convince him that the train would proceed quite safely without his presence on the engine's footplate. So he remained and during the journey insisted, under instruction, on handling the controls at frequent intervals. His scarlet coat became so dirty that he never again repeated the experience! After a 25 minute journey the royal special arrived at Paddington, not the magnificent station opened in 1854 that we know today, but a station of cramped proportions located at nearby Bishops Road. After her train ride, Queen Victoria made it known that she was 'quite charmed' by her new experience and Prince Albert's restrained comment was 'not so fast next time, Mr Conductor'. Quite probably the Prince was thinking of a horse drawn omnibus by using the term 'conductor'! Two weeks later, Victoria returned to Windsor, by train, taking her infant son Albert Edward (later Prince of Wales and King Edward VII). The story of royal railway travel had begun.

Although Queen Victoria liked train travel and the privacy it gave to her, compared with riding in carriages on dusty roads where, should one of the horses falter, a gathering crowd might discover the royal passenger, causing

The Prince and Princess of Wales (afterwards King Edward VII and Queen Alexandra) visited Wales on a three day tour in June 1896 and this picture shows the GWR royal train in which they were travelling, at Welshpool during a halt there in the late afternoon of 25 June en-route from Paddington to Machynlleth. Note the gathering of Cambrian Railways officials intent on the supervision of their railway's locomotive – lavishly decorated Aston 4-4-0 No 68 of 1893 – being coupled to the GWR's train. See the special train notice on pages 10 and 11. (Courtesy Ifor Higgon)

embarrassment at such close quarters, it soon became apparent that continued royal patronage could only be sustained if the Queen's wishes for her journeys were undertaken precisely as she had instructed. In the latter years of her reign, the conclusion of many of her journeys brought a sigh of relief to all concerned with the responsibility for planning and seeing them accomplished. As the network of railways spread, together with public acceptance and confidence, the Queen's own confidence did not. Although throughout her long reign of just over 63 years, she never declined to put off a journey where it was necessary to use the railway, there were occasions when she expressed strong concern on the safety of railways.

The year 1861 was a sad one for Queen Victoria in suffering two major family bereavements. In March, her mother died, followed in December by the loss of her beloved husband, Albert, who died of typhoid fever. But in the first weeks of that year, on 28 January, the Queen's physician, Dr Baly, was killed in a railway accident on the London & South Western Railway at Raynes Park, then known as Epsom Junction. The royal doctor was travelling in a first class carriage of a late afternoon Waterloo to Portsmouth express when the engine of the train was derailed as it passed over the junction points, derailing the rest of the train. Several carriages overturned including the one in which Dr Baly was sitting. In the rapid confusion Dr Baly fell through a broken door and immediately the carriage rolled over on top of him resulting in instant death. Following this tragedy the Queen was terrified that a railway accident should occur to a train in which she was travelling. Deeply concerned and shocked over the loss of a trusted confidant, the Queen expressed a wish that all trains henceforth should be run with the same meticulous safety precautions that applied whenever she made a rail journey. The wish was duly noted, but the Queen was never actually told that if such meticulous attention to safety was applied to the running of all trains, then few trains would run at all! Never for a moment did Queen Victoria ever fully understand that all her instructions, communicated to senior railway staff by members of her Household, always involved special working arrangements.

But the sad happenings of 1861 are nearly 20 years hence from Victoria's first train ride in 1842. The royal town of Windsor was to remain without a railway for several more years. Although Queen Victoria and Prince Albert spent much of their time at Windsor Castle, plans by railway promoters to put Windsor on the railway map were strongly opposed by the Queen herself, supported by Eton College. While undesirable visitors could not entirely be kept out of the royal town, it was believed that the existence of a railway would encourage such persons to visit this area of relative tranquility and spread evil influences among the pupils of Eton College. So for several more years to come the nearest railway stations to Windsor were over 2½ miles away at Slough, on the GWR, or 18 miles at Farnborough, on the LSWR.

An early royal journey of great international significance, highlighting the inconvenience of Windsor's lack of railways occurred in October 1844 when Louis Phillipe, the French King, arrived from France to visit Queen Victoria. He landed at Portsmouth (still unconnected by rail) and was met by Prince Albert and the Duke of Wellington. The Royal Party then

21

During the course of Queen Victoria's journey north from Windsor to Balmoral, on 22 May, 1880, the Queen presented the Albert Medal to Coastguard George Oatley, whose bravery in swimming to a stricken ship off the coast resulted in the safe return of the crew ashore, during a short ceremony at a temporary platform at Ferryhill Junction, Aberdeen. Watching the Queen pin the medal to Oatley's breast is Princess Beatrice and at the extreme right is the kilted figure of the Queen's loyal servant, John Brown. In this unknown artist's drawing, little authenticity is attached to creating the railway scene in that the locomotive would have been placed further from the Queen's saloon! (Authors Collection)

travelled from Gosport by the London & South Western line to Farnborough where they continued their journey to Windsor by road.

The railway promoters persisted in their campaign to serve Windsor and the prestige of attracting royal patronage. The determination of the rival companies, the GWR and the LSWR, eventually bore fruit with the GWR winning the race over the rival LSWR by less than two months. On 8 October, 1849, the GWR opened its branch from Slough to Windsor followed, on 1 December by the LSWR, with the extension of its line from Datchet. Originally with such strength of opposition in keeping railways out of Windsor, it is perhaps ironic that ultimately the two railway stations came to be built less than half a mile from the Castle boundary, with the GWR close to the west front of St George's Chapel and the LSWR in Home Park to the north of the Castle. Both railways can claim the title 'The Royal Road', the GWR for the first royal railway journey, and equally the LSWR since Queen Victoria set off on her visits to the Isle of Wight and the Continent from its station, now called Windsor & Eton Riverside. The South Western station was also used by visiting foreign royalty arriving in special trains. However, the honour was reversed in 1897 when the Great Western Railway truly celebrated Queen Victoria's Diamond Jubilee. To commemorate the 60th year of her reign, the Great Western's Board of Directors sanctioned, as the Company's gift to Her Majesty, the building of a new royal station alongside that used by the public, now known as Windsor & Eton Central. Not content with just giving the Queen a new station, the Great Western provided a splendid new royal train of six bogie coaches with gangway connection throughout, but more of this new train in chapter 8.

22

Between 1844 and 1862 the Royal Family acquired three country homes as retreats from the public gaze. The acquisition of these properties in the Isle of Wight, Scotland and East Anglia, in addition to the established official London residence of Buckingham Palace and the out of town fortified Windsor Castle, provided the opportunity whereby several railways were to be entrusted with the honour of conveying the Queen and her family over long distances when they wished to move from one house to another. It might also be said that the emergence of the railway age had encouraged the acquisition of the additional residences because of the ease by which the Household could be moved. For the most part, such journeys were of a private nature but additionally, there were occasions when official visits were made to various parts of the country. Unless these were to places on the line of route when moving from one royal home to another, there was usually the need for a separate railway journey to be made. The potential for royal railway travel, at a time when railways were a developing industry, was significant, and the railway companies in areas where royal residences had been established were eager to attract royal patronage. Where this was likely, money was spent on the construction or adaption of carriages for royal use. Sometimes, they looked more comfortable than they really were. Special waiting rooms, lavishly appointed, were also built.

Immediately after Louis Phillipe's visit from France in October 1844, Queen Victoria and Prince Albert went to recuperate at Osborne House in the Isle of Wight and later adopted it as one of their homes. Just across the Solent was Gosport, where Louis Phillipe had boarded the train on his journey to Windsor. Thus there was railway link over the greater part of the distance between the two royal residences. Osborne House, situated within sight of the sea, was close to Cowes where the Royal Family would arrive after crossing the Solent from Gosport. At Gosport a private station was later provided exclusively for Queen Victoria's use in what was called

After visiting Birmingham on 23 March, 1887, to lay the foundation stone of the Law Courts building, Queen Victoria returned to Windsor in the GWR royal train (Queen's coach third from the front) hauled by 2-2-2 locomotive No 55 Queen. This rare photograph of a moving train of that period, was taken at Olton station, on the outskirts of Birmingham; on this part of the GWR system the 7ft broad gauge had been abandoned for some years, as shown by the wide space between the tracks. (Courtesy Charles Lines)

the Royal Clarence Victualling Yard. The station consisted of just one curved single line and platform with an overall roof. At the seaward end of the station was a waiting room connected with a pontoon used for transference between the royal yachts (there were then two) and the royal train. It was the Queen, herself, who decreed whether this station should be used by anyone else of importance but such incursions were infrequent. Completion of the journey on the Isle of Wight would be from East Cowes through lush green countryside to Osborne House. Railways did not come to the Isle of Wight until 1862 when a line of 4½ miles was opened from Cowes to Newport on the west side of the Medina river. In 1875 another line, from Newport to Ryde, was opened with a station at Whippingham to serve Osborne House. By now Queen Victoria, who had expressed a wish for a private station at Whippingham, was accustomed to her relaxing country drive from East Cowes and her request for a station, close to Osborne, was that the facility would be available should she wish to travel to other parts of the island. Also, the Queen was probably advised that her use of the financially ailing Ryde & Newport Railway (part of the Isle of Wight Central Railway from July 1887), would cause further embarrassment in finding a suitable train. The use of Whippingham station, in relation to Osborne House, was mostly confined to those summoned by Royal command to visit, and the comings and goings by members of the Queen's Household. In later years it was opened for use by the public.

However, in 1888, Queen Victoria noted in her Journal for Saturday 11 February that she had made her first journey on an Isle of Wight train. The occasion was an afternoon visit by the Queen to the Royal National Hospital for Consumption at Ventnor. Accompanied by her daughters, the Princesses Beatrice and Victoria and an entourage of senior members of the Queen's Household, Her Majesty travelled in a special train from Whippingham station to Ventnor and back again. The journey involved travelling over both the Isle of Wight Central and Isle of Wight companies' lines, with reversal of the Island's first royal special taking place on the outward and return journeys at Ryde St John's Road. Your author has been unable to ascertain specific details of the carriages and locomotives used, but it seems likely that the more prosperous Isle of Wight Railway would have assisted the less prosperous Isle of Wight Central Railway in the provision of some kind of saloon for the Royal party and several other carriages to accommodate the entourage. Evidence of this appeared in the following day's Court Circular, recording the visit in detail: 'Mr. Horace Tabourdin, chairman of the Isle of Wight Railway, Messrs. F. W. Slade and J. M. Stobert, directors, and Mr. Hicks, the secretary, accompanied the Royal train.' For the section of journey, between Whippingham and Ryde St John's Road, over the Isle of Wight Central, an IWCR locomotive was used while, after reversal at Ryde and for the longest section of the journey between there and Ventnor, one of the Isle of Wight Railway's Beyer Peacock 2-4-0 tank locomotives, painted dark red with shining brasswork, would have been a natural choice. Whether or not Queen Victoria was impressed or even enjoyed her first Isle of Wight railway journey, remains a matter of conjecture. However the Court Circular continued: 'The Royal train over the Isle of Wight Central Railway was in charge of Mr. H. Simmons, and from Ryde to Ventnor on the Isle of Wight Railway in charge

(facing page)
Even after the invention of photography, published pictures showing royalty relaxing in saloons, used as 'palaces on wheels' are unknown. However, the unknown artist of this drawing, from about 1875, portrays Queen Victoria and Princess Beatrice travelling in the saloon carriage of the London & North Western Railway returning from Balmoral to Windsor. (Author's Collection)

A detail of Queen Victoria's LNWR 1869 saloon now in the National Railway Museum, York. (Crown copyright, courtesy National Railway Museum)

(overleaf)
The ornately produced train plan printed in mauve, purple, silver, gold, blue, green, brown and red, showing the names of those travelling on Queen Victoria's funeral train, including the train crew and railway officers. (Courtesy G. M. Kichenside)

GREAT · WES

FUNE

HER · LATE · MOST · GRAC

ARRANGEMENT

Paddington to Windsor

ENGINE.	BRAKE VAN.	SEMI-SALOON.	COMPART-MENTS.	SALOON.	SALOON.	RO
				Lt Col. Sir A. Bigge.	Col. H. H. Mathias.	
				Lt Col. Rt Hon. Sir F.I. Edwards.	Col. W. Aitken.	
				Col. J. Brocklehurst.	Col. E. T. Hutton.	
				Lt Col. The Hon. W.P. Carington.	Capt Sir E. Chichester.	
				Lt Col. A. Davidson.	Capt E. S. Poë.	
				Lt Col. Hon. H. C. Legge.	Capt Count F.C. Metaxa.	
				Capt F. Ponsonby.	Capt W. H. May.	
				Sir J. Reid.	Col. B. G. D. Cooke.	
ROYAL	Guard. T. King.		Mr A. Hubbard.	Lord Suffield.	Col. Lord Blythswood.	
SOVEREIGN.		ROYAL	Mr Robinson.	Lord Lawrence.	Col. J.H. Rivett-Carnac.	
	Mr W.H. Waister.	FOOTMEN		Lord Churchill.	Col. J. Stevenson.	
				Lord Colville of Culross.	Col. Earl of Harewood.	
Mr J. Armstrong.	Mr E. Rendell.	AND	Mr T.I. Allen.	Col. Brabazon.	Col. Duke of Beaufort.	
Inspt W. Greenaway.		ATTENDANTS.		Col. H. Ricardo.	Col. C. B. Bashford.	
Driver. D. Hughes.			Mr W.A. Hart.	Capt Holford.	Col. Earl of March.	
Fireman. G. Bayliss.				Col. J.C. Cavendish.	Col. Duke of Montrose.	
				Col. Sir R. Ogilvy.	Brevet-Col. T.F.D. Bridge.	
				Col. Duke of Northumberland.	Col. H. N. Mc. Rae.	
				Col. Marquis of Londonderry.	Col. H. G. Dixon.	
				Col. Earl of Haddington.	Col. G.L.C. Money.	
				Col. Viscount Galway.	Capt Hon. H. Lambton.	
				Col. C.P. Le Cornu.	Capt C. Campbell.	
				Col. J. Davis.	Capt A. Mac Leod.	
				Col. W. Martin.	Capt A. A.C. Parr.	
				Col. W. Bell.	Capt G. L. Atkinson.	
				Col. W. Campbell.		

(right-hand column, rotated:) Maj. Gen. Sir H. Ewart. Maj. Count Gleichen. Capt H.S.H. Plouis of Battenberg. / Maj. Gen. Sir J. Mc.Neill. Vice-Admt Sir J. Fullerton. Admt Sir M. Culme Seymour.

EARL
G.K.

T. I. ALLEN, Supt of the Line.

...RN · RAILWAY.

...L · OF

...S · MAJESTY · THE · QUEEN.

...ROYAL · TRAIN.

...m. Saturday 2nd Feby 1901.

...OON.	SALOON.	SALOON.	SALOON.		SEMI-SALOON.	COMPART-MENTS.	BRAKE VAN.
...of ...olk. ...E ...IS ...of ...oke. Viscount Valentia. Sir J. Acland Hood, Bart. W. Cavendish, Esq. Lord Belper. Duke of Buccleuch. Earl of Waldegrave. F.M. The Rt Hon Viscount Wolseley. Lt Col. H.T. Fenwick.	**H.M. THE KING.** **H.M. THE QUEEN.** H.R.H. Duke of Connaught. H.R.H. Ds. of Fife. H.I.M. The Kaiser. H.R.H. Ps. Victoria. H.R.H. Duke of Saxe Coburg. H.R.H. Ps. Charles of Denmark. Crown Prince of Germany. H.R.H. Ps. Christian. Prince Arthur of Connaught. H.R.H. Ds. of Argyll. Prince Henry of Prussia. H.R.H. Ps. Henry of Battenberg. Crown Prince of Denmark. H.I.H. Ds. of Saxe Coburg. Prince Charles of Denmark. H.R.H. Ds. of Connaught. H.R.H. Ds. of Albany. H.R.H. Ps. Adolph of Schaumberg-Lippe.	H.R.H. Duke of Cambridge. H.M. King of the Hellenes. H.H. Prince Ed. of Saxe Weimar. H.M. King of the Belgians. H.R.H. D. of Baden. H.M. King of Portugal. H.R.H. P. Arnulf of Bavaria. H.R.H. Prince Christian. H.R.H. D. of Wurtemberg. H.R.H. G. D. of Hesse. H.R.H. P. of Waldeck Pyrmont. H.R.H. D. of Sparta. H.S.H. Hereditary P. Hohenlohe-Langenburg. H.R.H. C.P. of Norway & Sweden. H.R.H. P. of Hohenzollern. Crown Prince of Roumania. H.R.H. P. Philip of Saxe Coburg. K.T. & R.H. Archduke of Austria. H.H. D. of Mecklenberg Strelitz. H.R.H. D. d'Aosta. H.H. Hereditary P. of Saxe Meiningen. H.I. H.G.D. Michael. H.H. D. Ernest Gunther. H.R.H. C.P. of Siam. H.H. P.F.C. of Hesse. H.S.H. D. of Teck. H.S.H. P. Francis of Teck. Prince Henry of Reuss. H.H. P. Leopold of Saxe Coburg. Duke of Fife. H.H. P. Mohammed Ali Pacha. H.R.H. D. of Saxony. H.S.H. P. Ernest of Saxe-Altenburg. H.S.H. P. Adolph of Schaumberg-Lippe. H.H. P. Albert of Schleswig Holstein. H.S.H. P. Hohenlohe-Langenburg. H.S.H. P. Alexander of Teck.	Duc. D'Alencon.	Ds. of Buccleuch. Countess of Lytton. Miss Phipps. Lady Suffield. Miss Knollys.	Non-Com. Officers and Men of German Army Deputation.	Earl Cawdor. Mr J.L. Wilkinson.	Guard, W.J. Fowler. Interpreters, Lieut. Hambly. Messrs W.F. Wilson. R.M. Gregory. F. Hylands. A. Bauert T.P. Llewellyn. L.W. Meadows.

...hairman.
...retary.

J. L. WILKINSON, Gen. Manager.

of Mr. H. Day.' Such recognition could be taken that Her Majesty was well pleased with the Island's railways.

While Osborne House was a favourite home of Queen Victoria, second only to Balmoral, her love of Osborne was not shared by her son, King Edward VII, who succeeded to the throne on his Mother's death in 1901. In defiance of his late Mother's desire that Osborne should be retained as an official residence for her son, King Edward donated Osborne to the nation; thus its use as a royal residence was abandoned. Consequently, together with the development of motor transport, the opportunity for running royal trains on the Isle of Wight in future years was bleak. Cowes and the town's association with yachting continued to attract royalty, particularly for that great event in the yachting calendar known as Cowes Week and, less frequently, naval reviews in the Solent. But the need for a royal special was only justified if such visits were official. During Cowes Week, it was not unknown for some Royals to travel unrecognised by the ordinary service trains. Andrew Britton in volume two of his book, *Once Upon a Line* recalls, in fascinating detail, the story told to him by a now retired railwayman of a day when our present Queen, as Princess Elizabeth, and her sister, Princess Margaret, were children and accompanied by a lady-in-waiting, travelled by one of the normal service trains from Cowes to Newport. That childhood train journey is known to be still remembered by the Queen. She may have been further reminded of the occasion when a letter, addressed to Her Majesty and carried by one of the last trains to pass through Whippingham station on Sunday, 24 January 1971, outlined the Wight Locomotive Society's plans for the now established Steam Centre at Havenstreet station. The Buckingham Palace letter of reply expressed Her Majesty's delight in receiving from the Island's railway devotees, a communication 'so imaginatively conveyed'. The closure of all but one of the Island's railways for everyday use has now virtually eliminated any future possibility for royal railway travel. However, on 26 January 1976, a great grandson of Queen Victoria, Earl Mountbatten of Burma who was Governor and Lord Lieutenant of the Isle of Wight, and so tragically killed in 1979, visited the preserved Isle of Wight Steam Railway. During his visit, Earl Mountbatten took a hand at the controls of the surviving Class O2 0-4-4 tank locomotive No 24, *Calbourne*, built by the LSWR in 1891 and transferred from the mainland to Island duties in April 1925. It hauled the Earl's special train between Havenstreet and Wootton and part of the same line over which Queen Victoria rode between Whippingham and Ryde in 1888.

In 1848 Queen Victoria took a lease of Balmoral House in the Scottish Highlands, which four years later she bought outright. By 1855 the present 'castle' was completed from designs by Prince Albert, so firmly establishing their Scottish retreat over 600 miles north of the Isle of Wight and another opportunity for railway travel. On 28 September, 1848, Queen Victoria made her first railway journey from Scotland to England. With heavy fog over the East Coast, the planned evening departure south on board one of the royal yachts was considered too risky. Hurried arrangements were made for a special train to run between Montrose, then the most northerly railhead of the Aberdeen Railway, and London. The first stage of the 50 mile journey to Perth, via Forfar, was made in less than two hours. Next

The royal train replica of 1897 in the Royalty and Empire display has just arrived at Windsor with 4-2-2 No 3041 The Queen at the head. (Author)

A setting in the Madame Tussaud's Royalty and Empire display at Windsor & Eton Central station showing Queen Victoria, and Prince Edward and Princess Alexandra in the royal waiting room. (Author)

morning, departure from Perth was at 10.30 for a journey of just over four hours to Carlisle. Eventually, Crewe was reached at about 7pm where the Queen spent the night. The following day, 30 September, the Queen's special train left Crewe soon after 7am and reached London at about 11am. The train consisted of a combination of six carriages and trucks and Queen Victoria travelled throughout the long tiring journey in an ordinary four-wheel first class carriage belonging to the Aberdeen Railway.

In August, 1850, during a journey on the East Coast route from London to Edinburgh, Queen Victoria and Prince Albert attended ceremonies to celebrate the opening of Newcastle Central station and the completion of the Royal Border bridge, spanning the Tweed, at Berwick. There is a story that following the Queen's visit to Newcastle, on subsequent journeys she pulled down the blinds of her carriage whenever her train passed through Newcastle because the bill for the festivities, including a banquet, for the opening of the Central station, was later sent to Buckingham Palace. This is reputed to have so incensed the Queen that she vowed never to look upon Newcastle again. However, four years later when her train was travelling northwards, she noticed a large fire on Newcastle quayside. The Queen ordered that the train should stop to acquaint Her Majesty of the seriousness of the fire. Later, the Queen sent a large donation by way of relief. In later years, when the royal train ran on journeys to Scotland from Gosport or Windsor by the Great Western route via Leamington and Solihull to Bushbury Junction, just north of Wolverhampton, the Queen is known to have lowered the blinds in her carriage between Birmingham and Wolverhampton to save her from the distress of seeing the industrial landscape of smoking chimneys and grimy buildings in which she knew the harsh conditions that many of her loyal subjects were condemned to live.

In 1862, a country home was bought for Prince Albert Edward (later King Edward VII) at Sandringham, eight miles north-east of King's Lynn in Norfolk. By the time of the Prince's marriage to Princess Alexandra of Denmark, in March 1863, a railway from King's Lynn to Hunstanton had been completed nearly six months previously. Several days after their wedding, the Prince took his bride to Sandringham for the first time on 28 March, 1863 for an extended honeymoon. It was on this occasion that the first royal train arrived at the nearby station of Wolferton drawn by Sinclair 'W' class 2-2-2 engine No 284 painted in a special livery of cream, decorated with red roses and garlands. Until then, Wolferton had been just a wayside station of little importance, but with the establishment of a royal home nearby, Wolferton became *the* station on the Hunstanton line. However, the Hunstanton & West Norfolk Railway was one of the very small local railway companies that existed at that time and it was not until 1876 that a new station building was provided on the single track railway incorporating royal waiting rooms. The line was absorbed by the Great Eastern Railway in 1890 and eight years later, in 1898, when the line was doubled from King's Lynn to Wolferton, the station was rebuilt in mock Tudor style with an additional specially-designed royal building erected to accommodate the now frequent comings and goings for Sandringham House. This new building then formed part of the down side platform, with the original 1876 building providing facilities for the up side for departures to King's Lynn and London.

Mention has already been made of Queen Victoria's journeys to her Scottish home at Balmoral and it is significant now to turn attention to the opening of yet another railway and station that might never have been built had there not have been a royal residence and the obvious prestige of providing for royal needs. The Queen and Prince Albert usually paid a summer visit to Balmoral, but after Prince Albert's death, in 1861, the Queen felt the need of more seclusion as one of the many ways in which she tried to cope with the loneliness of widowhood by visiting Balmoral twice a year in the spring and autumn. In October 1866, the Deeside Railway (which became part of the Great North of Scotland Railway in 1875) completed the last section of its 43 mile line from Aberdeen to a terminus at Ballater, close to the Balmoral estate. Previously, Aberdeen had been the railhead for royal journeys, but the Deeside Railway's gradual extension westward towards Balmoral was to make it possible for the Queen and her family to get closer to their Scottish retreat by rail. In August, 1860, for the first time, Queen Victoria travelled through to Aboyne, 32 miles from Aberdeen. Seven years later, on Friday, 23 August, 1867, Her Majesty made her first use of Ballater station and thus started a long association with royal journeys lasting until October 1965.

Some of Queen Victoria's journeys appear to have been less than pleasant experiences for the railway staff concerned. At best there was always welcome relief when a journey had been completed with little or no adverse comment by the Queen's Household. At worst, it could only be said that the same misfortunes should not be repeated in spite of all the meticulous planning involved in every journey. Frequently, there was

After visiting Aberystwyth on 26 June, 1896 the Prince and and Princess of Wales, continuing their tour, left Machynlleth at 9.45am, for South Wales. On Saturday, 27 June, their train was hauled over the Cambrian system from Moat Lane (where reversal took place) to Talyllyn Junction, near Brecon, by another Aston 4-4-0, No 63 shown here. Note the bowler hatted official, left, the splendidly uniformed guard (below footplate) and other staff who appear proud to be on duty for the occasion. The Cambrian stop signal and house (partly clad in ivy) add some atmosphere to the scene which, quite probably, was taken after the royal personages had departed; they would have been too nervous to pose beforehand! (Courtesy C. C. Green)

A view by an unknown photographer of the GWR royal train, built to celebrate Queen Victoria's Diamond Jubilee, taking the Queen from Windsor to Paddington on Monday, 21 June, 1897, hauled by 4-2-2 locomotive No 3041, The Queen, suitably decorated with crowned headlamp and royal arms. (Author's Collection)

The Great Western Railway royal train of 1897, specially built for Queen Victoria's Diamond Jubilee celebrations, headed by 4-2-2 locomotive No 3041, The Queen, a posed photograph in the vicinity of Swindon Works. (British Rail/OPC Collection)

friction between senior railway officers and members of the Queen's Household as recalled by the London & North Western Railway's Superintendent, George P. Neele who, on retirement in June 1895 had made 112 journeys with the royal train. In his *Railway Reminiscences*, published in 1904, he refers to his encounters with the Queen's favoured Scottish servant, John Brown, whom he called the Queen's 'coarse phonograph'. It seems that Neele, in spite of detailed explanations in answer to Brown's prefaced words 'the Queen says', could never fully satisfy her trusted servant on, for example, the unpleasant smell caused by an overheated axle bearing. In making the arrangements for each journey, the Queen's likes and dislikes were well known, but John Brown could never be satisfied, supposedly acting on the Queen's instructions; or was he? He died in March 1883.

Neele continued to serve in attendance on the Queen's journeys until his last one on 21 June 1895, when the Queen and several members of her family travelled south from Balmoral. Before the departure from Ballater, Prince Henry of Battenburg ushered Neele into the royal saloon for his formal meeting with Queen Victoria whereupon she thanked him for his personal care to her and her family on the many occasions he had supervised the working of the royal train. At last, he received Royal thanks and could retire, happy in the knowledge that, amid all those turbulent exchanges of earlier years with John Brown, when on one occasion he ordered the train to be stopped because no candles had been placed in the Queen's saloon when she wished to read, he was now being thanked formally, yet in the privacy of Her Majesty's carriage with Prince Henry and Princess Beatrice looking on. Before leaving, the Queen gave him an engraving showing the whole Royal Family as a group at Windsor in 1887. Later, he was sent another souvenir in the form of a large silver tray engraved to acknowledge his long service to royal railway travel. The Royal Household also gave him a silver bowl on which were engraved over 30 names, including ladies-in-waiting to the Queen. The name of John Brown was not among them. However, a successor to Brown did have his name included – Munshi Abdul Karim, a young Indian servant of whom Queen Victoria was extremely fond.

The historic Diamond Jubilee celebrations took place in London on Tuesday, 22 June 1897 when Queen Victoria drove from Buckingham Palace, through cheering crowds along gaily decorated streets for a brief service of thanksgiving at the steps of St Paul's Cathedral. To enable the elderly Queen to prepare for this happy, but tiring day, she had rested overnight at Buckingham Palace. On the previous day, it had been the proud honour for the Great Western Railway to convey Her Majesty and Suite from Windsor to Paddington in the new royal train, supposed to have been a gift to Queen Victoria but which she never actually owned, and estimated to have cost around £40,000. As this was an occasion for public rejoicing, advance knowledge of the Diamond Jubilee royal special was widely known; certainly the Great Western wished to show-off its 'gift' of the company's loyalty to the Crown. What a magnificent sight it must have been as this very special royal train, drew slowly away from Windsor across the River Thames afloat with decorated boats, drawn by one of William Dean's 4-2-2 engines, No 3041 *The Queen*, decorated with crowned headlamp and large colourful cast metal royal coats of arms on the sides of engine and tender leading the six gleaming rich chocolate brown and cream coloured carriages. What were the Queen's own thoughts as she sat in the serene surroundings of her saloon, finished in satinwood with cream and green silk upholstered furnishings, sedately progressing onward through Slough, Southall, Hanwell and Acton to Paddington past groups of cheering well-wishers gathered behind lineside fences? Now nobody can really say. It is very likely that she recalled that very first train journey with Prince Albert all those years ago in 1842, over the same line.

Your author invites the reader to step back in time, nearly 90 years, and become one of the crowd gathered outside the Great Western station at Windsor several days before the Queen's Diamond Jubilee celebrations take place in London. The station is decorated with flags and bunting and under the gently curved glass roof, spanning the roadway outside the new Royal Station, are 70 men drawn from the 2nd Battalion of the Coldstream Guards. Waiting at the station entrance is an Ascot Landau with four Windsor Greys and postillion outriders. Watching the scene is a lady leaning on her bicycle, an old man in an invalid chair with his family, another family, mother and father and their baby in a perambulator, and many other of the Queen's loyal subjects. Impressed by this patriotic spectacle is a small barefooted waif boy, who rests for a few minutes by leaning on his broom, but knows he must soon wield that broom along Windsor's streets hoping to earn a penny or two. All are eagerly waiting for Queen Victoria and the Prince and Princess of Wales to emerge from the opulent Royal Waiting Room where the Queen is seated on a sofa awaiting the arrival, from Paddington, of her eldest daughter, the Empress Frederic of Prussia and her son Prince Henry of Prussia. At the red carpeted platform the Royal Train has just arrived and there is a first glimpse of part of the Great Western's new royal carriages, upon which no expense has been spared. Up front Driver David Hughes, (later to drive the Queen's funeral train in 1901 and subsequently honoured with membership of the Royal Victorian Order for service to the Queen) dressed in special royal train uniform, has taken out his pocket watch and is proud to discover that

Madame Tussaud's 'Royalty & Empire' exhibition, Windsor. Driver David Hughes checks his watch 'recording a one minute early arrival from Paddington'. The Empress Frederic of Prussia and her son, Prince Henry of Prussia, prepare to leave the royal train to be 'greeted by Lord Emlyn, GWR Chairman, on the left, and the Stationmaster, Mr Johnson'. Outside the Royal Waiting Room, 'Queen Victoria and her daughter, the dowager Empress of Prussia prepare to board an open landau for the drive to Windsor Castle, while the Guard of Honour presents arms.' On the right is a barefooted boy, resting awhile on his broom, witnessing the spectacle. (Author)

33

The LNWR Royal Train of 1897 – a posed photograph with three-cylinder compound 2-2-2-2 locomotive No 2053, Greater Britain, *painted in scarlet livery to celebrate Queen Victoria's Diamond Jubilee of 1897. (Courtesy National Railway Museum)*

Madame Tussaud's 'Royalty & Empire' exhibition, Windsor. In an anteroom of the Royal Waiting at the GWR's Windsor station, Queen Victoria's favoured Indian servant Abdul Karim, better known as 'the Munshi' waits with teapot and china teaset. (Author)

his polished green engine, named *The Queen*, with every inch of brass and copper gleaming brightly in the summer sunshine, has arrived a whole minute early on the 21¼ mile run down from Paddington. A little further back along the platform, at the entrance to the Queen's saloon, Lord Emlyn, Chairman of the GWR, and the Stationmaster, Mr Johnson, stand with slightly bowed heads as the widowed Empress Frederic of Prussia, closely followed by her son, Prince Henry of Prussia, prepares to alight.

Through one of the saloon windows can be glimpsed other distinguished Royal visitors, all of whom have come to stay with the Queen at the nearby Castle, to share with her in rejoicing in the achievement of having reigned on the Throne for 60 glorious years, her Diamond Jubilee. But this scene can be witnessed today, for history has come alive through the enterprise and skill of Madame Tussaud's, whose wax exhibition in London is world famous, and who in 1983 opened a permanent exhibition at Windsor & Eton Central station at first entitled 'Royalty & Railways' and now 'Royalty & Empire'. With the aid of a little imagination the exhibition visitor becomes infected with Diamond Jubilee excitement as a poorly dressed news boy invites all to buy the latest edition hot from the press, with the repeated call 'Empress of Prussia arrives in Windsor, read a'l a'bt it'. Yes, even the replica 4-2-2 engine No 3041 *The Queen* has all the atmosphere of the original with the wisp of steam and sound from inside this beautiful example of a graceful Great Western locomotive. To be truthful the whole exhibition, with the exception of the renovation of the Royal Station, unused by royalty for many years, and the discovery of one of the original 1897 saloons in use as a holiday home on the West Wales coast, has been created from scratch.

Not wishing to be completely outshone by the Great Western's loyal actions in Diamond Jubilee year, the mighty London & North Western, in whose train Queen Victoria travelled the longest distances, sprang a unique surprise upon the railway scene with the appearance of two express passenger engines painted in somewhat startling colours. Two of Francis

Webb's controversial compound 2-2-2-2 engines were chosen to show, as it were, the North Western flag. No 2053 *Greater Britain* was turned out in what was officially termed scarlet, a shade similar to Post Office red, with yellow and black lining. However, Queen Victoria must have been quietly amused at the choice of colour for the second engine, No 2054 *Queen Empress*. It was painted in a rather impractical livery of soft creamy white, edged with lavender, including the smokebox and chimney! The celebrations over, these two engines were quickly repainted in work-a-day Crewe blackberry black.

Shortly before the Diamond Jubilee celebrations, Queen Victoria went north from Windsor to Balmoral, during May, to seek the tonic effect of seclusion in the Scottish Highlands to sustain her for the strenuous Jubilee events of the following month. During her journey to Ballater, the Queen had accepted an invitation to visit Sheffield on Friday, 21 May. It was to be her last major public appearance before the Diamond Jubilee. Arriving at the Midland Station in sunny weather at 5pm, Her Majesty

During Queen Victoria's two hour visit to Sheffield the LNWR royal train was taken to nearby Wicker goods station where this photograph was taken showing some of the railway staff posing with this important train headed by the elegant Johnson Midland 4-4-0, No 2209. The Queen's horse drawn carriage, for her use at Balmoral, is being carried on a flat truck – the second vehicle from the locomotive. (Courtesy National Railway Museum)

LNWR Notice, May 1897, cover. (Author's collection)

stepped from her saloon in the LNWR royal train, leaning heavily upon a stick and assisted by her Indian servant Munshi Abdul Karim (known as the Munshi). After formal presentations, she drove in an open carriage to open Sheffield's new Town Hall and later to Norfolk Park to join several thousand children having a jamboree. A little over two hours later, at about 7.15pm and slightly behind schedule, the Queen's visit ended when she rejoined the royal train from a specially erected platform adjacent to the Cyclops steel and iron works of Messrs Cammell where she had watched the rolling of an armour plate for the battleship *Ocean*. Three days short of her seventy-eighth birthday, the Queen, according to contemporary accounts, was visibly fatigued as, helped by the Munshi, she entered her saloon and prepared for the journey that lay ahead, through the night, to arrive at Ballater, the following morning, at 8.20.

The journey from Windsor to Sheffield, as the reader can see from the timetable extracts reproduced, was by a devious route after leaving the GWR at Leamington, going via Nuneaton and Market Bosworth to join the Midland main line south of Burton-on-Trent. While the *official* document is precise over matters of route, timings and whose royal train, of the several companies involved, will be used, it does lay down that those companies will be responsible for making their own operating arrangements including the provision of locomotives and guards. Research has revealed details of some of the locomotives used and other information of interest.

Less than 24 hours before the royal train was to pass Fenny Compton, on the GWR line between Banbury and Leamington, a goods train was derailed there through a broken axle on a truck carrying stone. This occurred between 7 and 8pm on the evening of Thursday, 20 May, and as both up and down lines were blocked, it was thought that the Queen's train might have to be diverted after passing Oxford, to travel via Moreton-in-Marsh, Honeybourne, Stratford-upon-Avon and Birmingham. However, by early on the morning of Friday 21 May, both lines were cleared, but, quite possibly, Her Majesty noticed several of the damaged trucks lying at the trackside as her train passed slowly over the new track, which it had been necessary to lay because of the damage caused by the derailment. If the Queen did see those damaged trucks, her thoughts may have been of her physician, Dr Baly, who as already related died in a railway accident in 1861.

On the other hand, she may have been pleased to know that the engine taking her from Windsor to Leamington carried the name *Empress of India*. As a retired local railwayman recounted to the author many years ago, the GWR had chosen to use its 4-2-2 engine No 3040 bearing the name of her allegiance to India and the knowledge that several of the Queen's Indian servants, who were not popular with other members of the Royal Household, would be accompanying the Queen on this occasion. It is known that Queen Victoria, in spite of protests among some of her Household, insisted on being attended upon by people of darker skins, to whom she was attracted. So the Great Western's choice of engine was appropriate. At Leamington, a spa town dignified by the prefix 'Royal' when the Queen, as Princess Victoria, with her mother, the Duchess of Kent, had rested in the town's Regent Hotel in August, 1830, the royal train was shunted under GWR supervision to No 1 Exchange Line and where GWR Guard Murphy, in whose charge the train had been from Banbury to Leamington, handed over to his LNWR counterpart. Standing proudly on the Exchange Line between the two stations of the GWR and LNWR, was the scarlet painted LNWR Webb 2-2-2-2 compound, No 2053 *Greater Britain*. Few ordinary members of the public can have witnessed the sequence of getting the Queen's train from the lines of one railway company to another, let alone have caught a glimpse of their Queen whose picture adorned the 'best' room of most homes, for paragraph 31 of the time table, issued by the LNWR General Manager's Office, decreed that 'all stations must be kept perfectly clear and private during the passage of the Royal Train and no persons except those properly authorised, the Company's Servants on duty, and the Police, where their services are required, are to be admitted.' Possibly the best view of seeing this colourful engine puffing away from Leamington would have been from the banks of the River Leam as the train, all 16 carriages – a mixture of uneven looking bogie and six-wheel vehicles in the North Western's standard coach colours of carmine lake and off-white – moved slowly across the gently curving solid viaduct towards Kenilworth, Coventry and on through the depressingly drab mining landscape of Bedworth and Nuneaton en route to Derby. In not choosing the creamy white coloured *Queen Empress*, whose name would have been more appropriate to complement that of the Great Western's choice for this journey, did the LNWR hierarchy feel apprehensive that an engine of such colour might arrive on foreign Midland Railway metals at Derby streaked with grime, had the day turned out to be wet, and after passing wagon loads of coal standing in colliery sidings that lay along the route? It is quite probable that this was the reason for the choice of the scarlet *Greater Britain* to contrast with the Midland Company's two crimson lake liveried Johnson 4-4-0s which took over for the rest of the journey to Sheffield.

Although garish, it was supposed not to cause Midland officials to think that the North Western was seeking to show off, as in fact it really was! However, quite naturally, the Midland had as its allies the Sheffield local press which reported 'Not the slightest mishap or delay occurred on the railway journey during the time it was being worked by the officials of the Midland Company'.

The year 1897 passed and an air of Indian Summer, in time, emerged as the memories of the Diamond Jubilee very gradually receded into history. With renewed enthusiasm, in March 1898, Queen Victoria set out from Windsor in the GWR's 1897 train to travel over the South Western Railway to Portsmouth where she boarded the Royal Yacht *Victoria and Albert* for Cherbourg and what had become almost an annual visit, at this time of year, to the south of France.

In the following year on 11 March Queen Victoria made her last journey to Nice, in the South of France. Previously, the favoured route from Windsor had been to travel to Portsmouth and sail from there to Cherbourg. However, on this particular occasion there appears to have been a desire to reach the channel port of Folkstone with some degree of haste. Shortly before 11.00am the Queen and her party boarded the Great Western royal train at Windsor for a non-stop journey to Folkestone. The

LNWR Notice, May 1897, page 3 listing instructions at Leamington, Kenilworth etc. (Author's collection)

GWR Badminton Class 4-4-0 No 3297, Earl Cawdor, appropriately decorated and equipped for working the royal train non-stop from Windsor to Folkestone on 11 March, 1899. The tender is provided with additional water carrying capacity for the long run. (British Rail/OPC Collection)

engine chosen to make the run was Duke class 4-4-0 No 3297 *Earl Cawdor*, decorated with the royal coat of arms on engine and tender. For this unusual journey the tender was fitted at the rear with extra water tanks. The Court Circular records that the train was routed by way of Addison Road (now Kensington Olympia), to gain the South Eastern line, arriving at Folkestone Pier at 1.15pm. Although not recorded, clearly the GW engine did not take the train down the steeply-graded harbour branch from Folkestone Junction. Moreover even on the SER main line, clearances must have been tight, for the royal saloon itself was four inches wider than the limits permitted by the South Eastern loading gauge. The Court Circular also records that the Queen embarked on the South Eastern steam packet *Calais Douvres* and, after a fine passage, reached Boulogne in 1 hour and 30 minutes. After the formal presentation to Her Majesty of various local officials including Messieur Sartiaux of the Northern Railway of France, the Queen's special train left for the long overnight journey arriving in Nice at 4.00pm on 12 March.

The twentieth century dawned, it was the year 1900, and the Victorian royal trains rolled on into a new chapter of history; Queen Victoria was in her eighty first year. For her spring holiday the Queen requested to go to Ireland and stayed at Viceregal Lodge, near Dublin; she had not been there since August, 1861, when Prince Albert accompanied her. Late on the evening of 2 April, the LNWR royal train left Windsor for the overnight journey to Holyhead, going by way of the GW route to Wolverhampton and then by the North Western to Crewe and on through Chester to arrive at Llandudno Junction at 3.45am, where it remained until 7.45am for the final part of the journey to arrive at the Admiralty Pier at 9.00am. Travelling overnight by train enabled Her Majesty to benefit from a daylight sea crossing to Kingstown (today's Dun Laoghaire) in the yacht *Victoria and Albert*.

While the Queen, whose Irish visit lasted nearly a month, confined her movements to carriage drives in and around Dublin, her grand-daughter, Princess Victoria Eugenie, who accompanied Queen Victoria, was invited to Inchicore Works of the Great Southern & Western Railway. What her grandmother thought of the visit is best not related here, but she did not really approve of the Princess, in her late teens, visiting what she considered so alien a place as railway workshops! However, the Princess thought otherwise and during her visit performed the ceremony of naming a new engine by her popularly known name *Princess Ena*, the engine concerned being a D11 class 4-4-0 No 304. Another engine of the same class, No 301, already carried the name *Victoria*, so the young Princess could now boast to her grandmother of *her* own engine. The engine *Princess Ena* survived until 1959, but Princess Ena, by then a very old lady, lived another 10 years.

Queen Victoria had expressed a wish that she might be spared a little time, so to speak, to see in the new century. She spent early summer at Osborne House and at the end of August crossed the Solent to Gosport for yet another journey north to Balmoral in her favourite LNWR train. On

An interesting picture taken at Llandudno station in 1899 when Prince George, Duke of York (later King George V) alighted from the eight-wheel LNWR Equerries' Saloon, 5153. An identical saloon, No 5131, was used, almost exclusively, by the Prince of Wales. (Gwynedd Archives Service)

Queen Victoria's last visit to Ireland to 1900 was an occasion when Her Majesty travelled overnight in the LNWR royal train from Windsor arriving at Holyhead on the morning of 3 April where this picture was taken. The locomotive is Jubilee class four-cylinder compound 4-4-0 No 1915 Implacable. *Second vehicle from the locomotive is a covered carriage truck which had conveyed the Queen's horse drawn carriage. (A. G. Ellis, courtesy of E. Talbot)*

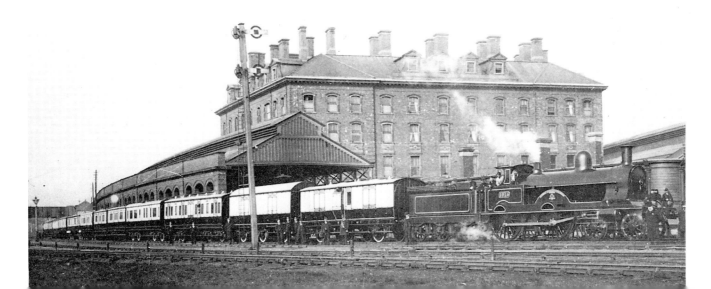

ROYAL TRAIN,
BALLATER TO WINDSOR,
6th and 7th November, 1900.

The fogs that prevail at this season of the year render it necessary that special precautions set forth in Circular No. 3033, relating to fogs and fog-signalling, should be strictly observed, so as to guard against the possibility of obstruction to the Royal Train on its journey from Scotland.

The Station Masters, Foremen, Platelayers, Signalmen, Gatemen, Shunters, Guards, and others concerned, are instructed to keep a strict watch on the shunting at Stations, and on operations in Sidings adjoining and on the Main Line, so as to prevent the possibility of any interference with the safe passage of the Royal Train.

FRED. HARRISON.

General Manager's Office,
Euston Station, 2nd November, 1900.

LNWR fog notice for what turned out to be Queen Victoria's last journey from Balmoral to Windsor in November, 1900. (Author's collection)

The royal train conveying Queen Victoria on her last journey from Balmoral to Windsor draws away from Ferryhill Junction, Aberdeen, following reversal there, headed by two Caledonian Railway Dunalastair class 4-4-0s on the late afternoon of Tuesday, 6 November, 1900. (Courtesy National Railway Museum)

the morning of Saturday, 1 September, the Queen's train drew into Perth station at 9.20 where Her Majesty alighted and had breakfast in the adjoining Station Hotel, something she had done on previous journeys, if a mid-day arrival at Balmoral had been desired. On other occasions the royal train had arrived at Ballater soon after 8.00am and then the Queen would breakfast at Balmoral. A little over two months later, on Tuesday 6 November, 1900, Queen Victoria left her Scottish home for the last time. Expressing a desire to join the royal train at Ballater privately and with the minimum of fuss, Her Majesty, dressed in deep mourning, did so and at 3.30pm her train left to begin the 588 mile journey to Windsor, arriving there the following morning at 8.45. Although this proved to be Queen Victoria's last visit to Scotland, loyal spectators gathered at Ferryhill Junction, Aberdeen, where reversal of the train took place, could not have known this to be so. During the five minute stop, while the two Great North of Scotland 4-4-0s were detached from one end and replaced at the other by two of the Caledonian Railway's Dunalastair 4-4-0s for the next stage of the journey to Perth, from the window of her saloon, Her Majesty was seen to smile in loving acknowledgement of those who had waited for an hour or more in the dreary drizzle of a late November afternoon. Then a railway employee appeared with two large black kitchen kettles of boiling water which he carefully handed into the train for the making of the time honoured afternoon tea. Moments later, the two engines eased the 14 carriage train forward and for those lucky enough to have watched the five minute spectacle, they would always be able to recount that they had said goodbye to their Queen.

During the first few days of 1901, it became known that Queen Victoria, who was now at Osborne House in the Isle of Wight, was unwell and her strength was ebbing. Early on the evening of Tuesday, 22 January, the Queen died. Her son, Edward, Prince of Wales, succeeded her as King Edward VII and his wife, Alexandra, was Queen. Queen Victoria's wish was to be laid to rest in the Frogmore Mausoleum at Windsor near where her dear husband, Albert, had rested after his tragic death in 1861. The responsibility for conveying the Queen's remains from the Isle of Wight to

LB&SCR B4 class 4-4-0 No 54
Empress, *which hauled Queen
Victoria's funeral train from
Fareham to Victoria Station,
London, on Saturday, 2 February
1901. A gilt crown on a crimson
cushion is mounted at the top of the
smokebox door in front of the
chimney with white and purple cloth
festoons along the side of the boiler.
The sombre occasion appears not to
have necessitated the then customary
LBSCR practice of whitewashing the
coal – its natural colour being
appropriate to the occasion!*
(Courtesy National Railway
Museum)

Windsor concerned three railway companies, the London & South
Western from Gosport to Fareham, the London, Brighton & South Coast
Railway from Fareham to London Victoria, and, finally, the Great Western
from Paddington to Windsor. The choice of the Brighton company's route
to London was that of King Edward VII, who no doubt thought that its
recently built royal train of 1898 for the King when Prince of Wales was
more in keeping with the times than either the South Western or London &
North Western could muster. However, Queen Victoria always refused to
travel on the Brighton company's line as she associated it with an early visit
to Brighton when she was almost mobbed by an over enthusiastic crowd in
the early years of her reign. Thereafter, she considered Brighton to be a rude
and vulgar place and disliked anything remotely connected with the resort!
But now Victoria was dead and her favoured South Western Railway was
not to be honoured with taking her remains to London. The Queen's coffin
was transported across the Solent from Cowes to Gosport on the smallest
of the royal yachts, *Alberta*, on Friday, 1 February. The next day the entire
journey from Gosport to Windsor took place. Thus on that morning at
Gosport, at the late Queen's private station in Clarence Yard, stood the
LB&SCR royal train which also included the GWR Queen's saloon (altered
in 1897 for the Diamond Jubilee) No 229, where the coffin was placed. The
interior had been transformed by the removal of some internal fittings and
lined with white cloth relieved by purple bands. Two LB&SCR first class
bogie carriages were also included making eight carriages in all. The
scheduled departure time from Gosport of 8.45am was delayed by eight
minutes, caused by the confusion of the large number of mourners,
including the German Emperor, in finding their allotted places, for the train
plan indicated the formation on arrival at Victoria. As reversal of the train
was necessary at Fareham, it meant that the train was the opposite way
round at Gosport. The platform, also, was of insufficient length to
accommodate the whole train and the lack of through gangway communication only made matters worse. For this oversight both the L&SWR and
LB&SCR blamed each other and the feud over this incident lasted in
railway circles for many years! The L&SWR was responsible for working
the train from Gosport to Fareham and provided an Adams A12 class 0-4-2
No 555. Further delay occurred at Fareham after attaching at the opposite

GREAT WESTERN RAILWAY.

TIME TABLE

OF

ROYAL TRAIN

CONVEYING

Their Majesties

THE

KING and QUEEN

And their Imperial and Royal Guests,

FROM

PADDINGTON to WINDSOR

AND BACK,

IN CONNECTION WITH THE FUNERAL OF

Her Majesty Queen Victoria,

ON

Saturday, February 2nd, 1901.

WYMAN & SONS, Ltd., Printers, 63, Carter Lane, Doctors' Commons, E.C.

SPECIAL INSTRUCTIONS FOR WORKING THE ROYAL TRAIN.

(TO BE KEPT STRICTLY PRIVATE.)

1. **SPECIAL WORKING AT PADDINGTON FOR DOWN ROYAL TRAIN.**—The Down Royal Train will start from No. 8 Arrival Line, pass along the Down Engine Line as far as Lord Hill's Bridge Box, and from there to Subway Junction along the Down Empty Carriage Line, passing on to the Down Main Line at Subway Junction. The speed over this portion of the Line must not exceed 10 miles an hour.

From 11.0 a.m. and until after the departure of the Royal Train all Up Trains must be worked to No. 7 Platform, and from 12.30 p.m. until after the Royal Train has passed all Down Light Engines and Empty Trains from the arrival side must be worked out from No. 7 Line over the Arrival Box and on to the Down Main Line at Westbourne Bridge Box.

2. **Preliminary Precautions.**—All Signal Boxes on the Route, which in the ordinary course might be closed, must be opened and the signals lighted at least one hour before the Pilot Train is due, and must remain so until "Train out of Section" for the Royal Train has been received from the Block Post in advance.

3. Goods Trains must not leave any station on the line on which the Royal Train will run unless they can reach the next station at which they can be shunted at least 30 minutes before the Royal Train is due at that place.

4. All shunting operations on the lines or Sidings adjoining the Line on which the Royal Train will run must be suspended 30 minutes before the Royal Train is due, and not be resumed until 5 minutes after it has passed, unless "Train out of Section" has been received from the Signal Box in advance for the Royal Train.

5. **Shunting or Stopping of Goods, Mineral or Cattle Trains and Light Engines** running over the next adjacent running line or lines.

(and further numbered instructions, 6 through 19)

18. Her Late Majesty's Saloon, which will be used as the Funeral Car, is to be taken out of the Train after arrival at Windsor, and sent specially to Slough, where it must be placed under cover in the Carriage Shed to wait further orders.

19. **Artificers.**—The Locomotive and Carriage Department will arrange for Artificers to accompany the Royal Train provided with all needful materials and appliances.

The Great Western Railway notice for the running of Queen Victoria's funeral train. (Courtesy G. M. Kichenside)

end the LB&SCR engine because of a minor fault in testing the brake, which resulted in a 10 minute late departure. The LB&SCR engine was No 54 *Empress*, a B4 class 4-4-0 designed by R. J. Billinton and released from Brighton Works in May 1900. The advance pilot engine of the same class, No 53 *Sirdar*, had already left 10 minutes ahead of the royal funeral train, so with a clear road the driver of the funeral train was asked if he could attempt to make-up the lost time, as King Edward VII, who was to meet the train at Victoria, disliked unpunctuality. A very fast run followed, during which a maximum speed of 80mph is thought to have been achieved, resulting in arrival at Victoria two minutes early. The late Queen would most certainly not have approved, and on a railway that included the name Brighton in its title! However, the German Emperor was very impressed when he alighted at Victoria and, through an equerry, expressed his appreciation to Driver Cooper and Fireman F. Way. He also commented on the performance of such a small engine compared with those of larger

3

20. **Guards.**—Two Guards will be in charge of the Royal Train; one to ride in the Front Brake Van, and the other in the Rear Brake Van.

21. The Head Guard must enter in his report the number of persons who travel by the Royal Train (other than the Railway Officials). The front Guard must keep his face towards the rear of the Train and be constantly on the look-out to observe any Signal that may be given by the rear Guard or attendants accompanying the Royal Train, and must communicate instantly to the Driver any Signal he may receive.

22. **Instructions as to reduction of speed at certain points.—Any instructions which may be in force with respect to slackening speed owing to New Works, Relaying Operations, Junctions, &c., applicable to the route over which the Royal Train will run, must be strictly observed.**

23. Detonators must **only** be used for the Royal Train in cases of emergency, and during Fogs or falling Snow, but must not be used to **call attention** to the Ordinary relaying operations or other works of which a written or printed Notice has been issued. The Enginemen of the Pilot Train, and of the Royal Train, before they commence the journey, must be supplied with all such Notices relating to the Line over which their Trains have to run, and the Locomotive Superintendent, before starting, must fully explain to them the instructions, and make them clearly understand between what points the Pilot Train and Royal Train must run at the reduced speeds mentioned in the Notices.

24. **Platelayers to signal Royal Train.**—The Engineering Department will station Platelayers along the Line, in good time before the Pilot Train is due, within signalling distance of each other, to signal the Royal Train. Additional men will also be placed at intervals inside the Company's fence on both sides of the Line, to prevent trespass.

25. Detonators and hand signals will be sent to the various Stations by the Divisional Superintendents, and must be handed to the Platelayers by the Station Masters, who will be responsible for seeing them returned after the Royal Train has run. The Gangers are responsible for fully instructing the Platelayers.

26. If all is right for the Royal Train to proceed, the Platelayers appointed for the purpose must exhibit a Green Hand Signal held steadily in the hand; if they wish to caution the Driver to reduce speed, a Green Hand Signal must be waved from side to side; and if it should be necessary to stop the Train, three detonators must be placed on the rails and a Red Hand Signal exhibited.

27. **Starting the Royal Train.**—Shortly before the Train is due to start the Locomotive and Carriage Superintendent, and the Divisional Superintendent, as regards their own Departments respectively, will each give an assurance to the Chief Traffic Officer in charge of the Train that everything is ready for the Train to proceed as soon as the Royal Personages are seated.

The Traffic Officer in charge will give the Signal to start to the Guards, who must act in strict accordance with Rule **171**, of the Book of Regulations, care being taken that the Royal Personages and all the members of the Suite, are seated before the Signal is actually given.

28. **Signalling the Pilot Train and the Royal Train.**—Immediately after asking "Is Line Clear" for the Pilot Train, the word "Pilot" must be telegraphed to the next Box in Circuit. The Royal Train must be signalled as an Express Passenger Train, and, in addition, immediately after the "Is Line Clear" Bell Signal has been given, the word "**ROYAL**" must be telegraphed to the next Signal Box in Circuit. The words "Pilot" and "Royal" must be sent on the Box-to-Box Single Needle Instrument; if no such instrument exists they must be sent on the Telephone, and in either case they must be repeated back by the Signalman receiving them.

29. "Train out of Section" must not be given for the Pilot Train until it has either passed half a mile beyond the Home Signal or has been shunted clear of the Line on which the Royal Train will run. Signalmen must not give "Line Clear" for the approach of the Royal Train from the Box in the rear until he has first received "Train out of Section" from the Signal Box in advance; but in foggy weather at places where no Fog-signalman is employed, he must not do so until "Line Clear" has been received from the Box in advance.

30. If the Block Signal "Train out of Section" or in foggy weather, at places where no Fog-signalman is employed, the Block Signal "Line Clear" has not been received from the Box in advance for the Pilot Train, the Royal Train must be stopped in accordance with the Block Regulations.

31. The Royal Train must not be allowed to enter any Block Section under Rule 5 of the Standard Block Regulations (Warning Arrangement), nor must any train be allowed to go forward under the "Warning Arrangement" on a line converging towards the line on which the Royal Train will run.

32. Signalmen must not give permission for a Train to follow the Royal Train either on the Main Line of rails or on Relief Lines, until the "Train out of Section" signal has been received for the Royal Train **from the Signal Box in advance**; and at Stations where two or more Signal Boxes exist at short distances apart, the Royal Train must have passed through the Station and into the outside section beyond, before any following Train is allowed to enter the Station.

33. A constant watch is to be kept on the Telegraph Instruments during the time the Pilot Train and the Royal Train are running between the Stations on either side, Up and Down. Where a Telegraph Clerk is not kept the Station Master must make special arrangements for watching the Instruments.

34. **Over Bridges.**—The following precautions must be taken at all Bridges carrying a Railway over the line of rails along which the Royal Train passes:—

Three (or more) Flagmen, each provided with a Red and a Green Flag, a Hand Signal Lamp and Detonators, must be on the bridge on the overhead railway 45 minutes before the Royal Train is timed to pass beneath it.

Twenty minutes before the Pilot Train is due to pass one Flagman must go down the Line and another up the Line on the overhead railway, each of them for a distance of three quarters of a mile from the bridge. The third Flagman must remain at the overbridge and also have with him two Hand Lamps.

As soon as the Pilot Train has passed, the Flagman at the bridge must wave his Red Hand Signal to the two distant Flagmen, who must acknowledge the Signal by repeating it, and immediately put down three Detonators ten yards apart on one rail of the line along which a Train would pass on its way to the bridge, and exhibit their Red Hand Signals towards any Train that may present itself. Should a Train approach and explode any of the three Detonators put down by the Distant Flagman, the Driver must draw on quietly towards the bridge until he is close to it, but he must not, under any circumstances, allow any part of his Train to pass on to or over the bridge. The Flagman at the bridge must also put down three Detonators on each side of the bridge, and exhibit Red Hand Signals in each direction, in such a manner as to stop any approaching Train before reaching the bridge.

After the Pilot Train has passed, no Train or Engine must be allowed on the bridge until the Royal Train has passed under it.

When the Royal Train has passed under the bridge the Flagman stationed there must wave his Green Hand Signal to the two distant Flagmen, who must acknowledge the Signal by repeating it to shew that they understand it, and take up their Detonators (if unexploded), exhibit their Green Hand Signals, and walk towards the bridge. Any Trains that may have been stopped must then be allowed to proceed.

Where there is a curve or any obstruction which prevents the man at the bridge and the men at the three-quarter mile point in either direction having a good sight of each other's Hand Signals, a man, or men, must be stationed intermediately, and the Hand Signals passed from man to man.

The distant men must keep a close watch for Signals from the man at the bridge, and at once acknowledge them by waving their own in a similar manner.

If, in accordance with these instructions, a Train is stopped at the bridge, the distant Flagman who has stopped it must protect it in the rear by placing three more Detonators 10 yards apart on the Rail, and he must continue to exhibit his Red Hand Signal until the Train has proceeded on its journey. It will not be necessary in such cases for the Guard to go back to protect his Train.

In the case of a Signal Box situated on or close to the bridge, only one Flagman need be provided, and he must stand on the bridge. In such circumstances it will be the Signalman's duty to block back to the Block Post on each side of him on the passing of the Pilot Train and not allow any Train or Engine to leave the rear Block Post in either direction until the Royal Train has passed.

The Flagman on the bridge will be responsible for advising the Signalman of the passing of the Pilot Train and Royal Train.

The Divisional Engineers will be responsible for arranging with the Engineers of any Railways, under whose Bridges the Royal Train will pass, for carrying out the instructions contained in clause 34.

35. **Stations to be kept clear and private**.—All the Stations must be kept perfectly clear and private during the passage of the Royal Train, and no persons (excepting those properly authorised, Passengers travelling in the opposite direction, the Company's Servants on duty, and the Police at those Stations where their services are required) are to be admitted to any of the Stations on the route. The Servants of the Company are to perform the necessary work on the platforms without noise, and no demonstration of any kind must be allowed.

36. **The Station Masters must be on duty, to watch the passage of the Pilot Train, and also the Royal Train.**

37. **Termination of Royal Journey.**—At the Windsor and Paddington platforms at which the Royal Personages will alight, a distinctive chalk mark must be made at the exact spot at which the Footplate of the Engine should be when the Train stops, and a man with a Red Hand Signal must stand on the Platform at the chalk mark to ensure the Train being stopped precisely at the appointed place.

38. **Information to be kept private.**—Under no circumstances is information to be given to any person (other than those who must necessarily be made acquainted with the arrangements) respecting the time of the running of the Royal Train, or any other circumstances connected therewith. Platelayers and all other men concerned must be strictly enjoined not to give any information to any one not concerned with the running of the Royal Train.

Note.—Station Masters and Heads of Departments must see that a copy of this Notice is handed to every person (and his receipt taken for it) who may be in any way engaged in connection with the working of the Train, including Drivers, Guards, Signalmen, Crossing Keepers, Flagmen, Fogmen, and all others concerned, who must read it carefully, and strictly act up to and obey the instructions contained therein. No want of knowledge of these instructions can be accepted as an excuse for any failure or neglect of duty.

Paddington, February 1st, 1901. **J. L. WILKINSON,** General Manager.

Receipt of this Notice to be acknowledged to Head of Department by First Train.

TIME TABLES
SATURDAY, FEBRUARY 2ND, 1901.

DOWN TRAIN.

Miles distant from Paddington. M.	C.	STATIONS AND SIGNAL BOXES.		Via Main Line Subway Junction to Slough. About P.M.
...		PADDINGTON ...	* dep.	1 0
	38¼	Westbourne Bridge	pass	—
	51¾	Lord Hill's Junction	,,	—
	71¾	Subway Junction	,,	1 6
1	12½	Green Lane	,,	—
1	30¼	Portobello	,,	—
1	66½	Ladbroke Bridge	,,	—
2	64	West London Jct. East ...	,,	1 8½
3	18¼	West London Jct. West ...	,,	—
3	53	Friars Junction	,,	—
4	13¾	Acton, East	,,	—
4	25¼	,, Middle	,,	1 10½
4	61	,, West	,,	—
5	48	Ealing	,,	1 12
6	47½	West Ealing	,,	1 14
7	24	Hanwell	,,	—
8	58½	Southall, East Junction ...	,,	—
9	2	,, East	,,	—
9	15½	,, Middle	,,	1 17
9	42	,, West	,,	—
10	70½	Hayes	,,	—
12	2¾	Dawley	,,	—
13	10	West Drayton East	,,	1 22½
13	33¼	,, ,, West	,,	—
15	3¼	Iver Box	,,	—
16	17	Langley	,,	—
17	25	Dolphin	,,	—
18	30½	Slough, East	,,	1 29
18	44	,, Middle ... ... * ...	,,	—
18	59½	,, Bath Road	,,	—
19	71	Eton...	,,	—
21	10	WINDSOR	arr.	1 35

Remarks.

PILOT SERVICE.—The Special Train from Paddington to Windsor, starting from No. 9 Line about 10 minutes in advance of the Royal Train will act as "Pilot" to that Train, and must occupy the same time in running between Stations as shewn for the Royal Train. The "Pilot" will be distinguished by Special Head Signals as specified in Clause 14 of the Special Instructions.

THE ROYAL TRAIN.—The Royal Train will start from No 8 Platform, and pass over the Empty Engine and Carriage Lines to Subway Junction, as shewn in Clause 1 of the Special Instructions.

The exact starting time of the Royal Train is somewhat uncertain, but at whatever time it starts it must occupy the same time in running between Stations as shewn in the Time Table.

* The time allowed at this point of the journey provides for the necessary slackening of speed in accordance with the special and standard instructions.

RETURN TRAIN.

Miles distant from Windsor. M.	C.	STATIONS AND SIGNAL BOXES.		Via Main Line from Slough. About P.M.
...		WINDSOR	dep.	3 30
1	19	Eton	pass	—
2	30½	Slough, Bath Road	,,	—
2	46	,, Middle .. * ...	,,	—
2	59½	,, East	,,	3 36
3	65	Dolphin	,,	—
4	73	Langley	,,	—
6	6¾	Iver Box	,,	—
7	56¾	West Drayton, West ...	,,	—
8	0	,, East	,,	3 42
9	7¼	Dawley	,,	—
10	19½	Hayes	,,	—
11	48	Southall, West	,,	—
11	74½	,, Middle	,,	3 46½
12	8	,, East	,,	—
12	31½	,, East Junc. ...	,,	—
13	66	Hanwell	,,	—
14	42½	West Ealing	,,	—
15	42	Ealing	,,	—
16	29	Acton, West	,,	—
16	64¾	,, Middle	,,	3 52½
16	76¼	,, East	,,	—
17	37	Friars Junction	,,	—
17	71¾	West London Junc., West ...	,,	—
18	26	,, ,, East ...	,,	3 55
19	23½	Ladbroke Bridge	,,	—
19	59¾	Portobello	,,	—
19	77½	Green Lane	,,	3 57
20	18¼	Subway Junction	,,	—
20	38¼	Lord Hill's Junction... ...	,,	—
20	51¾	Westbourne Bridge	,,	—
21	10	PADDINGTON	arr.	4 0

Remarks.

PILOT SERVICE.—Either a Pilot Engine, or one of the Return Specials acting as "Pilot" will start from Windsor for Paddington, about 10 minutes in advance of the Royal Train, and must occupy the same time in running between Stations as shewn for the Royal Train. The "Pilot" will be distinguished by Special Head Signals, as specified in Clause 14 of the Special Instructions.

ROYAL TRAIN.—The exact starting time of the return Royal Train is somewhat uncertain, but at whatever time it starts it must occupy the same time in running between Stations as shewn in the Time Table.

* The time allowed at this point of the journey provides for the necessary slackening of speed in accordance with the standard instructions.

The enclosed Form of Receipt for this notice must be forwarded to me in a foolscap envelope **BY NEXT TRAIN,** and the envelope marked outside, in red ink, "Receipt for Royal Train Notice," and the Guards must be instructed to personally deliver these letters immediately on arrival at Paddington.

An acknowledgment BY WIRE must also be sent, immediately the notice is received.

T. I. ALLEN,
Superintendent of the Line.

Paddington, *February 1st*, 1901.

proportions in Germany. From Victoria the late Queen's coffin was carried on a gun-carriage through London to Paddington station. Meanwhile the GWR royal saloon, which had conveyed the coffin from Gosport, was detached from the LB&SCR train and taken via the West London connecting line through Addison Road to be included in the GWR royal train. By the time the funeral cortège reached Paddington, it was waiting at platform 8 to take the remains of the late Queen on her final journey to Windsor. One of William Dean's newest type of 4-4-0 engines, No 3373 *Atbara*, had been renamed *Royal Sovereign* specially for the occasion and stood solemnly in Brunel's dignified station bearing a wreath of white immortelles surmounted with a purple draped crowned headlamp, a white disc over each buffer and one in front of the chimney, while on both sides where the large cast metal Royal Arms, also draped in purple. Preceding the funeral train were two special trains for guests, cabinet ministers and persons of ambassador and diplomatic rank. Departure was not until

*Queen Victoria's funeral procession
leaving the GWR station at Windsor
for St George's Chapel on Saturday,
2 February, 1901. (British Rail/OPC
Collection)*

*GWR admission tickets to
Paddington Station for the funerals
of Queen Victoria and King Eward
VII. (Courtesy: The Railway
Magazine)*

BLOCK **B**   No 117

GREAT WESTERN RAILWAY,
PADDINGTON STATION.

Funeral of Her Late Majesty the Queen,

SATURDAY, 2ND FEBRUARY, 1901.

ADMIT ONE PERSON TO STAND IN RESERVED ENCLOSURE.

ADMISSION ONLY BY STAIRCASE LEADING TO BRIDGE AT HOTEL END OF No I PLATFORM.

HOLDERS OF TICKETS SHOULD BE IN THEIR PLACES NOT LATER THAN 10 O'CLOCK.

Block **F** Hotel.
Standing only.
(SEE BACK.)   No. 234

NOT TRANSFERABLE.

GREAT WESTERN RAILWAY,
PADDINGTON STATION.

Funeral of His Late Majesty King Edward VII,

FRIDAY, 20th MAY, 1910.

ADMIT ONE PERSON TO COVERED ENCLOSURE AT END OF HOTEL.

Admission only through Hotel.

HOLDERS OF TICKETS SHOULD BE IN THEIR PLACES NOT LATER THAN **TEN** O'CLOCK.

Issued to

JAMES C. INGLIS, General Manager

1.40pm, instead of the planned time of 1.32pm. Immediately the GWR guard had locked the doors of the funeral saloon, King Edward was heard to say to the German Emperor, 'Come along, hurry up, we are 20 minutes late already,' whereupon the Royal party, apparently shocked by the King's command, uttered against the back-ground strains of bands playing the Funeral March, quickly entrained. The line from Paddington to Windsor was guarded throughout by men selected from all grades of the Great Western Railway, positioned on both sides at 25 yard intervals. The weather was bitterly cold and frosty and on arrival at Windsor the hawsers of the gun carriage, provided by the Royal Horse Artillery, were frozen up. The horses too had become restive and could not be used. In attendance was a naval Guard of Honour and realising the situation, a naval officer sought the help of the Stationmaster for some rope, but none was available. Then one of them thought of the idea of using communication cords, several lengths of which were quickly cut and removed from ordinary passenger coaches, twisted together and improvised into making the necessary drag ropes and away went the cortège towards St George's Chapel, pulled by the sailors, for the funeral service. The situation was saved.

The funeral was marked across the country. As an example an extract from a North Eastern Railway notice, issued on 31 January, 1901 read: 'At the hour of the funeral (2–3pm) all movement must cease for 10 minutes. Trains to be brought to a stand and remain motionless, and every servant on duty to stand quietly and reverently in his place for the period named.'

The locomotive used by the Great Western Railway for Queen Victoria's funeral train from Paddington to Windsor, No 3373 Atbara, specially renamed Royal Sovereign *for the journey on the afternoon of Saturday, 2 February, 1901. On the smokebox door, below a purple draped crowned headlamp, is a wreath of white immortelles. (Courtesy National Railway Museum)*

45

KING EDWARD VII
Reigned 1901–1910

The LBSCR Royal Train taking King Edward VII to Epsom Downs for the Derby Day race meeting in 1906 approaches Hackbridge hauled by aptly decorated B4 class 4-4-0 No 42 bearing the name, His Majesty. (From the E. T. Vyse/Wentworth S. Gray collection, courtesy J. H. Price)

A new reign, a new century and a king instead of a queen. King Edward VII could at last wield the power to bring about the changes which his Mother, Queen Victoria, had steadfastly refused even to consider. The railway companies quickly sensed this new era of optimism for it presented them with the opportunity of placing at the King's disposal all the very latest improvements in railway carriage design and construction. No more oil lamps for lighting, for although electricity had been installed in the LNWR and GWR Royal Trains, Queen Victoria declined to avail herself of it and continued to use in her personal saloons the trusted oil lamps. For the first time in railway history, royal trains could now go faster by Royal approval! It was to become a golden era in very many ways and for the railways in particular. While King Edward was keenly interested in and used the new motor cars which were appearing on the roads as rivals to horse power, he never abandoned his love of travelling stylishly, which at that time only a railway train could provide. Indeed your author's opinion is that as we advance towards the twenty first century, it is still only a well-appointed air-conditioned railway carriage which can give the traveller the tranquillity of moving over long distances from one place to another. Of easygoing disposition, which generated among people an atmosphere of ease and gaiety, King Edward nevertheless liked things to be done well and would not tolerate slipshod methods in his own life, but was prepared to accept reasonable argument for shortcomings which might occur.

The most pressing desire on the part of King Edward and more importantly the London & North Western Railway, was to replace the motley collection of antiquated saloons which formed the only royal train capable of providing facilities for long distance overnight journeys should the King and Queen wish to make such a journey with a large Suite in attendance. The LNWR royal train was no longer suitable; the North Western knew it and, if truth be known, King Edward hated it. To him its continued existence and use epitomised memories of the stern domination by Queen Victoria that overshadowed his earlier life. The Great Western's 1897 royal train was acceptable to the King with the exception of the outline appearance of the late Queen's saloon, referred to in the last chapter. However, fitted with electric lighting and some slight alterations to the furnishings, suggested by Queen Alexandra, these improvements went some way towards pleasing His Majesty; the train was thus used for several long journeys on other railways where overnight accommodation was not required. One such occasion was on 11 May, 1903, when four of the GW coaches and three East Coast Joint Stock teak-bodied vehicles were used for a special train taking the King on a day-time journey from King's Cross to Edinburgh hauled by one of the then latest type of Great Northern bogie

Another view of the LBSCR Royal Train in 1908, near Banstead, taking King Edward VII to Epsom Downs headed by I2 class 4-4-2T No 15. Note the whitewashed coal in the bunker! (From the E. T. Vyse/Wentworth S. Gray collection, courtesy J. H. Price)

singles, No 263, as far as Grantham.

But the King already had a relatively new royal train built specially for him when still Prince of Wales in 1897. The London, Brighton & South Coast Railway served a number of places where horse racing took place such as Epsom, Goodwood and Lewes. The King's passion for going to the races was well known, but as Prince of Wales, this form of relaxation was frowned upon by Queen Victoria. Imagine her reaction to the decision of the railway company which included in its title the name of Brighton, a town she refused ever to visit again, as related in chapter two, now actually encouraging her son by building a train for him to indulge his passion against her wishes! The 'Brighton royal train', as it became known, comprised five coaches, – two brake-firsts, two saloons for the Household and railway officers, all eight-wheeled bogie carriages, and the fifth carriage, for Edward, and occasionally used by Alexandra, 52ft long and carried on two six-wheeled bogies. The interior of this carriage was decorated in masculine style with the main saloon containing furniture upholstered in buttoned-in dark green morocco leather. The plate-glass windows were framed in green-grey brocade curtains. Electric lighting was provided throughout and the whole interior resembled a club-like atmosphere. When consulted during the design period, the Heir Apparent expressed his wish that he preferred not to be accessible to the entire number of persons on the train and for that reason, no vestibule gangway connection between the carriages was provided. Externally, the clerestoried carriages were finished in a colour of richly polished mahogany with gold lining. Royal use of this train ceased, as will be told in the next chapter, upon the formation of the Southern Railway.

Nevertheless the LNWR, as befitted the 'Premier' line, felt it needed to replace what undoubtedly was the principal royal train of Victorian years. In 1899, the LNWR had built at its Wolverton Carriage Works a 57ft long four-wheel bogie self-contained saloon for The Duke of Sutherland. He was a Scottish landowner of considerable wealth and owned a sizeable portion of the Highland Railway on which he exercised his right to travel in his own train in the form of the saloon just mentioned, hauled by a locomotive which he also owned and kept at Dunrobin Castle, between

It was the design of the LNWR built private saloon for the Duke of Sutherland in 1899 which influenced the ultimate outline of the LNWR royal saloons. The Duke exercised his right to run the saloon, No 57A, (bottom) now in the National Railway Museum, together with his own locomotive, shown below, an 0-4-4 tank engine named Dunrobin, on the former Highland Railway. On the expiry of the Duke's right to run the locomotive and saloon on what had now become a nationalised railway the engine and the companion four-wheel saloon were moved to New Romney, Kent, in 1950 and housed in a shed alongside the 15in gauge Romney, Hythe & Dymchurch Railway. In March 1965, Dunrobin and the four-wheel saloon were sold to a collector in Canada. (J. H. Aston, Lens of Sutton, G. M. Kichenside)

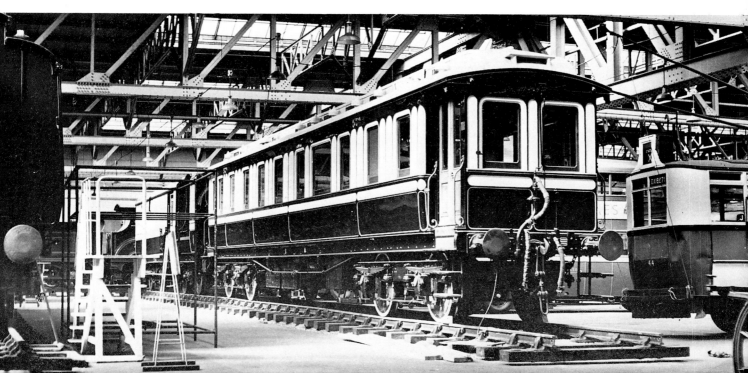

GREAT NORTHERN RAILWAY

Circular No 17,942a.

INSTRUCTIONS

To Station Masters, Inspectors, Engine Drivers, Guards, Platelayers. Signalmen, and others concerned.

JOURNEY OF

Her Majesty the QUEEN

AND SUITE

From WOLFERTON (G. E.) to BALLATER

ON

Friday, 14th August, 1903.

NOTE. These Instructions must be kept strictly private, and must only be communicated to those persons in the service of the Company who, in the discharge of their duty, require to know and act upon them; and those persons must not give any information whatever to anyone respecting the hours or other arrangements set forth in these Instructions.

On **FRIDAY, 14th AUGUST, 1903,**

A Special train conveying Her Majesty the Queen and suite will be run as under :—

		P.M
Wolferton (G. E.)	dep.	10 0
Peterboro' (G. E.)	arr.	11 10
" (G. N.)	dep.	11 15
" (G. N.)	pass	11 18
Grantham	"	11 52
Newark	"	12 7
Retford	"	12 27
Doncaster	"	12 45
Shaftholme Junction	"	12 50
Selby	"	1 5
York	arr.	1 22
	dep.	
Darlington	pass	
Newcastle	arr.	
	dep.	
Berwick	pass	
Edinburgh	arr.	
Aberdeen	pass	
Ballater	arr.	

G. E. Co.'s engine will work from Wolferton (G. E.) to Peterboro (G. E.), G. N. Co.'s engine from Peterboro' (G. E.) to York, and N. E. Co.'s engine from York.

1.—A Pilot engine will leave Peterboro' at 11.3 p.m., 15 minutes before the Royal train, and arrive at Doncaster at 12.31 a.m. The Driver must run at the speed indicated by the accompanying Time Table, in order that he may occupy the same time from station to station as the Royal train, and uniformly maintain the interval of 15 minutes throughout the journey.

No. 760 (8.45 p.m. from King's Cross) down express will act as the pilot train from Doncaster to York, and the down main line between Doncaster and York must not be fouled between the passing of No. 760 (8.45 p.m. from King's Cross) down express or the pilot engine if run, and the Royal train.

If No. 760 (8.45 p.m. from King's Cross) down express does not reach Doncaster in time to leave that station 20 minutes in advance of the Royal train, the pilot engine, instead of terminating at Doncaster, must go forward to York.

The Royal train will be formed as follows, and all vehicles fitted with the automatic vacuum and Westinghouse brakes :—

> ENGINE.
> Brake Third.
> Drawing Room Car.
> Sleeping Car.
> Sleeping Car.
> BRAKE VAN.

2.—The engine of the Royal train must carry special distinctive head lamps, shewing white lights as under :—

One on chimney.
One on smoke box.
Two on buffer beam (one at each end).

thus—

3.—The Royal train will be worked by two East Coast Conductors, and will be accompanied by the following :—

A representative from the Locomotive Department.

A representative from the Traffic Department.

A third Guard, provided with hand lamp and detonators, whose duty it will be to go back and protect the train if needful, in accordance with the regulations. This additional Guard must ride with the rear Conductor.

A fourth Guard, provided with hand lamp and detonators, whose duty it will be to go forward, if needful, in accordance with the regulations. This Guard must ride with the front Conductor of the train. The Conductors will go through to Edinburgh, but the G. N. Guards will work to York only. N. E. Co. will provide two guards from York to Edinburgh.

Brakes—The Royal train being fitted throughout with the **automatic vacuum and Westinghouse brakes.** The vacuum brake will be worked between Peterboro' (G. E.) and York in accordance with the instructions applicable to the working of that brake as contained in the Appendix to the Working Time Tables.

4.—The signal for starting the Royal train must be given to the Engine Driver by the front Conductor exhibiting a green hand-signal, but this signal must not be given until the front Conductor has received a similar signal from the rear Conductor, whose duty it will be to obtain authority to start the train from the Station Master or other person in charge of the Station, who, before giving such authority, must satisfy himself that all the passengers who have to proceed by the train have taken their seats, and that the examination of the train and testing of the brake has been completed. The head Conductor must see that the communication between the passenger and driver is in proper working order.

5.—The Royal train must be signalled in accordance with the general regulations for Absolute Block Telegraph working, a special distinctive code of **NINE** strokes on the bell (thus—3, pause, 3, pause,3) being given as the " IS LINE CLEAR " signal for the Royal train.

GNR notice of journey by Queen Alexandra from Wolferton to Ballater, 1903. (Author's collection)

Inverness and Helmsdale. The Duke used this saloon to entertain many crowned heads of Europe including, King Edward VII. This saloon had been designed by the North Western's Carriage Superintendent, C. A. Park and was to become, in general styling, the precedent for the new royal train. When consulted over matters of interior design and furnishings, King Edward's frequently quoted reply was 'make it as like a yacht as possible.' No one knows if these were his exact words, but his love of the sea was well known and, as we shall see, the King's wish was heeded. Under the direction of C. A. Park and the skill of the craftsmen at Wolverton Works, there appeared in December 1902 two saloon carriages for the use of King Edward and Queen Alexandra. An American railway paper reported the event: 'King Edward of England received from the London and North Western Railway Company a remarkable Christmas gift, which was nothing less than a luxuriously furnished special train with a new specially designed engine. The train is perfectly equipped, and will be used only for transporting the King and members of the Royal Family. The cost of the railroad company's present is given as 300,000 dollars.'

From this interesting report are two facts that were purely speculative. No locomotive was, of course, ever built for the sole purpose of hauling the royal train. Secondly, the cost quoted was a guess and no information of this kind was made public. It would seem that the first use of the new saloons, about two weeks before Christmas, gave some journalist an idea for a romantic story of the King getting what most boys, and some men, would have wished – a real train of their very own. The reality was and always has been in Britain, with the sole exception of The Duke of Sutherland's saloon, that while the railway companies provided carriages for the exclusive use of royalty, such carriages have always remained in railway ownership with royalty being charged the normal first class fare for each person travelling, including the Household, plus the appropriate rate per mile for the cost of running a special train.

The American report that the train was 'perfectly equipped' was true but gave no real idea as to the magnificence of what, at the time the report appeared, were just two carriages. Identical in external appearance, 65ft long and each carriage on two six-wheel bogies they were and have remained, in almost every way, the finest railway carriages ever to have been built for British use. The accompanying photographs can probably tell the reader more than all the eloquent words that have been spoken and written of these masterpieces of the coachbuilders' craft. In part, as a tribute to their original quality and the care they have always received, these two examples of the Edwardian period have survived and can be seen on display in the National Railway Museum at York. The Duke of Sutherland's saloon is also in the same museum; as a privately owned vehicle, it was purchased for the National Collection by the former British Railways Curator of Historical Relics in 1957 for £350, a real bargain, for it cost £5,000 to build!

In 1890, as Prince of Wales, King Edward VII travelled on what was then a very different kind of railway. On 4 November he formally opened London's first deep-level electric railway, the City & South London tube. The Prince, accompanied by the Duke of Clarence, was taken through the tunnel from Clapham Common to the Oval. It is now part of the London

Underground Ltd Northern Line. With continued interest in the development of the London Underground railway network, the Prince, in the year before he became King, declared open on 27 June 1900 the Central London Railway (now the Central Line) travelling from Bank station in the City of London, to Shepherd's Bush.

Having been born in 1841, King Edward grew up simultaneously with the railways. He was 18 years old when, for example, his Father, Prince Albert attended the inauguration of the Cornwall Railway, on 4 May, 1859, by travelling in a train across Brunel's single line bridge spanning the Tamar estuary at Saltash. Of mature age at 38 Edward would clearly remember the destruction during a severe storm of the first Tay Bridge in December 1879 which, six months earlier, Queen Victoria had crossed, by her own request, when returning south from Balmoral. By his own hand, on 4 March, 1890, he applied a silver key to the riveting apparatus ceremoniously securing the last rivet that marked the opening of the Forth Bridge in Scotland. Some years later, and with the responsibilities of kingship upon his shoulders, King Edward, accompanied by Queen

King Edward VII and Queen Alexandra leave the LNWR royal train at Newcastle-on-Tyne in July, 1906, to carry out engagements in the area. (Courtesy National Railway Museum)

The only photographic evidence which could be traced of King Edward VII opening the King Edward Railway Bridge, Newcastle-on-Tyne, was this less than perfect postcard. Against a background of the LNWR royal train, the King is pulling a small lever at the opening ceremony which took place on 10 July, 1906. (Courtesy Newcastle City Libraries)

49

Two days after the bridge opening ceremony some 800 yards up the river, King Edward and Queen Alexandra return south aboard the LNWR royal train which is seen here on the High Level Bridge, across the Tyne at Newcastle, hauled by gaily decorated North Eastern Railway 4-4-2 No 1792 on 12 July, 1906. (Courtesy National Railway Museum)

The Great North of Scotland Railway royal train in which King Edward VII and Queen Alexandra travelled from Ballater to Aberdeen to visit Marischal College on 27 September, 1906. The fourth vehicle from the locomotive is the carriage adapted by the GNSR for royal use, as referred to in the text, which has survived to be preserved. (GNSR Association)

Alexandra, travelled to Newcastle-upon-Tyne in the LNWR royal train where, on 10 July, 1906, he declared open the King Edward railway bridge.

King Edward VII was not as fond of Balmoral Castle as his Mother, Queen Victoria, for he only went there once a year. However, during his reign, the Great North of Scotland Railway made the prestigious gesture of collecting together six vehicles for a royal train. In 1902 the GNS upgraded a 48ft long bogie saloon, with a clerestory roof, to the status of royal use. During Edward's autumn visits to Balmoral the GNS royal train was used for several journeys between Ballater and Aberdeen, the most notable and colourful being on 27 September 1906, for on that day, with Queen Alexandra, the King travelled to Aberdeen to open the new building at Marischal College on the occasion of Aberdeen University's Quatercentenary celebrations.

Before the L&NWR had fully completed its semi-royal saloons to accompany those it had built at the end of 1902 for the King and Queen, the Great North of Scotland royal train made the only trip of its career south of the Border into England in September 1903. The Great North of Scotland Company claimed that the use of its train had been commanded by the King, but the reality of the situation was a written request from the General Manager of the Great Northern Railway requesting the use of the GNS royal train. During the first two weeks of September, it was used to take the King, first from King's Cross to Ollerton where the King stayed for a week at nearby Rufford Abbey, home of Lord and Lady Saville. During the King's stay there, the train was used on three occasions to take the King and his party, attending the races, from Ollerton to Doncaster and back. On 14 September the King finally left Ollerton in the GNS train, via the East Coast route, for Ballater.

50

The embarrassment of the Great Northern Railway in having to seek the assistance from the smallest of the Scottish companies was considerable, but, no doubt, more acceptable in financial terms than hiring for such a lengthy period the Great Western train or what at the time was available from the LNWR. The lack of suitable saloons for royal use on the East Coast route led to a joint decision being taken by the three railway companies, the Great Northern, North Eastern and North British, which had a shared ownership of the carriages used for ordinary service on Anglo-Scottish trains and collectively called East Coast Joint Stock (ECJS), to remedy the situation. As much as anything else the move was to impress the King and Queen that what the L&NWR could do with its sumptuous 12-wheelers from Wolverton, the combined forces of three railway companies could do as well or even better. However, the practical contribution for building an East Coast royal train was confined to the two English companies south of the Border, although on completion the North British had a share in ownership. The GNR and NER each built one saloon at their Doncaster and York works respectively, to the design and under the direction of Nigel Gresley, Carriage & Wagon Superintendent of the GNR, who later became Chief Mechanical Engineer of the LNER, and was knighted in 1935.

King Edward's reign lasted little more than nine years during which time he and Queen Alexandra travelled extensively on the railways of England, Ireland, Scotland and Wales on official tours, in addition to many journeys for private reasons. On a visit to Ireland, during the last week of July, 1903, Their Majesties travelled in four royal trains provided by the Great Northern of Ireland, the Midland Great Western, the Great Southern & Western, and Londonderry & Lough Swilly Railways respectively. Each railway built or adapted a vehicle for use as a royal saloon at the respective companies' works except for the one on the Londonderry & Lough Swilly 3ft narrow gauge line for a journey from Buncrana to Londonderry. The Londonderry & Lough Swilly Railway did not possess a carriage that could be transformed into a royal saloon and relatively short notice of the

In the Summer of 1903 King Edward VII and Queen Alexandra made a week long visit to Ireland and the first stage of their journey was in the LNWR royal train from Euston to Holyhead on 20 July; the royal train is seen speeding along past a group of wellwishers near Rhyl, drawn by two four-cylinder compounds Nos 1946 Diadem and 1970 Good Hope. Technically not a perfect photograph by any means, but does any other pictorial evidence still exist capturing the excitement of those gathered to watch the King and Queen speed past under Summer skies and the shade of parasols? (Clwyd County Record Office)

Great Northern Railway (Ireland) Q class 4-4-0 No 124 Cerberus, *built in 1902 by Neilson Reid, as prepared for working the royal train from Dublin (Amiens Street) to Newtownards on 25 July, 1903. (Watson Collection, courtesy C. P. Friel)*

intended journey by the King and Queen left the Company with insufficient time to get one built. An approach was made to the Belfast & Northern Counties Railway for assistance which promptly obliged by loaning one of the saloons used on the Ballymena & Larne section, suitably refurbished and decorated for the occasion.

King Edward's request for royal trains to go faster has already been noted, and the Great Western did just that when his reign was little more than a year old. On 7 March 1902 King Edward and Queen Alexandra visited Dartmouth to lay the foundation stone of the Royal Naval College, that eventually superseded the use of the training ships *Britannia* and *Hindustan*. Using five coaches from the GWR royal train, including Queen Victoria's saloon, they travelled non-stop from Paddington to Kingswear via Bristol, a distance of 228½ miles, in 4 hours 23 minutes – 20 minutes ahead of the scheduled time. From Kingswear the royal party crossed the River Dart to Dartmouth in the GWR steamer *Dolphin*. After carrying out other engagements in the area, the King and Queen returned to London on March 10 when the royal train left Millbay Docks station, Plymouth for a non-stop run to Paddington, which took 4 hours 44 minutes for the 246½ miles. The two journeys were the first non-stop runs ever made over these distances on the line and achieved only by the combined confidence of the Great Western and the encouragement of King Edward who took a personal interest in the whole affair. The locomotive, responsible for this outstanding achievement, was Atbara class 4-4-0 No 3374, *Baden Powell*, but renamed *Britannia* for the two royal workings.

On the return journey from Plymouth, by special request from His Majesty, the train slowed down while passing Swindon Works to give an

The cover of the timetable and map of the journey by King Edward VII and Queen Alexandra to Dartmouth and Plymouth in 1902. (Courtesy G. M. Kichenside)

GREAT WESTERN RAILWAY.

THE TRAIN BY WHICH

Their Majesties

THE KING AND QUEEN

AND SUITE

WILL TRAVEL ON

Friday, March 7th, 1902,

WILL RUN AT THE FOLLOWING TIMES:—

PADDINGTON STATION	- *depart* 10 30 a.m.	KINGSWEAR STATION	- - *depart* 4 10 p.m.
KINGSWEAR do.	- *arrive* 2 55 p.m.	PLYMOUTH (NORTH ROAD) STATION	- *arrive* 5 30 p.m.

J. L. WILKINSON,
General Manager.

opportunity for the men employed there, who were briefly allowed to leave their work, to stand at the lineside and watch the royal train go past. Equally, and in addition to acknowledging the acclaim of the railwaymen gathered to watch, King Edward, and it is believed Queen Alexandra too, wished to catch a glimpse of the Works which had produced the engine behind which they were riding and making railway history in non-stop running. A significant point, marking the new reign, was the absence of an advance pilot engine during any part of the outward and return journeys, although for several more years yet pilot engines for longer journeys were still run on other railways, particularly on journeys to and from Scotland. Indeed the Caledonian Railway often used its celebrated (and since preserved) 4-2-2 No 123 in just such a role.

Over a year later on July 14, 1903, another record was achieved by the Great Western Railway, when the Prince and Princess of Wales (later King George V and Queen Mary), travelling to Cornwall, were passengers on the fastest run ever made at that time from Paddington to Plymouth when their train was recorded to have reached a maximum speed of 87mph near Wootton Bassett, west of Swindon. The train was really the first part of the Cornishman express consisting of three coaches from the royal train and two ordinary passenger coaches, and hauled by one of the very latest City class 4-4-0s, No 3433 *City of Bath*. For this run there had seemingly been requests at the highest level for a 'good run' for evidence of this is clear in that two prominent railway enthusiasts of the day, Charles Rous-Marten and the Rev W. J. Scott, had been invited to travel in a reserved compartment on the train. Although the locomotive's performance on this run has been the subject of many written words and further detailed description is outside the context of this book, one fact, of general interest, should be mentioned. The royal special, leaving at 10.40am, had been scheduled to travel the 245¾ miles from Paddington to North Road station, Plymouth, in 4 hours 30 minutes. Running non-stop, with Driver Burden at the controls, who was also the driver on the two non-stop runs the previous year, he succeeded in accomplishing the journey in 3 hours 53

The GWR royal train, conveying King Edward VII and Queen Alexandra on 10 March, 1902, leaves Plymouth for Paddington, via Bristol, which was achieved in the record time of 4 hours 24 minutes hauled by Atbara class 4-4-0 No 3374 Baden Powell, but specially named Britannia *for working the royal train to and from Devon.* (Plymouth City Museum & Art Gallery)

Royal special on the Mumbles Railway when King Edward VII visited King's Dock, Swansea, on 20 July, 1904. (The National Library of Wales)

King Edward VII and Queen Alexandra leaving the special train to view Birmingham Corporation's waterworks scheme in the Elan Valley, near Rhayader on 21 July, 1904. (Scott Russell, courtesy C. C. Green)

Great Central Railway royal special and the crew at Chester (Northgate) await the Prince and Princess of Wales who were travelling to Stockport and back on 7 July, 1908. The decorated locomotive is GCR class 8E compound 4-4-2 No 259 King Edward VII. (Collection of E. B. Woodruffe Peacock)

minutes! It was a quite unprecedented royal train journey with not a hint of disapproval from the Royal passengers.

It was not always the large main line railways which could boast their pride of royal patronage as on at least two occasions during King Edward's reign two unusual railways claimed the prestige of royal trains. During a visit to Wales in 1904, the King and Queen Alexandra rode on the world's oldest passenger railway, the Swansea & Mumbles (closed in 1960), for on July 20, they made a brief journey after arriving in the royal yacht to cut the first sod of the new King's Dock, Swansea. They travelled in a lavishly decorated bogie trailer, formerly an experimental battery car, hauled by a dock-owned steam engine. Another royal visit to the Swansea & Mumbles took place some years later on 19 July 1920, when King George V and Queen Mary came ashore from the royal yacht at Mumbles Pier and travelled to Swansea for the opening of the Queen's Dock. But in 1904, King Edward and Queen Alexandra, on the day following their visit to Swansea, 21 July, made a nine-mile return journey on a temporary railway, built for Birmingham Corporation's waterworks scheme in the Elan Valley

Watched by railway employees from the nearby works, the GWR royal train takes the Gloucester line out of Swindon station, carrying King Edward VII to the Royal Agricultural Society Show at Gloucester on 23 June, 1909 hauled by locomotive No 4021 King Edward. (British Rail/OPC Collection)

54

The interior of Queen Victoria's GWR saloon as altered to a hearse carriage to convey the coffin of King Edward VII from Paddington to Windsor on 20 May, 1910. Note the four leather straps which were used to secure the coffin to the catafalque during the journey. (British Rail/OPC Collection)

The scene at Paddington Station on 20 May, 1910 before the departure on the left from platform 8 of the Funeral Train conveying King Edward VII's remains for burial at Windsor. (By gracious permission of Her Majesty The Queen)

55

near Rhayader. The King wished to view the Craig Goch dam and the rough mountain tracks were unsuitable for the motor car that had brought the royal party to the area, so the King and Queen sat in a special train of two four-wheel saloons and a brake van with a small saddle tank steam engine provided jointly by the Waterworks Department and the contractor.

King Edward VII died at Buckingham Palace on 6 May, 1910 following a short illness. After lying in State in Westminster Hall, during which time thousands of people filed past the catafalque to pay their final respects to a much loved and popular King, the coffin containing his remains were conveyed by train from Paddington to Windsor, for burial in St George's Chapel, on Friday, May 20. Somewhat ironically the Great Western used Queen Victoria's personal saloon as the hearse vehicle, also used to convey the late Queen's coffin in 1901. Although not too fond of riding in the saloon and the memories it created of his Mother's resistance to change, it really was the only practical choice available at short notice and there was not the remotest idea that some senior Great Western official who, not approving of King Edward's relaxed style of kingship, was seeking, so to speak, to get his own back, for 'dear' Edward was too popular a monarch for that. The interior of the main saloon area, where the late King's coffin rested on a catafalque almost a yard high, was carpeted in a delicate shade of lavender. All daylight was excluded by the insertion in the window-frames of heavy purple curtains, with subdued electric lighting for illumination. The walls were draped in purple and white. At each of the four corners where the coffin rested, were circular chairs upholstered in purple and white where, during the journey, military officers sat keeping

GWR Funeral Train of King Edward VII as used for the journey from Paddington to Windsor on 20 May, 1910 headed by Star class four-cylinder 4-6-0 No 4021 King Edward adorned for the sad occasion by purple draped royal arms. The hearse vehicle is fourth from the locomotive. To accommodate the large number of mourners it was necessary to supplement the royal train formation by using ordinary saloon carriages, one of which is the second vehicle from the front. (British Rail/OPC Collection)

guard over the body. The rest of the 11 coach train consisted of all the GWR 1897-built royal saloons, plus first class saloon coaches which were needed to accommodate the large number of mourners who included not only members of the British Royal Family, but many of the crowned heads of Europe and the extrovert German Emperor, Kaiser Wilhelm II, cousin to the acceding King George V. Never before, or since, have so many heads of state travelled in one train, whereby a serious error on the driver's part could dramatically have altered European and world history during that half hour journey. The engine chosen to take the funeral train down to Windsor was the appropriately named No 4021, *King Edward*, a 4-6-0 four-cylinder member of the Star class designed by G. J. Churchward and not quite one year old. It was driven by Driver W. Butcher and left Paddington a little after 12 noon. The journey proved to be the last time Queen Victoria's saloon was used, and stripped of its guise as a hearse, was banished to Swindon Works away from view where it lay until being broken up in 1912. However, an end section of the satin wood interior was saved and survives to this day in the National Railway Museum, York. The Edwardian era, on which it was said, the sun would never set, was over, but sunset did not come for a while yet.

The Funeral Train taking the remains of King Edward VII from Paddington to Windsor hurries through Acton, headed, appropriately, by GWR 4-6-0 No 4021, King Edward, on 20 May, 1910, watched by a gathering of onlookers on the opposite embankment. (By gracious permission of Her Majesty The Queen)

4

KING GEORGE V
Reigned 1910–1936

ROYAL TRAIN NOTICE

NOTE.—These instructions must be kept strictly Private, and must only be communicated to those persons in the service of the Company, who, in the discharge of their duty, require to know and act upon them; and those persons must not give any information whatever to anyone respecting the hours or other arrangements set forth in these Instructions.

Cambrian Railways.

No. 142.   TRAFFIC MANAGER'S OFFICE,
R/7/11   OSWESTRY, JULY 8TH, 1911.

TIME TABLE

FOR THE JOURNEY OF

THEIR MAJESTIES

The KING and QUEEN

AND SUITES,

FROM

Afon Wen to Machynlleth, Friday, July 14th,

Machynlleth to Aberystwyth and back, July 15th,

AND

Machynlleth to Whitchurch, July 17th, 1911

(En route to Edinburgh.)

MONDAY, JULY 17th, 1911.

	Pilot Engine.	Royal Train.	
	a.m.	a.m.	
Machynlleth .... dep	9 40	10 0	(Down Platform) The 9.5 a.m. ex Aberystwyth will be held at Dovey Junction until the Royal Train has left.
Cemmes Road .... ,,	9 48	10 8	
Llanbrynmair .... ,,	9 59	10 19	
Talerddig .... ,,	10 10	10 30 / 10 31	Banking Engine to be detached.
Carno .... ,,	11 18	10 24	
Pontdolgoch .... ,,	10 18	10 40	
Caersws .... ,,	10 26	10 46	Pass 8.15 a.m. ex Oswestry.
Moat Lane .... ,,	10 22	10 49	
Newtown .... ,,	10 29	10 49	
Abermule .... ,,	10 36	10 56	
Montgomery .... ,,	10 41	11 1	
Forden .... ,,	10 44	11 4	
Welshpool .... ,,	10 51	11 10	8.10 a.m. ex Aberystwyth to be shunted for Pilot engine and Royal Train to pass.
Buttington .... ,,	10 53	11 13	
Pool Quay .... ,,	10 56	11 15	
Four Crosses .... ,,	11 4	11 23	
Llanymynech .... ,,	11 11	11 31	Pass 10.0 a.m. ex Whitchurch.
Pant .... ,,	11 9	11 29	
Llynclys .... ,,	11 11	11 31	
Oswestry .... ,,	11 16	11 35	
Whittington .... ,,	11 22	11 42	
Ellesmere .... ,,	11 31	11 51	
Bettisfield .... ,,	11 39	11 58	
Fenn's Bank .... ,,	11 44	12 4	
Whitchurch .... arr	11 50	12 10	

The 11.20 a.m. Tanat Valley Train must not be despatched from Oswestry until the Royal Train has passed.

The Royal Train will consist of Brake Van, Two Saloons, Queen's Saloon, King's Saloon, Dining Car, Three Saloons, and Brake Van, all London and North Western Stock.
(Weight, 321 Tons.)

The Royal Train will be worked by two Engines in front, assisted by an Engine in the rear from Machynlleth to Talerddig.

To be worked by Guard J. Williams in charge, with Guard J. Phillips, Aberystwyth, as Assistant.

The following special speed restrictions must be carefully observed :—
Glandulas Bridge, between Machynlleth and Cemmes Road, 10 miles per hour.
Kilkewydd Bridge, between Forden and Welshpool, 5 miles per hour.

The Pilot Engine to run on to the Chester Branch at Whitchurch, over Siding points, and back into No. 2 Siding.

The Royal Train will draw up at Whitchurch Platform at the point indicated by the Station Master, viz., with the leading Van well clear of the Chester Bay points. The Engines will then be detached and run forward on to the Chester Branch clear of Siding points, and the L. & N.W. Engine, which will stand in the Chester Bay, will then be attached.

After the departure of the Royal Train, the Cambrian Engines will work back as per General Notice No. 141.

CHAS. L. CONACHER,
TRAFFIC MANAGER.

OSWESTRY, JULY 8th, 1911.

Please acknowledge receipt, by first train, on the accompanying form, addressed to the Traffic Manager.

The carefree years of King Edward VII's reign lingered after his death like an Indian Summer into the reign of his son, Prince George, Duke of York and Prince of Wales, when he succeeded to Kingship and became King George V in May 1910. Britain's railways were at their peak and most colourful, but already the era of the motor car was dawning. The shadows were imperceptibly lengthening on a tranquil British way of life to be abruptly transformed, within a few years, by a world conflict that would erupt and be known as the Great War. Meanwhile, the new King and his wife Queen Mary were keen to acquaint themselves with their people and to travel widely in doing so. King George liked trains, and although not strictly speaking a railway enthusiast, he enjoyed travelling by train and was always interested in the railways' progress, especially the introduction of new types of locomotives. The King and Queen inherited the use of five royal trains all of which as described in chapters nine and ten, were comparatively new. They were built and owned by the L&NWR, GWR, SE&CR, LB&SCR while the fifth train was built jointly by the GNR and NER for use on the East Coast route. Together with Queen Mary, King George made extensive use of the various royal trains available to them. The King and Queen, as described later, also paid visits to the two major railway works at Crewe and Swindon, something no previous reigning monarch had ever done. Several other railway companies, where the need to accommodate royal travellers did not occur frequently, owned one or two saloons, either specially built or adapted, and with the addition of standard dining and first class carriages a creditable royal special could be mustered.

Soon after the Coronation ceremony, in Westminster Abbey on 22 June 1911, King George V and Queen Mary made extensive use of the LNWR royal train. For the Investiture of their eldest son Prince Edward as Prince of Wales at Caernarvon Castle on Thursday, 13 July, the royal train was divided and ran in two parts from Holyhead, with an interval of 40 minutes between them, to Griffith's Crossing, just outside Caernarvon. This arrangement was necessary to coincide with the times of various processions and for the convenience of train working at such a small station. The investiture ceremony took place on the day after the King and Queen had arrived at Holyhead from Dublin upon the conclusion of a state visit to Ireland, their Majesties spending the night on board the yacht *Victoria and Albert*. Almost a week earlier the LNWR royal train had taken the King and Queen, accompanied by Prince Edward, northwards from Euston to Holyhead, drawn by two of the North Western's George the Fifth class superheated 4-4-0s Nos 5000, *Coronation* and 2663, *George the Fifth*, with non-superheated 4-4-0 No 2664, *Queen Mary*, running as

the advance pilot engine. On the day of the Investiture, the first train from Holyhead (Admiralty Pier) left at 12.15pm conveying the Prince of Wales, hauled by two London & North Western 4-6-2 tank engines, arriving at Griffith's Crossing at 1.10, with the King and Queen arriving in the second train at 1.50. After the ceremony the Royal party returned to Holyhead in the royal train, now remarshalled as one train. On July 14, after spending the night on the royal yacht, the King and Queen with the Prince rejoined the royal train and travelled to Bangor to visit Bangor College. During the next three days, the Royal party visited Portmadoc, Machynlleth and Aberystwyth with locomotives being provided by the Cambrian Railways in the shape of two 4-4-0s built in 1895, of William Aston design, Nos 81 and 83. The royal party's departure from Wales was over the Cambrian main line from Machynlleth via Welshpool and Oswestry to Whitchurch, where the LNWR again took over for the journey to Edinburgh via Crewe for a State visit to Scotland. The King was deeply appreciative of the admirable arrangements made by the LNWR in connection with the

The first major occasion, following King George V's Coronation in June, 1911, where rail transport had a significant involvement, took place the following month when his eldest son was invested as Prince of Wales in a ceremony at Caernarvon Castle on 13 July. Here the royal train conveying the Prince arrives at the temporary station at Griffith's Crossing, near Caernarvon, behind two LNWR 4-6-2 tank locomitives. (LNWR/courtesy H. R. Stones)

On 14 July, 1911 King George V and Queen Mary visited Bangor College and the royal train is seen drawing into Bangor station hauled by George V class 4-4-0 No 5000 Coronation. A refreshment room lady in white apron (extreme right) appears eager not to miss seeing Their Majesties step off the train! (LNWR/courtesy H. R. Stones)

(opposite) Cambrian Railways notice for 1911 journeys by King George V and Queen Mary and the last page showing timetable of the final journey over the Cambrian system by King George V and Queen Mary in 1911. (Ifor Higgon)

Investiture of the Prince of Wales and shortly afterwards the LNWR General Manager received a letter from the King's Private Secretary expressing appreciation to all who had been involved, and mentioning that all the various journeys, and the arrangements for them, had been carried out during a period of unusually hot weather. Presumably there was a similar appreciative letter sent to the Cambrian Railways which was entrusted with the LNWR royal train and whose two 4-4-0 engines, of simple graceful outline, in lined out black livery and the insignia of the Prince of Wales on their tenders, looked every bit as smart as the North Western's lined out blackberry black products from Crewe!

By contrast when the King and Queen returned to this country from India, in February 1912, after attending the Coronation Durbar at Delhi in December 1911, the weather was bitterly cold and snow lay on the ground as they stepped ashore from the P&O ship *Medina*, at Portsmouth. Greeted by the Prince of Wales, who accompanied the King in the inspection of a guard of honour on the South Railway Jetty, they travelled in the LBSCR royal train to Victoria, hauled by decorated 4-4-2 No 39. Apart from the annual outing, when the King visited Epsom Races, the LBSCR train was to see little further use. The lack of vestibuled connections between the coaches proved increasingly unpopular with the King and his household. Upon the formation of the Southern Railway in 1923 the LBSCR royal train became available for use by first class passengers travelling by a morning business service from Eastbourne to London Bridge, returning in the late afternoon. At first the coaches were in their original condition, but after a time the SR replaced the comfortable seating, once used by royal posteriors, with something much less opulent.

King George V, followed by the Prince of Wales, inspects a Royal Marine Guard of Honour on the South Railway Jetty, Portsmouth, before boarding the LBSCR royal train for Victoria upon the King and Queen's return from the Delhi Durbar in India, on 5 February, 1912. (By permission of Hampshire County Library)

In bitterly cold weather, on 5 February 1912 with snow on the ground, the LBSCR royal train steams gently away from Portsmouth's South Railway Jetty and past the ship, HMS Medina *in which the King and Queen had just arrived from India. Reassuringly, a man displays a green flag, indicating to the driver of the locomotive, Class H1 4-4-2 No 39, that the line ahead is clear. (By permission of Hampshire County Library)*

*(opposite)
A corner of Queen Victoria's 1869 saloon showing an occasional table, chair and the edge of a sofa. Note the matching deep blue furnishing materials, curtains, drapes and quilted partition. (Courtesy National Railway Museum)*

(left)
Decorated for working the royal train with crowns surmounting the headlamps and on the chimney lamp bracket is LB&SCR 0-4-2 Gladstone, now in the National Railway Museum, York. (Crown copyright, courtesy National Railway Museum)

(below left)
The LB&SCR royal train portrayed during the reign of King Edward VII on a journey from Victoria to Epsom near Banstead hauled by 4-4-2T No 15. (From an F. Moore postcard, Ian Allan/LPC)

(below right)
The recipient of this postcard would surely have been delighted to have received what the caption describes as 'A Royal Train Southern Railway (S. E. & C. Section)'. Printed after the formation of the Southern Railway, in 1923, it depicts the South Eastern & Chatham Railway's Edwardian royal train drawn by that company's Class E 4-4-0 No 516, with the 1903 King's saloon No 1R third from the locomotive. (Author's Collection)

A ROYAL TRAIN.

SOUTHERN RAILWAY
(S. E. & C. SECTION.)

The LBSCR royal train near Mitcham Junction en-route from Portsmouth to Victoria conveying King George V and Queen Mary on their return from India on 5 February, 1912, hauled by 4-4-2 No 39. The leading two vehicles, ahead of the royal coaches, are a six-wheel brake van and an eight-wheel bogie first carriage. (LCGB/Ken Nunn Collection)

(opposite)
By comparison with the heavily draped interior of Queen Victoria's 1869 LNWR saloon (see page 61) the 1902 saloons built by the LNWR for King Edward VII and Queen Alexandra were much simpler in style though gracefully elegant with white enamel decor on partitions and ceilings, decorated with gilded mouldings. This is the King's bedroom in the LNWR 1902 saloon as subsequently fitted out for use by King George V; note the thermometer on the wall above the bed. George V was known to be a stickler for the temperature of 60 degrees fahrenheit to be maintained as nearly as possible whenever he travelled. Note also the electric light fitting in the clerestory, the wall lights, and the fan; the loudspeaker was a later addition. (Crown copyright, courtesy National Railway Museum)

The Midland Railway royal train, soon after its formation in 1912, passing Hendon on 12 August in that year, hauled by Class 2 4-4-0 No 502, taking King George V and Queen Mary to visit the Duke of Devonshire at Bolton Abbey, Yorkshire. (LCGB/Ken Nunn Collection)

In 1913 the King and Queen made new ground in getting more deeply acquainted with their people by visiting and seeing for themselves how they lived and worked. In particular they were keen to visit industrial areas resulting in a new image of the King and Queen instead of the traditional picture of their Majesties riding in horse-drawn carriage processions with no real contact between ordinary folk and their monarch. To undertake many of these visits, train journeys played a major part. On one extended tour to Lancashire in the summer of 1913, the King and Queen were away from Buckingham Palace for a week, staying as guests of Lord Derby at his Knowsley home near Rainford. Their visit commenced on Monday, 7 July, by travelling in the LNWR royal train from Euston to Warrington, completing the remainder of the day's engagements by road. Each morning, except on Sunday during the week long tour the Royal party set off from Knowsley, sometimes as the Court Circular of the day recorded 'proceeded by Motor Car' or 'left Rainford Halt', where a special platform had been erected for their convenience. From the late afternoon of Tuesday 8 July, until the evening of Thursday 10 July, the King and Queen's rail journeys in the LNWR royal train were handled by the Lancashire & Yorkshire Railway over whose territory they travelled. The Court Circular recorded that they 'travelled by special train on the Lancashire & Yorkshire Railway', departing and arriving at various stations on the L&Y system including Blackpool (Talbot Road), Bolton, Rochdale and Colne. It was a great honour for the L&Y to be loaned the use of such a magnificent set of royal carriages from the neighbouring LNWR. The L&Y Chairman, Sir

(opposite)
The LNWR royal train hauled by L&Y 4-6-0s Nos 1514 (pilot) and 1525, passing Chorley en-route from Rainford Halt to Colne on 9 July, 1913 during the tour of Lancashire by King George V and Queen Mary. The double-heading was a precaution against possible water shortage in the tenders due to lack of water troughs on the particular route followed to Colne. (Courtesy National Railway Museum)

Exterior of Rochdale station decorated on 9 July, 1913, when King George V and Queen Mary rejoined the royal train there to return to Rainford Halt during their intensive road and rail tour of Lancashire towns. (Courtesy National Railway Museum)

A lone policeman keeps guard over the LNWR royal train standing at Blackpool (Talbot Road) with spick and span L&Y 4-6-0 No 1514 waiting to take King George V and Queen Mary to Rainford Halt in the late afternoon of Tuesday, 8 July, 1913 during a tour of Lancashire towns. Strangely, throughout the period the LNWR train ran on L&Y metals the royal headlamp code was not used, but the normal express code displayed as shown. (Courtesy National Railway Museum)

George Armytage and the better known General Manager, Mr (later Sir) John Aspinall, were both presented to their Majesties during their travels on L&Y metals.

Preparations for these journeys had been going on for several months and for the actual visit senior officials and their lesser beings were tuned to concert pitch, reassuring themselves that if anything might go wrong, it could only be by some mischievous act of divine providence and nothing at all to do with them! Three L&Y engines were specially prepared for the royal journeys. Two of George Hughes' four-cylinder 4-6-0s Nos 1514 and 1525, of Sandhills and Blackpool sheds respectively, were specially overhauled and given a highly decorative polished finish to their standard lined black livery. Both engines were fitted with eight-wheel tenders with greater water capacity than normal, since on one journey from Rainford Halt to Colne, there were no water troughs en route. The third engine, selected to act as advance pilot, was one of Aspinall's 4-4-0s, No 1229, designed when he was Chief Mechanical Engineer, before becoming the L&Y General Manager in 1899. This engine was temporarily attached to Bolton shed with Mr C. Burchall as its driver. The two drivers specially chosen for engines 1514 and 1525 were Messrs W. Wing of Sandhills, near Liverpool, and J. Southworth of Blackpool. All concerned were keen to demonstrate, not least to the London & North Western, that the Lancashire & Yorkshire Railway, whose bread and butter living was for the most part the carriage of raw materials and merchandise, textile mill workers and Blackpool trippers in a good natured but harsh industrial area, could also convey the King and Queen on home territory safely, respectfully and with the dignity the occasion demanded. In addition to the customary town hall receptions by robed and chain-clad local dignitaries, the King and Queen visited a diverse range of industrial premises which included textile mills and factories where soap and glass were made. There was also the apparent thrill for the Royal visitors of pressing electric switches to commemorate and unveil tablets. In Rochdale, famous as the home of the Co-operative Movement, music hall star Gracie Fields, and several well-

known Liberal politicians, the King unveiled a tablet in a new ward of the local Infirmary. In Southport, he opened a new park, while in Blackburn the King opened a new public hall and later unveiled, at Bolton, another tablet at the town's Nurses Home, all by pressing electric switches!

One of their earliest industrial tours was, so far as this book is concerned, to Crewe when the King and Queen visited the locomotive works there in April, 1913. It was also the first time that a British reigning monarch had ever visited a railway works, although there had been a previous royal visit to Crewe Works when the King's father, as Prince of Wales (later King Edward VII), did so in January 1866 to see the then new Bessemer steel plant, but saw little of actual locomotive construction. So on the afternoon of Monday 21 April the King and Queen arrived in the LNWR royal train at Crewe station at 2.30 where they were met by local town officials and introduced to the Chief Mechanical Engineer of the LNWR, C. J. Bowen Cooke. Appropriately the Mayor of Crewe that year, who also greeted their Majesties, was Mr F. Manning, a signalman who, between mayoral duties, worked in the nearby Basford Hall Junction box. The royal train, drawn by engines Nos 2663, *George the Fifth*, and 5000, *Coronation*, left the station for the locomotive works to arrive at a temporary platform near the new fitting shop at the western extremity of the works, where the King and Queen alighted. Nearby, for the royal party to inspect were several interesting locomotives and carriages. These included a full-size model of the *Rocket*, Queen Adelaide's coach, built by the London & Birmingham Railway in 1842 and, for comparison, one of the latest LNW bogie brake composite coaches. Leading this cavalcade of rolling stock, in pristine LNWR lined out blackberry black paint, was the recently-built four-cylinder 4-6-0 express engine No 2222 *Sir Gilbert Claughton*, which Mr Bowen Cooke, who had designed the engine, was proud to show King George. The Royal visitors, with the LNWR Chairman, Sir Gilbert Claughton who accompanied Queen Mary, then continued their tour of the

The Royal Daimler has just arrived at Talbot Road Station, Blackpool where Queen Mary, followed by King George V, is greeted by railway officials before joining the LNWR royal train to travel to Rainford Halt on the late afternoon of 8 July, 1913. The saloon is semi-royal eight-wheel vehicle No 5071 which later became LMS No 803 and used in Prime Minister Winston Churchill's train during World War II. (Courtesy National Railway Museum)

Visit of King George V and Queen Mary to Crewe Locomotive Works, on 21 April 1913. Here Mr C. J. Bowen-Cooke, Chief Mechanical Engineer, (on the right) escorts the King (Queen Mary follows behind) past the first of the Claughton class locomotives No 2222, Sir Gilbert Claughton. (Courtesy The Science Museum)

The LNWR royal train arriving at Crewe Locomotive Works on 21 April 1913, for the visit of King George V and Queen Mary, hauled by George class 4-4-0s Nos 2663 George the Fifth (pilot) and 5000, Coronation. (By kind permission of J. B. Radford)

various workshops and travelling around the works area in two specially cleaned and prepared four-wheel vehicles known as Crewe 'cabs' hauled by a Ramsbottom 0-4-0 saddle tank No 3001. The Crewe 'cabs' really looked like well wagons with rectangular open sided cabs placed amidships which gave a low ground loading facility. They rarely attracted publicity, normally being used for general transport of bulky items or as ambulances for the movement of workers injured in accidents to the Works Hospital. For the Royal visit two carriage type upholstered seats had been fitted in each 'cab'. The King and Queen left the works by car for Crewe Hall where they stayed as guests of the Marquis and Marchioness of Crewe. In the evening, the Superintendent of the Line, Mr Robert Turnbull, was summoned by Royal Command to Crewe Hall, where the King conferred on him the honour of knighthood. The following two days, Tuesday and Wednesday, were spent touring the Potteries, and on Thursday the King and Queen left Crewe station, at 1.00pm to return in the royal train to Euston.

Sir Robert Turnbull's knighthood was the second occasion within a year in which a senior railway officer had received such an honour, for on 22 July 1912, during the opening ceremony of the Great Central Railway's Immingham Dock, the King, without prior knowledge of the majority of people gathered to witness the occasion, borrowed his equerry's sword, and laid it upon the shoulder of Sam Fay, the General Manager, requesting 'Sir Sam' to rise. Earlier the King and Queen Mary had arrived at Immingham Dock in the East Coast royal train hauled by GCR compound 4-4-2 No 364 *Lady Henderson*, named after the wife of the Great Central Chairman.

The outbreak of the Great War in August 1914, lasting until November 1918, changed many things and the lives of very many people including the Royal Family. One of the greatest changes was the social upheaval where women left their traditional occupations of working in their own homes and as domestic servants in the large houses of the aristocracy to work in munitions factories, on the land, and even the railways as cleaners and porters and so replacing their menfolk who had left to join the armed

forces. Significantly this was to change for all time the future pattern of royal railway travel. In travelling around the country on morale-boosting visits to review troops, four munitions and other factories, and give words of encouragement to wounded men and others in hospitals, the King and Queen decided that it was no longer desirable or practicable to stay, as they had normally done, as guests of their friends in the area they were visiting, and so cause embarrassment to their hosts whose domestic staff was quite probably depleted. In their determination to make a contribution to the war effort, their Majesties enforced a strict discipline on themselves and their staff. One of the many practical things they did was to use the LNWR royal train as a 'palace on wheels', whenever it became necessary to spend one or more nights away from Buckingham Palace or one of their other homes at Windsor Castle or Sandringham. The King's Scottish home of Balmoral Castle was closed for the duration of the war and the Royal Family did not return there for a holiday until August 1919. The adoption of the LNWR train as a mobile home was obvious, for each of the two main saloons used by the King and Queen already had sleeping accommodation. Other coaches in the train also provided dining and sleeping facilities for the staff of the Royal Household and the small number of railway staff who always travel on the train. In 1915, silver plated baths, encased in mahogany, were installed in the dressing rooms of the two saloons used by the King and Queen. A bath was also fitted in a sleeping car for the Royal Household staff, which was further altered to form three separate flatlets.

So began the now long-established practice for the Royal Family to use trains as complete mobile homes, sometimes for several days at a time. Following the cessation of hostilities and the armistice in November 1918, there was general dissatisfaction among workers in many industries, including the railways, concerned with pay and conditions. This general unrest came to a head with a nine-day national railway strike in 1919, lasting from 26 September until 5 October. During the railway strike, the King and his Court, staying at Balmoral, wished to return to London. Although some trains did run during the strike with volunteer labour, King George, not wanting to cause embarrassment to railway management and staff alike, decided to make the southbound journey from Scotland by road, in a relay of motor cars with an overnight stop at Lowther, Lord Lonsdale's home. A happier post-war association of royalty with railways took place on 21 March 1922, when Queen Mary, deputising for King George V who was indisposed, formally opened the newly reconstructed Waterloo Station by cutting a ribbon across the steps leading to the Victory Arch.

Quite probably with a lingering happy memory of his visit to Crewe Locomotive Works in 1913, the King, accompanied by Queen Mary, was pleased to accept an invitation to visit the Great Western Railway Works at Swindon, on Monday, 28 April 1924, during the first official Royal visit to the town. Arriving shortly after 2.00pm at Swindon station from Windsor in the GWR royal train, in which luncheon had been served en-route, their Majesties first drove to the town's Cenotaph, then to the Town Hall and later to the Victoria Hospital before proceeding to the Works. On arrival at the Sheppard Street entrance of the Carriage Works, the King and Queen were received by Mr C. B. Collett, Chief Mechanical Engineer, who then presented his Assistant, Mr W. A. Stanier and the Manager of the Carriage

Standing on the adjacent track, a look-out man holds a green flag indicating to the driver on the sharply curved exit from No 1 platform at Paddington, that the line ahead is clear for Star class 4-6-0 No 4023 King George, to take the GWR royal train in which King George V is travelling to Shrewsbury to visit the Royal Agricultural Show there on 3 July 1914. (GWR Magazine)

Towards the end of the long overnight journey from Euston taking King George V and Queen Mary to Balmoral for their Summer holiday, the LNWR royal train draws away from Aberdeen behind two Great North of Scotland Railway Class F 4-4-0s Nos 50 Hatton Castle *and 47* Sir David Stewart *on the morning of 19 August, 1922. (LCGB/Ken Nunn Collection)*

& Wagon Works, Mr E. T. J. Evans. The Royal visitors were shown the various stages of carriage manufacture. Queen Mary was particularly interested in watching the women in the sewing and trimming shops and in inspecting the kitchen of one of the latest dining cars built and designed at Swindon. Escorted by the GWR Chairman, General Manager and senior officials, the Royal Party then crossed to the opposite side of the main line to visit the Locomotive Works which commenced by inspecting the Iron Foundry. Here their Majesties saw a foundryman casting a welcome message in white hot molten metal. The casting can still be seen on a wall of the same building, at the time of writing in use for the repair of diesel engine units, but in 1985 listed for closure.

Continuing their visit, the Royal visitors stood to watch a 4300 class 2-6-0 running at full speed on the stationary test plant. Using a shield to protect his eyes, the King watched acetylene welders at work. In the Erecting Shop the King and Queen looked upward as a completed locomotive was hoisted by an overhead travelling crane high above their heads. The most memorable and well known part of this visit came at the conclusion of the tour when the King and Queen came to inspect the newly completed Castle class 4-6-0 No 4082 *Windsor Castle*, in steam, coupled to the royal train, standing near the Weighbridge House, ready for the return journey to Windsor. A temporary platform had been placed alongside the engine to enable the Royal visitors to mount the footplate, meet the driver and fireman and inspect the controls. Moments before the King and Queen boarded, so to speak, the engine of *their* train, the works' hooter sounded and employees quickly gathered to watch what was to become a happy event in the history of Swindon Works. King George was visibly thrilled to be actually standing on an engine footplate and when asked, with the encouragement of the publicity-minded General Manager, Sir Felix Pole, if he might like to drive the engine, the King gleefully replied 'yes please'.

70

Driver Rowe and Fireman Cook then gave the King some elementary instruction about the engine's controls and invited him to take the regulator. With Queen Mary, smiling approvingly and thoroughly enjoying the prospect of a ride 'up front', the King correctly waited for the signal from the guard before moving off. When this was given, just before 5.00pm, His Majesty opened the regulator and the royal train gently steamed away from the siding, enthusiastically cheered by employees from the Works, for the short journey of approximately one mile to Swindon station. Here the King and Queen, with some reluctance, climbed down from the footplate to rejoin their saloon in the royal train for a ride 'on the cushions' back to Windsor.

Soon after the grouping of the railways in 1923 into four large companies, the LMS decided that one of its most prestigious ideas for publicity would be to repaint the former LNWR royal train in the new crimson lake livery then being applied to ordinary passenger coaches. Formal notice was given to Buckingham Palace, but King George V did not agree, much to the amazement of the LMS officials whose idea it was! The King, being rather fond of the ex-LNWR train, politely replied that if it was necessary for the train to be repainted, then it should be in the existing 'plum and spilt milk' colours, and so it remained in the two-tone LNWR livery until the outbreak of the Second World War, in 1939. Then the whole train was painted in standard LMS all-over crimson livery and less conspicuous from possible identification in air raids by enemy planes. This episode also illustrates that there was not always a cosy relationship between the King's Household and the railways.

Indeed, there was an occasion, just after the first world war, when relationships between the LNWR Superintendent of the Line and the King's lifelong friend and equerry, Sir Charles Cust, became strained concerning some detail in the planning of an overnight journey from London to Scotland. On such occasions a change of engines was normally made at Crewe and it was customary for Sir Charles Cust to climb down from the royal train in such a manner to imply that it was he who must supervise this operation regardless of the railway staff present! With the co-operation of the locomotive department at Crewe it was arranged that on this particular journey northwards the two Claughton class 4-6-0s to take over the royal train at Crewe should bear appropriate names that might remind the King's equerry of his difficult manner when consulted by the railway company's officials. On the night of the journey, when the royal train arrived at Crewe, Sir Charles, as expected, left the train to satisfy himself that the engine changing was carried out satisfactorily. There was an air of tension as the two engines from London were uncoupled and slipped away into the darkness leaving, for a very few minutes, the royal train engineless. Then out of the gloom came the two replacement engines backing slowly into the flickering gas-lit platform. The aristocratic looking figure of Sir Charles stepped a few paces forward to catch a glimpse of the train engine's name. Spotting that the brass plate of No 207 read *Sir Charles Cust* and, for a few seconds, thinking that the railway company had forgiven him, he bounded a few more paces to look at the name on the pilot engine No 2430, coupled ahead. In the dim station light he saw that the polished brass plate read *Vindictive*. At that precise moment the Line Superintendent, L. W.

A famous photograph seen by millions, but the title of this book renders its inclusion almost obligatory! It is the scene on the footplate of GWR Castle class 4-6-0 locomotive No 4082 Windsor Castle, of Their Majesties King George V and Queen Mary immediately after their visit to Swindon Railway Works on Monday, 28 April, 1924. Accompanied by senior Great Western officials, the King displays a boyish smile at the prospect of driving Windsor Castle, *while Queen Mary smiles cautious approval while clutching the cabside with a white cloth!* (BR/OPC Collection)

The LNER royal train near Ganwick, Hertfordshire, en-route from King's Cross to Wolferton, sometime towards the end of King George V's reign, hauled by Super-Claud Class D16 4-4-0 No 8783, one of two such locomotives specially selected for royal duty and painted green with white cab roof, copper-capped chimney, brass beading and allocated to Cambridge shed. (BR/OPC Collection)

Horne, who had encountered much of the friction with Buckingham Palace, came forward. For a moment there was silence. Sir Charles then broke into a smile and made a gesture that he understood the implied situation. The two gentlemen shook hands and the platform scene ended. However, the King's train still departed with the engines in order reading *Vindictive Sir Charles Cust*!

King George V and Queen Mary celebrated the Silver Jubilee of their reign in May 1935, but less than a year later the King died at his Sandringham home in Norfolk. For Christmas 1935 as was customary, the King and Queen had left London by train for the festive season and a break from routine at his favourite country home. It was to be the King's last journey by train as a reigning monarch. For sadly, after a short illness, King George V died peacefully late on the night of 20 January 1936. The sad, but proud duty, of conveying the late King's body from Sandringham to London, to lie in State and later for burial at Windsor, fell to the London & North Eastern and Great Western railways. The LNER first class saloon No 46 which had been used as a hearse coach for the late Queen Alexandra from Wolferton to King's Cross in November 1925, was also used on this occasion. On the day after the King died the coach was quickly found and sent to Stratford works, in east London for the necessary alterations to carry the King's coffin.

Within 24 hours, the interior fittings, chairs, tables and settees, had been removed and a centre partition taken out. The centre saloon part of the coach had been lined throughout with black and mauve velvet on the walls,

72

a black velvet carpet covered the floor, and a catafalque erected in the centre of the saloon. All windows were painted black to exclude light and black velvet curtains were hung at the doors and the end corridors. The catafalque area was lit by subdued lighting. The coach exterior was painted black with the raised mouldings of the bodywork finished in mauve; the roof was left white. The 10 coach train included an ordinary LNER brake first, a full length van, four first class saloons, East Coast royal saloons Nos 395 and 396 and the LNER royal train brake van No 109. On the morning of Thursday, 23 January the body of the late King was carried on a gun carriage, followed by his white pony, Jock, for the 2½ mile journey to Wolferton station. Here, against a background of music from Chopin's *Funeral March*, his coffin was placed aboard the funeral train for the first stage of the journey to King's Cross. At 12.5pm the train, hauled by ex-Great Eastern Railway class B12 4-6-0 No 8520, built in 1914, slowly and almost silently left for King's Lynn where reversal was necessary before continuing to London. At King's Lynn, as the train passed near to the playing fields of King Edward VII Grammar School, the boys and their masters stood caps in hand. The first engine which had brought the train from Wolferton, was taken off and replaced by Sandringham class 4-6-0 No 2847, *Helmingham Hall* for the journey onwards to King's Cross, via Ely, Cambridge and Hitchin, arriving there at 2.45pm.

In the following week on the morning of Tuesday, 28 January after the Lying-in-State for four days in Westminster Hall, the final journey from London to Windsor took place. The coffin, carried on a gun-carriage drawn by a naval gun crew based at Chatham, made a solemn procession from Westminster Hall, past silently mourning crowds, to Paddington station. The cortège entered the station by way of the approach slope leading down

The funeral train conveying King George V's body from Wolferton to King's Cross passes a silent crowd gathered at Welwyn station to pay their token of respect to a much loved King on 23 January, 1936. Sadly, just over a month later, the driver of the locomotive in this picture, Sandringham class 4-6-0 No 2847 Helmingham Hall, Frederick W. Collis, who had taken over the train at King's Lynn, died suddenly after reporting for duty at Cambridge where he was based. Aged 55, driver Collis had been an LNER employee for 38 years and had often driven the royal train when the late King was travelling between London and his Norfolk home at Sandringham. (The Illustrated London News)

G R

THIS ENGINE
Nº 4082 WINDSOR CASTLE WAS BUILT AT
SWINDON IN APRIL 1924
AND WAS DRIVEN FROM THE WORKS TO THE STATION BY
HIS MAJESTY KING GEORGE V
ACCOMPANIED BY QUEEN MARY
ON THE OCCASION OF THE VISIT OF THEIR MAJESTIES
TO THE GREAT WESTERN RAILWAY WORKS AT
SWINDON ON APRIL 28TH 1924.

WITH THEIR MAJESTIES ON THE FOOTPLATE WERE
VISCOUNT CHURCHILL.   CHAIRMAN.
SIR FELIX POLE.   GENERAL MANAGER.
Mʀ C.B.COLLETT.   CHIEF MECHANICAL ENGINEER.
    LOCOMOTIVE INSPECTOR.   C.H.FLEWELLEN.
    ENGINE DRIVER.   E.R.B.ROWE.
    FIREMAN.   A.W.COOK.

INSCRIPTION PLATES AFFIXED TO SIDES OF ENGINE ABOVE.

from Praed Street to the cab-rank space between platforms 8 and 9. A stand for guests of the GWR was built over the buffer stops of platform 9 and 10 which, together with the tall slender roof supporting columns and advertisement hoardings, were draped in purple and black. The funeral train left from platform 8, as did the funeral trains of Queen Victoria and the late King's father, King Edward VII. Before the funeral procession arrived four special trains conveying guests for the funeral service at Windsor, had already left the station. A fifth special guest train left from platform 9 after the cortege had arrived, but several minutes before the King's funeral train departed. Earlier in the morning, at 10.35, the funeral train had arrived at platform 8 from Old Oak Common carriage depot. It was the same train belonging to the LNER that had been used for the journey from Wolferton to King's Cross, except that the full length luggage van had been removed from the formation. With the exception of the funeral saloon, specially painted black, all the coaches were in LNER varnished teak livery. A few days earlier, the train had been transferred to the GWR to enable a rehearsal run to be made to Windsor and back with the *foreign* company's stock! The engine selected to haul the funeral train, was No 4082 *Windsor Castle* which, as we have seen, the King himself had driven from Swindon Works to Swindon station in 1924 with Queen Mary on the footplate. For the funeral journey the engine bore the Royal Coat of Arms, made at Swindon in 1897 for Queen Victoria's Diamond Jubilee, but now draped in purple.

To the strains of Handel's *Dead March in Saul*, rendered by the band of the Household Cavalry, the long procession entered the station. Some few minutes elapsed before the gun-carriage bearing the late King's body arrived and stopped on the sand strewn roadway between platforms 8 and 9, directly opposite a large red carpet that led to the open doors of the black hearse saloon. While the coffin was being borne into the train, the band of the Coldstream Guards played *Blest are the Departed*. The tired and sad figure of His Majesty King Edward VIII watched as his father's coffin disappeared into the darkness of the train. Then King Edward, with Queen Mary, the Royal Dukes and Duchesses and visiting Kings and Princes entered the funeral train to find their places in the various saloons. With the station in virtual silence, several minutes slipped by and then the funeral train was signalled and at 12.33pm slowly drew away from the platform to the piping lament of *The Flowers of the Forest*. During the 35 minute journey, thousands of people watched from the sides of the track and overbridges, as the train steamed through the winter countryside to the King's final place of rest at Windsor, reached at 1.9pm. Following the funeral service in St George's Chapel, King Edward VIII and members of the Royal Family and Guests returned to Paddington in the royal and guest trains during the afternoon.

King George V, respected and loved by many, was dead, but his name was not forgotten. In 1927, King George graciously gave permission for the GWR to name its new 4-6-0 express passenger locomotive *King George V*. This well known locomotive, No 6000, has survived to be preserved in working order. Ironically, *King George V* and the other 29 members of the King class were rarely used on royal trains, particularly during GWR ownership before nationalisation.

Great Western Railway publicity recording for posterity that its locomotive No 4082 Windsor Castle, which King George V had driven in 1924, drew the late King's funeral train from Paddington to Windsor in January, 1936. (BR/OPC Collection)

The funeral train of King George V, on 28 January 1936, from Paddington to Windsor steams by on an embankment beside a muddy farm track, near Iver, watched by a boy and two people perched on the roof of their Ford car for an elevated view of GWR locomotive No 4082 Windsor Castle and the blur of LNER varnished teak coaches moving nearer the late King's resting place. (F. R. Hebron/Rail Archive Stephenson)

5

KING EDWARD VIII
Reigned January – December 1936

With the death of King George V, a father figure of kingship, there was a feeling of loss among his subjects. His solidly traditional way of life, supported by Queen Mary, gave reassurance to those who found difficult times in the depression years of the early 1930s. Now his eldest son, the Prince of Wales, loved and admired by many, had succeeded to the throne. He was christened with seven names and it was the last of these, David, that was used by his family and close friends. However, he was proclaimed by the first of his Christian names to become King Edward VIII. His popularity as Prince of Wales was a bonus in helping him bear the responsibilities that, as King, he now had to face.

As Prince of Wales, King Edward VIII had travelled extensively on Britain's railways as well as on various railways abroad during extended tours. In March 1920, he left home shores in the battle-cruiser, HMS *Renown* for a world-wide tour of the Empire. Overland journeys were made in special trains and although royal train journeys abroad do not form part of the principal theme of this book, it is of significant interest to mention just one incident which might have caused serious injury or worse. In Western Australia, on 5 July, the royal train was approaching Bridgetown when the Prince's carriage and the one ahead of it became derailed and were dragged a short distance before they both turned over and slid down an embankment. Luckily, the Prince was unhurt and made an undignified exit by climbing through a window of the overturned carriage. The cause of the derailment was attributed to heavy rain which had weakened the track.

Some months later, on 11 October, when the Prince stepped ashore at Portsmouth there was the reassuring sight, at the South Railway Jetty, of his grandfather's LBSCR royal train waiting to take him to London's Victoria station and home to Buckingham Palace. The Class B4 4-4-0 No 46 *Prince of Wales* carried front-end decoration in the form of the Prince of Wales feathers as a welcome home tribute. But, as events in later years were to prove, the Prince felt these trimmings belonged to a bygone age and were of no practical value. As a very young man of 21, at his own insistence, he saw active military service as an officer in the Grenadier Guards in France during the 1914–18 war and the experiences subsequently changed his outlook with requests for simplicity which, when he became King, made a significant impact on the style of his railway journeys.

To commemorate his visit as Prince of Wales to Derby Locomotive Works on 22 February 1928 the London Midland & Scottish Railway named one of its newly completed Fowler 2-6-4 tank engines, No 2313, *The Prince*. One can speculate if the Prince, himself, really approved of the gesture. The hand painted white name on the tank sides disappeared during

76

Southern Railway royal special of Pullman Cars, conveying the Prince of Wales (soon to become King), leaves the South Railway Jetty, Portsmouth, for London, hauled by T9 class 4-4-0 No 729, after the naming ceremony of HMS Duke of Gloucester in 1935. (The News, Portsmouth)

the engine's first repaint and without any official announcement for the de-naming. However, during the visit, the Prince was accompanied by the LMS President, Sir Josiah Stamp, and it appears that an understanding with His Royal Highness was reached in which Sir Josiah agreed to make his personal saloon available, on reasonable notice being given, for any journey which the Prince might wish to undertake on the company's system. The saloon concerned was built in 1920 by the LNWR at Wolverton for its chairman's use. In later years, as LMS No 45000, it was included in the LMS royal train. Indeed, at the time of writing, this saloon, now renumbered 2911, is still in active service and frequently to be seen in the royal train as reformed in the Queen's Silver Jubilee Year of 1977. It is used as accommodation for senior railway staff.

While still Prince of Wales, and only a short time before becoming King, Prince Edward was the chief guest at a banquet held to celebrate the centenary of the formation of the Great Western Railway, in 1935. The banquet took place on the evening of 30 October at Grosvenor House, Park

An official photograph of LMS 2-6-4 tank engine No 2313 newly completed at the time of the visit by the Prince of Wales (later King Edward VIII) to Derby Locomotive Works on 22 February, 1928. Named The Prince *to commemorate his visit, the white painted name was not perpetuated and disappeared during the engine's first repaint.* (Courtesy National Railway Museum)

Lane, London. It might have been expected that such a grand occasion would have taken place at the company's own establishment, the Great Western Hotel adjoining Paddington station, for in 1854 it received a royal opening performed jointly by Prince Albert and the King of Portugal. But at the time of the centenary the hotel was in the midst of major alterations. Nevertheless, the Great Western received a royal accolade when the Prince referred during his speech to the company's many associations with royalty, in particular for serving Windsor, and honoured the railway with the title 'The Royal Road.' The publicity conscious Great Western exploited the honour to maximum effect. In 1936, it published another of its popular books in the 'For boys of all ages' series, written by W. G. Chapman, called *Loco's of "The Royal Road"*, and hundreds of copies were sold from station bookstalls all over the GWR system. One comparatively little known facet following the honour was that from then on, supervisory staff wore on their uniforms buttons with the company's initials surmounted by the Imperial Crown. Some years after nationalisation, several older members of staff were still to be seen proudly wearing these buttons, for the Great Western boast of tradition and service lasted for many years under the auspices of state ownership!

Sadly, by 1935, the GWR no longer had its own royal train. The clerestory saloons of 1897 had been quietly removed from the scene as it had now become the practice to borrow the two remaining complete royal trains from the LMS for long distance overnight journeys, and from the LNER for day-time use. However, the GWR could still muster a very presentable set of saloons as it did on 29 November 1934, when the Duke and Duchess of Kent, following their wedding, travelled from Paddington to Birmingham on their honeymoon journey in a special train which included several of the super-saloons, built for the Plymouth transatlantic boat trains and named after members of the Royal Family. On that occasion the Duke and Duchess rode in the coupé compartment of the saloon *King George*, hauled by King class 4-6-0 No 6000, *King George V*.

After King George's death, at the beginning of 1936, it seemed that the future of the elderly ex-LNWR royal train was in doubt. King Edward VIII had, by then, firmly established his travelling habits. For many of his day journeys he preferred to use an aeroplane or for shorter journeys a motor car. Where an overnight journey was necessary, he asked to use a first class sleeping car which could be reserved and attached to a normal service train. He is believed to have been embarrassed at the thought of one person, accompanied by only a very few members of his Household, having the exclusive use of a whole train. The King is known to have disliked the turgid formalities surrounding the use of the ex-LNWR train, which he never used during his short reign. Several of the carriages were loaned by the London Midland & Scottish Railway to the Southern Railway to form a special train conveying the Maharajah of Mysore from Portsmouth to Torquay on 9 August, 1936 and hauled by ex-LSWR T9 class 4-4-0 No 122. A rare photograph of the Maharajah's special passing Exeter Central station, taken by A. Earle Edwards, appeared in *The Railway Magazine* for December, 1936.

The King did not share his father's love of Sandringham House and rarely went to the Norfolk home, for, by then, he had his own country retreat of Fort Belvedere, near Windsor, with journeys to and from there by car. So the future of the East Coast royal train, belonging to the LNER, was also in doubt. However Queen Mary continued to use saloon No 395 as her personal carriage, of which she was fond, and frequently travelled in it to many parts of the country, often attached to ordinary service trains when the running of a complete royal special was not required.

The annual pilgrimage of the Court to Balmoral in 1936 was almost a non-event. It was not until 19 September that the King, together with his brother, the Duke of York, arrived at Ballater station about 9.00am. After

Photographs of King Edward VIII, as King, in a railway setting are rare and he is known to have disliked intensely the formality of the LMS ex-LNWR royal train. However, shortly before his abdication he made what became his much publicised two-day tour of South Wales in November, 1936, using a special train of GWR saloon and ordinary coaches. Here the King has just alighted from his train – not at a station platform with red carpet but as the King himself would have wished via a temporary stairway and across a siding in the goods yard of a small station 'somewhere on the King's itinerary.' (The Photo Source/ Fox)

only a short holiday, lasting barely two weeks, he returned to London on 1 October, this time accompanied by the Duke and Duchess of Kent. The special train of eight carriages, which almost certainly included at least one or two of the ex-LNWR semi-royal saloons, left Ballater during the early evening for Aberdeen where they were attached to the front of the ordinary 7.47pm train for the overnight journey to Euston. The shortness of the Balmoral visit was an ominous indication that King Edward VIII preferred to spend his leisure time with an established circle of friends nearer to London. At about this time, there were rumblings of gossip about a particular friend of the King, Mrs Wallis Simpson, frequently seen in the King's company. The subsequent development of this relationship into marriage, which made it necessary for the King to abdicate the Throne, is now well-known history.

King Edward VIII's abdication took place on 10 December 1936, but only a very short time before that unhappy event he made what became his famous two-day tour of the mining and industrial areas in the South Wales valleys, designated the South Wales Special Area. The tour took place on 18 and 19 November and is believed to have been the last time he travelled, as King, by train. The King's wish to visit this area was to see for himself the conditions of dereliction and poverty following the early 1930s depression years, in an attempt to boost the people's morale. His overnight journey from Paddington by special GWR train included the two 1930-built special saloons, Nos 9004/5, a sleeping car and ordinary first class coaches, and was made with the minimum of ceremony. After arrival at the tiny station of Llantwit Major on the first day the King travelled by car for much of the tour, but using the train as a travelling headquarters where he spent the night at Usk. The formal language of the Court Circular read: 'The Royal Train, at Usk, Monmouthshire, Nov. 18' indicating that the King had completed the first day of his tour and that in the evening he had dinner aboard the train in the company of a small number of local civic and other officials whom the King had invited. The second day of the King's tour commenced with the arrival of his special train at Cwmbran where he was handed by his Equerry a letter signed by Mr C. H. Thomas on behalf of local unemployed men expressing pleasure at the King's interest in their problem area. The conclusion of the tour, later in the day, came when the King rejoined his special train at Rhymney station and returned to Paddington, arriving there at 7.00pm.

In later years, as Duke of Windsor, he made periodic visits to England from his exile home in France accompanied by the lady for whom he renounced the throne to marry, by then Duchess of Windsor, but never accorded the title Her Royal Highness. A typical newspaper headline, 'Windsors arrive in London,' would be the first knowledge of their otherwise incognito arrival at Victoria station on the Night Ferry service from Dover. On one occasion, 3 December 1957, the Duke came alone to attend a memorial service in London for his former Equerry and friend, Major 'Fruity' Metcalfe. Having travelled on the Night Ferry a news photographer photographed him leaving a dingy side entrance of Victoria station acknowledging the salute by a London policeman – almost the only welcome for the return of an ex-king to the capital which had once acclaimed him.

KING GEORGE VI
Reigned 1936–1952

If King Edward VIII's reign had cast an uncertain cloud over the future of conventional royal trains, his abdication cast a potentially more dangerous cloud over the future of the British Monarchy. With little preparation for the role of king, Edward's brother, Albert, Duke of York, now succeeded him as King. Known to his family as 'Bertie' he chose the last of his four Christian names, George, and thus the reign of King George VI had begun. As Duke of York he had performed two significant railway engagements in addition to making numerous train journeys. The most noteable of these took place on 1 and 2 July 1925, when the Duke and his wife, the Duchess of York (formerly Lady Elizabeth Bowes-Lyon, now Queen Elizabeth the Queen Mother) attended the centenary celebrations of the opening of the Stockton & Darlington Railway. Just over a year later, on 6 August 1926, the Duke of York, as patron, was visiting a boys' camp near New Romney, in Kent, where construction of the 15in gauge Romney, Hythe and Dymchurch Light Railway was at an advanced stage.

Before his visit, the Duke had expressed a wish to visit the railway, whereupon efforts were made to complete a section of line in time for the royal visit. Although not officially opened for nearly another year, sufficient

King George VI and Queen Elizabeth bid farewell to workers at the Austin Motor Plant at Longbridge, near Birmingham as the former LNWR royal train is about to leave the works sidings for the short journey to Birmingham where Their Majesties arrived at New Street LMS Station on 1 March, 1939. (Birmingham Post & Mail)

progress had been made for the Duke to drive the first passenger train, carrying about a hundred of the Duke's guests and friends, for nearly two miles from the boys' camp to New Romney and back again. With Captain J. E. P. Howey, promoter of the line, the Duke sat in the cab of the miniature Pacific locomotive *Northern Chief*. Behind him, sitting cross-legged on the back of the engine's tender and thoroughly enjoying himself, was Nigel Gresley (later Sir), the LNER Chief Mechanical Engineer whose full-size A1 Pacifics served as the basis for the miniature engine's design.

It was truly a valuable piece of publicity for Captain Howey and his railway which could proudly boast that its first train was driven by royalty. Incidentally, your author's very first knowledge of this miniature railway was as a young boy being shown a photograph by his mother, who told him 'our King', as he had now become, 'is driving that little engine with the flags on'. A simple story but, perhaps, this book really originates from the telling of that story!

King Edward's abdication brought a reprieve for the ageing ex-LNWR royal train. King George VI and Queen Elizabeth and their two young Princesses, Elizabeth and Margaret, soon discovered the convenience and comfort that it gave to a family on extended tours or for going on their summer holidays to Balmoral. The King's Coronation ceremony took place on 12 May, 1937 – the date originally intended for Edward VIII's Coronation. The new King with his Queen and their Princesses caught the imagination of their people in helping them to cast aside the unhappy memories of the recent abdication crisis. The mood of the nation was truly captured when on 5 July, 1937 the LMS introduced its new streamlined train, called the Coronation Scot, between Euston and Glasgow. It was immortalised by Vivian Ellis whose music *Coronation Scot*, was the familiar signature tune to the BBC radio thriller 'Paul Temple'. The LNER at the same time introduced its new streamlined train, the Coronation, between King's Cross and Edinburgh.

After the Coronation and engagements in England, the King and Queen then made use of the ex-LNWR royal train to pay State visits to Scotland (5–11 July), Wales (13–15 July) and later in the month, for journeys between Euston and Stranraer to visit Northern Ireland (27–29 July).

During the latter part of Their Majesties' Welsh tour, several incidents embarrassed the LMS officials after taking over responsibility for the train from the GWR at Afon Wen. John M. Dunn tells in his book, *Reflections on a Railway Career*, of the time at Llandudno Junction shed a few days before the Royal visit, when a Great Western locomotive official from Swindon came to have a friendly look round and to see the Stanier 2-6-4 tanks, Nos 2492 and 2493 which were to take the royal train from Afon Wen to Caernarvon and on to Bangor. The man from Swindon was not impressed since cleaning had not even been started and Mr Dunn, who had been instructed by an autocratic superior to act as guide, felt embarrassed when told by his Great Western visitor that *their* engines, selected for the GW part of the journey, had been sent to Swindon Works for all the bright parts to be removed, cleaned and burnished, and then refitted. Eventually some attempt was made to prepare the LMS engines for the big day, but the results of such meagre effort was obvious to all, not least the high ranking LMS officials gathered at Afon Wen station. Two absolutely gleaming

GREAT WESTERN RAILWAY

Journeys of Their Majesties
THE KING AND QUEEN
and Suites

NOTICE OF
ROYAL TRAINS

Paddington to Portskewett
on
TUESDAY, JULY 13th

Portskewett to Newport
and
Swansea (H.S.) to Pencader
on
WEDNESDAY, JULY 14th

Pencader to Aberystwyth
and
Aberystwyth to Afon Wen
(en route to Caernarvon and Euston)
on
THURSDAY, JULY 15th, 1937.

THE L.M. & S. COMPANY'S ROYAL TRAIN WILL BE USED THROUGHOUT THE JOURNEYS SHEWN IN THIS NOTICE. THE TRAIN WILL CARRY TWO G.W. STANDARD PATTERN WHITE PAINTED TAIL LAMPS.
(IMPORTANT—See paragraph 2, page 25.)

WORKING OF EMPTY TRAIN—JULY 13th.
The empty (L.M. & S. Company's) Royal Train, which will be due Kensington (Addison Road) at 11.6 a.m., July 13th, to be worked forward to Old Oak Common at the following times :—
Kensington (Addison Road) .. .. dep. 11.15 a.m.
Old Oak Common .. .. arr. 11.30 a.m.
The Train to be stabled at Old Oak Common on No. 16 Shed Road and to leave Old Oak Common at 8.40 p.m. for Paddington.

WORKING OF ENGINE FOR ROYAL TRAIN.
The engine (No. 4082) to work the Royal Train from Paddington to Portskewett and Portskewett to Newport to leave Old Oak Common (East Box) at 9.35 p.m. for Paddington.

ALTERED PLATFORM ARRANGEMENTS AT PADDINGTON.
9.50 p.m. Paddington to Penzance to start from No. 2 Line. Empty coaches to leave Old Oak Common at 9.0 p.m. (following 9.25 p.m. train engine).
Coaches of 11.0 a.m. Paddington to be placed in No. 2 Line opposite the Royal Saloons immediately after departure of 9.50 p.m. train.

CLEARING STATION PLATFORMS AND APPROACHES—PADDINGTON.
Station Master to arrange for the platforms and approaches at Paddington to be cleared 30 minutes before the Train is due to leave.
Nos. 2 and 3 Platforms to be closed to the Public after departure of 10.0 p.m. train until the Royal Train has left No. 1 Line.

FORMATION *(FROM ENGINE)* **OF ROYAL TRAIN LEAVING PADDINGTON :—**
BRAKE FIRST .. .. No. 5154
SLEEPING SALOON .. .. .. „ 461
DINING SALOON.. .. .. .. „ 77
SALOON .. .. „ 806
SLEEPING SALOON .. .. .. „ 495
SALOON .. .. „ 807
DINING SALOON.. .. .. .. „ 76
H.M. THE KING'S SALOON
H.M. THE QUEEN'S SALOON
SALOON .. .. „ 805
BRAKE FIRST .. .. „ 5155

ADVICE OF DEPARTURE TIME OF TRAIN AND MEASUREMENTS FROM PADDINGTON.
Station Master, Paddington, to advise Station Master, Portskewett, and Mr. Trevor Roberts, Newport, the time the Train leaves. Station Master, Paddington, also to advise Station Master, and Mr. Trevor Roberts, Newport, the distance from the centre of the footplate of the engine (as indicated by a brass arrow) to the centre of the door of the King's Saloon, and from the centre of the door of the King's Saloon to the rear end of the Train.

2

GWR royal train notice for the 1937 Coronation Tour of Wales. (top) The cover and (below) train information and Paddington departure arrangements. (Courtesy Ifor Higgon)

GWR 4-4-0 Dukedogs, in all their Swindon splendour, arrived with the royal train from Aberystwyth, where the King and Queen had opened the new National Library of Wales.

More misfortune was to beset the LMS, for when the two shabby-looking 2-6-4 tanks sporting the four-lamp royal headcode drew into Caernarvon, the Bangor footplate crew, no doubt plagued by nerves, somehow failed to stop at the appointed position. As a result the entrance of the principal saloon, from which Their Majesties were to alight, was some distance past the red carpeted area of platform, and a group of perplexed looking dignitaries hurriedly repositioned themselves to greet the King and Queen before they even had time to set foot on the bare surface of the platform! Worse was to come at Bangor station where some choirs had assembled at the position on the platform where it was planned that the two royal saloons would halt while engines were changed. This time the royal train stopped short of the appointed place and the intended entertainment for Their Majesties while the 2-6-4 tanks were replaced by a Royal Scot 4-6-0 for the homeward journey to Euston, did not materialise. Subsequently, those responsible for the arrangements were summoned to Crewe to receive severe reprimands and, officially, the matter closed, but most definitely was not forgotten!

When the King and Queen, together with Princess Elizabeth and Princess Margaret, left Euston station on the evening of 3 August, 1937 to travel north for their summer holiday at Balmoral, the misfortunes of the LMS during the recent Welsh tour were forgotten in a few brief moments of glory. For standing proudly coupled to the ex-LNWR royal train, by now looking very much a period piece of Edwardian charm with carriages in the two tone 'plum and spilt milk' of the LNWR, was one of the newest and most modern looking LMSR steam locomotives ever to have been used for a royal train. No wonder the King and Queen, and their Princesses, showed so much interest in the locomotive which was to take them on the first stage of the journey to Carlisle. For they were standing beside an impressively sleek machine that had a vivid blue streamlined casing which hid the boiler from view. Horizontal silver lines stretched along the length of the casing converging into a 'V' at the sloping front end. It was, of course, the second of William Stanier's 4-6-2 Pacific locomotives built for working the Anglo-

GWR royal train notice extract for July 15, 1937 of the journey by King George VI and Queen Elizabeth, from Aberystwyth to Afon Wen. (Courtesy Ifor Higgon)

During the 1937 Coronation Tour of Wales Their Majesties King George VI and Queen Elizabeth visited Aberystwyth where they formally opened the new National Library of Wales. Later on the same day, 15 July, they travelled to Caernarvon and the royal train is seen heading north towards Barmouth hauled by two GWR Dukedog class 4-4-0s Nos 3210 and 3208 which took the train to Afon Wen, where two LMS 2-6-4 tank engines continued the journey. (Ifor Higgon)

The overnight royal train from Perth to Euston nearing journey's end passing Headstone Lane, in the London suburbs, on the sunny morning of 2 July, 1938 hauled by LMS streamlined 4-6-2 No 6226 Duchess of Norfolk, *painted crimson with gold lines.* (LCGB/Ken Nunn Collection)

The royal train entering Bangor station, at 6.10pm, on 15 July, 1937 hauled by LMS Stanier 2-6-4 tank locomotives Nos 2492 and 2493 which had not been cleaned to perfection (see text). (H. A. Coulter/ kind permission of E. N. Kneale)

The King and Queen returned to Euston from Bangor in July 1937 with the royal train hauled by Royal Scot class 4-6-0 No 6152 The King's Dragoon Guardsman. (H. A. Coulter/kind permission of E. N. Kneale)

Scottish Coronation Scot service, already mentioned. With a horizontal cast nameplate which read *Queen Elizabeth*, fixed half-way along the side of the streamlined casing to relieve the visual impact of the silver lines, No 6221 was sure to have featured in the young Princesses' notebooks of unusual and interesting things to be noted during this particular train journey. It is known that *the two Princesses*, as they were frequently referred to, enjoyed immensely the adventure of travelling overnight in a train built for their Great Grandfather, King Edward VII. There is the story of a railwayman at Euston, suddenly finding himself with a Royal Command, so to speak, when a few coppers were pressed into his hand by a boisterous Princess Margaret, encouraged by her elder sister Elizabeth, to buy their favourite comic paper from the station bookstall before the royal train departed. The passage of time has, quite possibly, clouded the precise facts of this happy story. However, its substance proves that, like ordinary children, the young Princesses were excited by the prospect of a long train journey, but felt the need for something to look at before tucking up in bed, when it had become too dark to catch glimpses of town and country as they sped northwards.

By the beginning of 1939, the very real possibility of a second major conflict in Europe, resulting from the rise to power of the German leader Adolf Hitler, was being taken seriously. The circumstances leading up to the declaration of what was to become the second world war on 3 September 1939 are so well documented that further mention of them is unnecessary. However, the circumstances of war meant, as had been the case in the 1914–18 conflict, that royal railway journeys were to play an important role in assisting the King and Queen in travelling extensively to visit troops, factories engaged in the production of armaments, and later to areas devastated by German bombing raids. For the very obvious reasons of security all wartime royal train journeys were made under conditions of the strictest secrecy. It transpired after the war ended in 1945, that footplate crews were often unaware of their precise destination, and such information was only given at the last possible moment to ensure that nobody, except those whose necessary duty it was, should possess any knowledge which perhaps only by chance and unknowingly might be passed to persons of subversive intentions. Consequently, your author has seen only one wartime photograph which showed the LMS royal train, 'somewhere on GWR territory in the Midlands', photographed from an overbridge with a box Brownie camera by an off-duty station porter. Though now retired from

84

railway service and many years later, he still displayed emotions of guilty conduct when, from his wallet, he produced the soiled and fading snapshot of the royal train near his station which, since he was not on duty, he should not have known about! As photographic film for private civilian use was virtually unobtainable, the otherwise loyal GWR servant may have desired to use up the last piece of pre-war film, saved from a day out with his family at the seaside in happier times. For posterity, he could have chosen no more worthy cause than to record the King's train passing *his* station.

The declaration of the second world war with the threat of air raid attack caused concern that the ex-LNWR royal train, by now the only set of carriages painted in the conspicuous carmine lake and white colour was an easy target to spot from the air. Therefore, the LMS authorities suggested to the King that the whole train should be repainted in the standard colour of crimson lake as applied to ordinary passenger vehicles and making the royal train far less conspicuous from the air. His Majesty readily agreed and thus, 16 years after the London & North Western Railway ceased to exist, the threat of possible enemy attack became the reason for the change of colour. So for the second time the ex-LNWR royal train served as the wartime travelling home for a king and queen. In 1941, the silver plated baths, in each of the King's and Queen's saloons and installed in 1915, were replaced by more conventional and practical ceramic baths. At the end of each bath a horizontal red line was painted several inches above the waste outlet. This was the King's wartime five inch depth of water indication which following Government recommendations to the entire country to save water and fuel he is believed to have instructed to be applied to royal baths as an economy measure. However, there was still considerable concern for the safety of the King and Queen whenever it was necessary for them to spend long periods in carriages with a wooden body structure. The crimson lake colour, while making them less conspicuous, was no insurance should an incendiary bomb explode in close proximity as, frequently, Their Majesties insisted on travelling through areas which were known to be targets for enemy air raid attacks.

The onset of war thus hastened a decision by the LMS to replace the two ex-LNWR saloons used by the King and Queen. There is evidence that as early as 1938 it was planned to build a complete new royal train to replace the Edwardian vehicles. Thus the commonly held view that new saloons

The King's visit to the 'shadow factory' on 10 March, 1938 might have been secret, but the photographer who took this picture of the royal train, in which the King had travelled overnight from Euston, was in luck when he saw the prestigious looking ex-LNWR carriages standing in King's Norton station, a few miles from Birmingham, with one of the original Midland Railway 4-4-0 compound locomotives, No 1014, performing the royal duty as the four lamp headcode indicates. (W. Leslie Good/courtesy W. A. Camwell)

In 1938 the threat of war was being taken seriously and this picture shows King George VI alighting from the ex-LNWR royal train at Cofton sidings, on the outskirts of Birmingham, to make a 'secret' visit to the adjacent Austin aircraft 'shadow factory' on 10 March, 1938. (Birmingham Post & Mail)

E.R.O. 53360/3.

THIS TIME TABLE MUST BE KEPT STRICTLY PRIVATE AND MUST NOT BE GIVEN TO THE PUBLIC.

London Midland and Scottish Railway Company.

NOTICE OF

ROYAL SPECIAL TRAINS

LONDON (Euston) to BARNT GREEN

Tuesday Night, February 28th
and
Wednesday Morning, March 1st

BARNT GREEN to COFTON GROUND FRAME

COFTON GROUND FRAME to BIRMINGHAM

BIRMINGHAM to LONDON (Euston)

Wednesday, March 1st
1939

3

The following trains to be altered as shown:—

11. 5 p.m. "Q" Euston to Edinburgh, if run, to follow the Royal Train.

10.55 p.m. Empty Coaches, Down Carriage Shed to Euston, to leave at 11.10 p.m.

10.40 p.m. Parcels, Euston to Manchester, to follow, from Willesden, the Royal Train, and the 11.5 p.m. "Q" Euston to Edinburgh, if run.

WEDNESDAY, MARCH 1st, 1939.
ROYAL SPECIAL TRAIN—BARNT GREEN TO COFTON GROUND FRAME.

Miles.			
			a.m.
—	**BARNT GREEN**	dep.	**9 20**
1½	**COFTON GROUND FRAME**	arr.	**9 27**

BARNT GREEN.—The Royal Train will be drawn from the Coal Yard Road direct to the Up Slow Line at Barnt Green.

COFTON GROUND FRAME.—The Royal Train will arrive Cofton Ground Frame on the Up Slow Line, and must come to a stand with the cab of the leading engine opposite a point at which a man will be stationed exhibiting a hand signal.

After the Royal Train has come to a stand, the vacuum must be entirely destroyed and the brake held on the train until the driver receives instructions from the station-master to re-create the vacuum.

WEDNESDAY, MARCH 1st, 1939.
ROYAL SPECIAL TRAIN—COFTON GROUND FRAME TO BIRMINGHAM (New Street).

Miles.			
			a.m.
—	**COFTON GROUND FRAME**	dep.	**9 57**
1½	Halesowen Junction	pass	10 2
3¾	King's Norton	„	10 8
8	Camp Hill	„	10 20
10½	Proof House Junction	„	10 28
11¼	**BIRMINGHAM (New Street)** ... ... (No. 3-2 Down Platform).	arr.	**10 30**

The Royal Train will travel on the Main, Passenger or Fast line (where more than one line exists), unless shown otherwise on the following page:—

(above) *LMS royal train notice cover for journeys between Euston and Barnt Green by King George VI and Queen Elizabeth in 1939.* (below) *Extract from the LMS 1939 notice showing journeys Barnt Green (overnight stabling point) to Cofton (for visit to Austin Motor Works) and Birmingham (New Street) station.* (Author's Collection)

were built solely as a direct result of the elderly ex-LNWR saloons being thought to give insufficient protection, is not entirely true. The conditions of a nation at war certainly prevented the building of a complete new train with the result that just three new vehicles were actually built; a saloon each for the King and Queen and a service car. All three vehicles were completed at the LMS Wolverton Works in 1941. For obvious security reasons, no publicity whatever was given to their construction, although by the cessation of hostilities in 1945 their existence had become well-known to any observer lucky enough to catch a glimpse of the LMS royal train. The new saloons and service car were easily recognisable by their simplicity of appearance with flush steel panelling to the bodies, and, marshalled among the train of ex-LNWR carriages, many searching questions were asked of these austere-looking vehicles. Their existence was not made public until late in 1946 when the LMS publicity department officially acknowledged what to keen eyed observers had become common acknowledge for several years. A series of official photographs were circulated to the press at large. These wartime built examples of royal carriages were to set the general pattern of royal rail journeys for not only King George VI's reign, but also that of his daughter, Princess Elizabeth, when she succeeded her father to become Queen in 1952. The King and Queen's saloons, Nos 798 and 799 respectively, together with the service car, No 31209, had no precedent regarding appearance.

After King George VI's death in 1952 their use was inherited by our present Queen Elizabeth II, using her mother's saloon, No 799, while the former King's saloon, No 798, was used by HRH Prince Philip.

An anecdote of coincidence, concerning one of the wartime journeys by the King and Queen, was told to your author while researching for this book. 'Vic' was Nottingham born and bred and from an early age was fascinated by the engines of the old Midland Railway which passed near his boyhood home, a particular favourite being the compound 4-4-0s and the later examples of this type built after the formation of the LMS. His passion of religiously noting down all he has seen, now makes his well thumbed notebooks a potential source in solving unexplained mysteries of railway operation. While serving in HM Forces and returning to duty from embarkation leave, 'Vic', dressed in full battle order and laden with kit bag, spotted something to cheer him up momentarily when his train from Nottingham drew into St Pancras station in the dusk of early evening. Across a platform he saw two glossy black Compound 4-4-0s, his favourite engines, coupled to the LMS royal train. From his battledress pocket came a notebook in which he jotted down first the date, 'Tuesday, March 2, 1943', followed by 'St Pancras 7.00pm Nos 1060 (pilot) + 1042'. He enquired where might the royal train be heading for that night and would have been surprised to have received an answer to such a question which, in wartime Britain, he knew there was not much point in asking. He was not too shocked when told by a policeman on duty, 'sorry soldier, can't tell you that – there's a war on'. He had to wait a very long time for the answer – indeed, 40 years, when in 1983 your author met 'Vic' and told him 'that night the royal train was taking the King and Queen to visit Nottingham the following day!'

Not even the Buckingham Palace Court Circular recorded where Their

NOTICE No. 30.

PRIVATE.—For use of the Company's Servants only.

GREAT WESTERN RAILWAY.

NOTICE OF
ROYAL TRAINS

OCTOBER 22nd and 23rd, 1941

SPECIAL NOTE:—It is of national importance that the Staff must not, under any circumstances, give information to ANYONE not affected by the arrangements shewn in this Notice.

☞ THIS NOTICE, WHICH WILL BE DISTRIBUTED BY THE DIVISIONAL SUPERINTENDENTS CONCERNED TO ALL STAFF AFFECTED IN THEIR RESPECTIVE DIVISIONS, MUST BE ACKNOWLEDGED TO THE DIVISIONAL SUPERINTENDENTS IMMEDIATELY ON RECEIPT BY TELEGRAM AS FOLLOWS:—" ARNO. THIRTY."

TIME TABLE OF ROYAL TRAIN FROM MONMOUTH TO KINGHAM.
WEDNESDAY, OCTOBER 22nd.

FORMATION OF ROYAL TRAIN LEAVING MONMOUTH (TROY):—

ENGINES (Nos. 5516 and 5532)
BRAKE FIRST ... No. 5154
DINING SALOON ... 77
SALOON ... 806
SLEEPING SALOON ... 477   336 tons.
SALOON ... 807
DINING SALOON ... 76
H.M. THE KING'S SALOON ... 800
BRAKE FIRST ... 5155

The formation of the Royal Train arriving Kingham will be the reverse of that shewn above, and it will be worked from Ross-on-Wye by Engines Nos. 6917 and 6921.

5

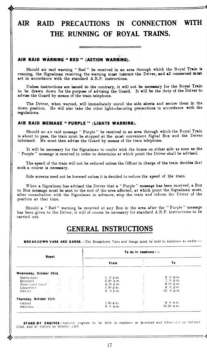

AIR RAID PRECAUTIONS IN CONNECTION WITH THE RUNNING OF ROYAL TRAINS.

AIR RAID WARNING "RED" (ACTION WARNING).

GENERAL INSTRUCTIONS

17

Majesties were going, except for a brief mention, a day or two later, which merely stated that the King and Queen had carried out a tour in the Midlands. That tour, to the provinces, was typical of many. According to *The Nottingham Journal* for Thursday, 4 March 1943, the day after the Royal visit, few local people knew the King and Queen were to visit their city, it being 'a well-guarded secret for security reasons'. The local paper gave much coverage of Their Majesties' visit to Nottingham and district without naming the various industrial and military establishments they actually visited. However, the paper did report that the King and Queen 'on the platform of the LMS station, Nottingham, last night, prior to entering the royal train, chatted to Civil Defence and first aid workers who told the Royal visitors of their experiences during the Nottingham blitz on the night of May 8–9, 1941'. Perhaps the King, on listening to the blitz stories, recalled an earlier blitz when he and the Queen were having dinner on the royal train and an air raid warning sounded. The story, as told by one of the train's former chefs, George T. Holmes, is that it was shunted into a tunnel. Soon after the 'all clear' sounded the train was shunted out into the open

GWR royal train notice of 1941 war-time journey by King George VI (left) The cover; (centre) extract from the GWR 1941 notice showing journey Monmouth to Kingham and train formation; (right) extract from the GWR 1941 notice showing Air Raid precautions. (Author's collection)

The King, Queen and two Princesses return home from their South African tour aboard an SR Pullman Car special seen here near Woking, en-route from Portsmouth Harbour to Waterloo behind Maunsell 4-6-0 No 850 Lord Nelson, on 12 May 1947. (LCGB/Ken Nunn Collection)

again. Moments later, the wailing sirens meant that the train was shunted back into the refuge of the tunnel. A short while later the 'all clear' sounded again and out steamed the train, the King and Queen still seated at table. Soon after, for a third time, the sirens sounded again. King George, by now had lost his patience. He summoned the officer in charge of the train and told him 'either we stay in the tunnel or we stay out'. 'And out we stayed', recalled Mr Holmes.

Peace eventually came on 8 May, 1945, when Victory in Europe was declared and followed, in August, by the ending of the war in Japan. But pre-war Britain was gone forever. There emerged what was termed a period of austerity that was to last for virtually the remainder of King George VI's reign. With serious shortages of fuel and raw materials the railways, like many industries, suffered in their attempt to recover from the ravages inflicted by war. It was at this time that the GWR, amidst its other post-war problems set about creating, once again, its own royal train. Four special saloons Nos 9001/2, built in 1940, and Nos 9006/7, built in 1945, intended for VIP use, together with the addition of ordinary brake composite coaches, were assembled to provide a train intended mainly for day use, although saloons 9006/7 did have sleeping accommodation. Also at this time all four of the main line companies faced uncertainty as a result of the overwhelming Labour victory in the July 1945 General Election. This resulted in a policy of nationalisation for strategic industries, and for the railway companies, the threat manifested into reality when the King signified his approval in giving the Royal Assent to the Government's Transport Bill to become the Transport Act of 1947. Thus on 1 January, 1948, the private railway companies under government control since the outbreak of war, now passed into state ownership under a newly formed British Transport Commission. The Royal Family's views on the railways' change of ownership are unknown. If they did have any doubts that state ownership might eclipse their use of royal trains, time has proved any such doubts were groundless. Indeed, it was not until 1954 – two years after the King's death – that the LMS royal train lost its private ownership colour of crimson lake to be repainted in the now familiar livery of 'royal claret'.

The colourful highlights of royal train journeys in the immediate post-war years occurred on the Southern Railway in 1947. In January and May, in connection with Their Majesties' departure and return for their tour of South Africa, two Royal Pullman Specials were run between Waterloo and Portsmouth Harbour. Towards the end of the year, in November, the wedding of the King's elder daughter took place when Princess Elizabeth and the Duke of Edinburgh, after their marriage, left Waterloo in a special train which included two Pullman Cars to begin their honeymoon in Hampshire. All three trains were hauled by Lord Nelson class locomotives decorated on the smokebox door with large circular coloured plaques. The post-war years saw the King and Queen resuming their more traditional provincial tours using, for the most part, the LMS royal train for long distance and overnight journeys, while for shorter journeys the LNER and newly formed GWR trains were used. From time to time members of the Royal Family other than the King and Queen made use of individual saloons of the LNER and GWR trains. On the Southern Railway and after nationalisation the Southern Region Pullman Cars were used, for unlike the

The post-war LNER royal train approaches Brookmans Park on the afternoon of 3 June, 1947 en-route from Cambridge to King's Cross, hauled by the locomotive then used for royal duty, Class B2 4-6-0 No 1671 Royal Sovereign. The Buckingham Palace Court Circular for 3 June recorded that the King and Queen had visited Cambridge for the celebration of the Fourth Centenary of Trinity College and where the King had once studied. The visit appears to have been private and the royal four-lamp headcode is not displayed – the train carrying the normal express passenger two-lamp display. (LCGB/Ken Nunn Collection)

war years peacetime travel on the Southern almost always involved trips of relatively short duration and rarely necessitated the need for overnight accommodation. This general pattern continued throughout the remaining years of the King's reign and lasted well into that of Queen Elizabeth II.

As the memories of war gradually faded to become part of history, the strain of the war years and the effect they had on the King's health became apparent. Reluctantly, His Majesty accepted the advice of his doctors involving a less strenuous programme of engagements, but to those who saw him, it was very clear to observe that the King was a sick man. He is known to have greatly appreciated the comfort of his 1941-built personal saloon, No 798, on what were now less frequent railway journeys. However, because of his failing health, it sometimes became necessary on overnight and long distance journeys for the King's equerry to request that speed should be reduced to minimise disturbing the King while he slept. In September, 1951, the King underwent a serious operation, and when in the middle of November the same year Princess Elizabeth and the Duke of Edinburgh arrived at Euston station from Liverpool on their return from Canada, the King had not recovered sufficiently to accompany the Queen, Princess Margaret and his excited grandson, Prince Charles, who were at the station to meet them. The boyish thrill of the young Prince Charles, on seeing the polished green engine, rebuilt Royal Scot No 46126 *Royal Army Service Corps*, steam into the platform with the ex-LMS royal train bringing his mother and father home, amused millions for the moment was captured on newsreel cameras and the sequence screened on television and in cinemas. Surely it brought joy to the King, himself, when it was shown to him.

That happy occasion at Euston followed by the public belief that the King's health had improved was to be short-lived. On the morning of 6 February, 1952, it was announced from Sandringham that the King had

(opposite) The Southern Railway notice for the honeymoon special for Princess Elizabeth and Lt Philip Mountbatten in 1947. (Courtesy Mike Christensen)

89

(this page: above) *Prince Charles looks a little bewildered at Euston Station when, with his grandmother, Queen Elizabeth, and aunt, Princess Margaret, he was there to welcome home his parents, Princess Elizabeth and the Duke of Edinburgh, from their Canadian tour on 17 November, 1951. A detachment of Royal Canadian Mounted Police form a Guard of Honour beside the ex-LMS royal train in which Princess Elizabeth and the Duke of Edinburgh had travelled from Liverpool.* (Courtesy National Railway Museum)

(facing page)

(top left) *The 12.45pm Victoria to Tattenham Corner royal Pullman Special on 7 June, 1947, taking the King and Queen to Epsom Races for the Derby, passing East Croydon hauled by new SR Bulleid-designed 4-6-2 No 21C157, subsequently named* Biggin Hill. (LCGB/Ken Nunn Collection)

(top right) *An important occasion at Brackley on the now closed Banbury – Buckingham line occurred at this small wayside station on 13 May 1950 when the Stationmaster, Mr Whitney, welcomed the King, Queen and Princess Margaret who arrived there while on their way to Silverstone and the first Grand Prix de l' Europe. The King is seen leaving one of the 1941 LMS saloons, whose portable steps fail to reach the very low platform, stepping onto a hastily acquired empty ammunition box!* (By kind permission of Mrs Whitney)

(centre left) *Exterior of Leamington Spa Station, reconstructed by the GWR in 1939, and shown here as decorated for the arrival by car from Warwick of the King and Queen on 5 April, 1951. At that time a small team from the Western Region's Publicity Unit would always lavishly decorate stations used for formal royal visits.* (British Rail/OPC Collection)

(bottom) *The Midlands visit of the King and Queen on 5 April, 1951 culminated in a drive from Warwick Castle, where the Royal party had taken tea, to Leamington Spa to board the royal train for Windsor. Here the King and Queen, accompanied by the Mayor and Mayoress of Royal Leamington Spa, Councillor and Mrs B. A. Fetherston-Dilke, have just arrived at the top of the stairway and are walking towards their waiting train at platform 3. Note the decorations and so called 'modern' gas lamp above the King.* (British Rail/OPC Collection)

Wolferton Station, on the Sandringham Estate, closed in 1969, but last used by Royalty in 1966 when King's Lynn became the railhead for royal journeys to and from Sandringham. Here on a crisp Winter morning in January, 1951, the ex-LNER royal train waits to take the King, Queen and Princess Margaret back to London after their Christmas holiday. The engine is ex-Great Eastern 4-4-0 No 62614. (Alan Howard/Eastern Counties Newspapers)

died, peacefully, in his sleep during the early hours of the morning. Far away in Kenya on tour with the Duke of Edinburgh, was Princess Elizabeth and it was there she received the sad news which also meant she was no longer a Princess but Queen Elizabeth II. For British Railways there was now the sad, but proud task of conveying the late King's remains from Norfolk to London, for Lying in State and later to Windsor for burial. The late King's father, King George V, had also died at Sandringham in 1936 and so the Eastern and Western Regions as successors under nationalisation to the LNER and GWR respectively, now had to put into effect what was, in reality, a re-run of the arrangements carried out in 1936. The funeral train was composed of ex-LNER coaches, still all in varnished teak livery, and including the two principal 12-wheel East Coast royal saloons. First class saloon, No 46, used as a hearse vehicle for the funerals of Queen Alexandra in 1925, and King George V in 1936, was again used to perform the same melancholy duty; as on the two previous occasions, it was

stripped of internal fixtures and adapted to carry the late King's coffin. Externally the body sides were painted black, with hatchments of the King's Coat of Arms mounted centrally on each side, while the roof was finished in white. The locomotives used for the journey on the Eastern Region from Wolferton to King's Cross on Monday, 11 February, were Class B2 4-6-0 No 61617 *Ford Castle* for the 6½ miles from Wolferton to King's Lynn, and after reversal there the first of the new Standard Class 7 4-6-2s, No 70000 *Britannia* with its cab roof painted white, took over for the remainder of the journey via Cambridge and Hitchin to King's Cross arriving punctually, at 2.45pm. The King's body was then taken in procession to Westminster Hall for Lying in State.

For the journey from Paddington to Windsor on Friday 15 February the ex-LNER train had been transferred to the Western Region. Unfortunately for the pride of the old Great Western Company, Castle class engine No 4082 *Windsor Castle*, the so called 'royal' engine used for King George V's funeral in 1936, had been sent to Swindon Works for scheduled repairs and overhaul only two days before King George VI had died. As the necessary work could not be completed in time for the journey to Windsor, it was decided to exchange name- and numberplates, together with the cabside plaques commemorating the footplate ride made by King George V and Queen Mary in 1924, with the most recently overhauled engine of the same class which happened to be No 7013 *Bristol Castle* completed at Swindon in July 1948. At the time, there was criticism that the commemorative

The funeral train conveying the body of King George VI to London for Lying in State seen here passing Finsbury Park on Monday, 11 February, 1952 on the journey from Wolferton to King's Cross drawn by BR Standard Class 7 Pacific No 70000 Britannia, *which took over after reversal at King's Lynn.* (J. A. G. H. Coltas)

93

The scene on platform 8 at Paddington Station on 15 February, 1952 as King George VI's coffin is placed aboard the funeral train for Windsor hauled by Castle class locomotive No 7013 Bristol Castle carrying the name and numberplates of Castle locomotive, No 4082 Windsor Castle, which King George V had driven in 1924, and which was used for his funeral journey to Windsor in 1936. The real 4082 was under heavy repair in Swindon Works on this occasion and could not be used. For a period before and immediately after the departure of the funeral and special guest trains, Paddington Station was closed for the arrival and departure of ordinary trains which were cancelled, or in some cases started or terminated at Reading and Oxford.
(British Rail/OPC Collection)

plaques, recording that King George V had actually driven *Windsor Castle* were now to be carried by an engine not entitled to boast of such distinction and, in particular, as the engine to carry the plaques was one built under the auspices of state ownership and never had the honour of displaying on its tender sides the magic words 'Great Western'! However, those officials at Paddington and Swindon responsible for the exchange of the engine identity, did so with the most honourable of intentions. For on that sunlit Winter day when an engine bearing the number 4082 named *Windsor Castle*, and decorated with purple draped Royal coats of arms, steamed gently away from Paddington's No 8 platform at 12.35pm, only the most knowledgeable and discerning railway observer would have detected the minor details of design telling of one engine masquerading as another. After the funeral journey, to appease the criticism, the cabside commemorative plaques recording King George V's 1924 trip were removed for safe keeping, but the engine's name- and numberplates were not exchanged back again. King George VI had been laid to rest, but the memory of his name remained, in the form of two curved brass nameplates, one on each side of the Swindon-built Great Western King class 4-6-0 No 6028.

7

QUEEN ELIZABETH II
Reign Commenced 1952

In contrast to previous chapters this one, covering the reign of Queen Elizabeth II is a continuing story and cannot be completed, your author hopes, for a very long time. Thus a resumé of the continuing saga is considered more appropriate.

At the beginning of Queen Elizabeth II's reign in February 1952 Britain's railways, indeed like many of those in other countries, were still largely worked by steam locomotives. It was only in electrified areas, as on some parts of the former Southern Railway, that one might begin to appreciate the future of the railway scene amidst ominous soundings that steam locomotives were inefficient and their replacement by electric and diesel power would be the answer to many of the railways' problems. Then in the early 1960s the name Beeching hit the railway scene, Dr Richard Beeching with a government mandate to arrest the heavy financial losses being incurred by British Railways. He produced a plan for making Britain's railways profitable, but at a price. That price was the closure of hundreds of stations and many lines, leaving a skeleton network of routes between large towns. At the same time the British Transport Commission and responsibility for the railways were vested in a newly created British

Early on the morning of 8 October, 1952 a triple train crash occurred at Harrow & Wealdstone Station, on the main line from Euston to the north-west, in which 112 people were killed. A week later, on 14 October, the Queen, accompanied by her children Prince Charles and Princess Anne and her sister Princess Margaret, returned to London from their Balmoral holiday on the royal train, seen here passing the scene of this tragic accident. Former streamlined 4-6-2 locomotive No 46245, City of London, hauls the Queen's train slowly through the damaged station and beneath a temporary footbridge replacing the span demolished in the crash. (The Photo Source/Keystone)

Princess Elizabeth stands beside the last Great Western designed Castle class 4-6-0 locomotive to be built, No 7037, which she has just named Swindon *during her visit to the Workshops there on 15 November, 1950.* (British Rail/OPC Collection)

Railways Board – an attempt to bring back a private style element into railway management. The aftermath of Dr Beeching's term of office is too well known to need further mention. His proposals, fortunately, were never fully implemented, but this did not save two stations regularly used by royalty from being victims of his axe. Those stations were at Ballater (for Balmoral) and Wolferton (for Sandringham). Not even the revenue generated from royal patronage was considered sufficient to save them and the prestige of having a 'royal' station on the railway system, was of little importance to the nationalised industry. And what of today's household BR marketing brand name 'Inter-City'? In the early years of the Queen's reign the Western Region, whose management still comprised enterprising ex-Great Western company men, already had a businessmen's express called, 'The Inter-City', taking the business tycoons from Paddington to Birmingham and Wolverhampton in the morning and back home again to the capital for early evening. On one fine spring-like day early in March 1954, The Inter-City received royal acclaim when HRH Princess Margaret, and her entourage, boarded the train at Leamington Spa and travelled to Paddington in the ex-GWR chocolate and cream coloured royal saloon No 9006 attached at the front, hauled by the Great Western 4-6-0 named after her late father, No 6028 *King George VI*.

While the Queen, herself, has never publicly pronounced her views on railways, Her Majesty, like any other of her subjects, obviously has likes and dislikes, and when she became Queen had already been on the footplates of a South African Beyer-Garratt locomotive in 1947, and at Swindon in 1950 during a visit to the Works there, a Star class locomotive bearing her name, *Princess Elizabeth*, numbered 4057. At the time of the

Queen's Coronation, in June 1953, Prince Charles was coming to the age when small boys are fascinated by railway engines. At the time of the Coronation, a popular women's magazine, in a series of articles on royalty, reported that the Queen was not particularly fond of railway travel. Such a statement could only be pure speculation. Of more recent years, it is a fact that not only the Queen, but also other members of the Royal Family, have used rail travel less often; two significant factors responsible for the decline are first, the smaller railway system, resulting from Dr Beeching's axing of station and lines, and second, for longer day journeys, where speed is essential, an aircraft of the Queen's Flight will suffice to leave more time for fulfilling a crowded diary of engagements. Probably, the Queen's attitude towards railways, quite apart from the very obvious one of affording privacy, relaxation and sleep, where speed is less important, goes back to the memories of her childhood and the excitement of overnight journeys to and from Scotland for the annual summer holiday at Balmoral. Even one of her first meetings with her future husband, Prince Philip, concerned a clockwork railway laid out on the floor of the room in which they met. Briefly, the situation was that it took place in July 1939 while King George VI and Queen Elizabeth were visiting the Royal Naval College at Dartmouth. During their parents' visit, Princess Elizabeth and her younger sister, Margaret, were taken to the nearby house of the officer-in-charge of the College. Among those called upon to help entertain the two young Princesses was a naval cadet, Prince Philip of Greece. For a time, the Prince is said to have entertained the Princesses with the clockwork trains. Were those trains real scale models, gauge O and made by Bassett-Lowke of Northampton? Perhaps it was just a simple Hornby tinplate set which really bore no resemblance to the engines of the royal train. However, when Princess Elizabeth eventually married Prince Philip, on 20 November 1947 and after their wedding in Westminster Abbey, they had a full-size train to take them on their honeymoon from Waterloo to Winchester, before being driven by road thence to the Mountbatten family home of Broadlands, Romsey. Their tea-time departure from London, in a five-coach special train which included two Pullman Cars, *Rosemary* (in which the

The special train provided by the Ulster Transport Authority for the 1953 Coronation tour to Northern Ireland of the Queen and Duke of Edinburgh. Hauled by Class W 2-6-0 No 102, painted black, the special train, painted in blue and cream, worked from Lisburn to Lisahally, near Londonderry, where the Royal Party left the train for a short trip upriver to Londonderry on 3 July. This proved to be the last time a royal train was run in Northern Ireland as all subsequent visits by Royalty have used air and road travel. (Ulster Folk & Transport Museum)

GREAT NORTHERN RAILWAY (Ireland)
and
ULSTER TRANSPORT AUTHORITY

NOTICE OF ROYAL TRAIN
conveying
Her Majesty Queen Elizabeth II.
and
His Royal Highness The Duke of Edinburgh
from
Lisburn to Lisahally
and
Return Arrangements
from
Londonderry (Waterside)
to
Belfast (York Road) or Larne Harbour

FRIDAY, 3rd JULY, 1953

The Royal Train

will be marshalled as under leaving Lisburn :—

U.T.A. Engine No. 102.
(A) G.N.R. Brake First No. 231.
(B) G.N.R. Dining Car No. 403.
(C) G.N.R. Corridor First No. 227.
(D) U.T.A. Saloon No. 3.
(E) G.N.R. Saloon No. 50.
(F) U.T.A. Saloon No. 8.
(G) U.T.A. Dining Car No. 87.
(H) G.N.R. Corridor First No. 225.
(I) U.T.A. Dining Car No. 90.
(J) G.N.R. Brake First No. 232.

The total tare weight of the train behind the engine is 308½ tons, and the over-all length of the train is 672 feet.

The principal doorway will be that at the leading end of Coach (E), G.N.R. Saloon No. 50, and the distance between the middle of the engine footplate and the middle of this doorway is 281 feet 9 inches.

To facilitate the seating of those travelling, each Coach, except D, E and F, will bear an identifying lettered plate at each end.

A pilot train will precede the Royal Train, running approximately twenty minutes in advance of the latter.

Both trains will be worked throughout by U.T.A. engines and enginemen with G.N.R. pilot drivers from Belfast to Antrim.

The detailed timings of the pilot train and the Royal train are as follows :—

			Pilot Train.	Royal Train.
			a.m.	a.m.
Belfast (Gt. Victoria St.)		dep.	10 0	10 15
Lisburn		arr.	10 15	10 30
Lisburn		dep.	10 35	10 55
Knockmore Junction		pass	10 38	10 58
Brookmount		,,	10 46	11 2
Ballinderry		,,	10 49	11 9
Glenavy		,,	10 54	11 14
Crumlin		,,	10 56	11 18
Aldergrove		,,	11 2	11 22
Antrim		,,	11 12	11 32
Cookstown Junction		,,	11 18	11 38
Ballymena (Passenger)		arr.	11 28	11 50
				p.m.
Ballymena		dep.	11 40	12 5
Cullybackey		pass	11 48	12 13
Glarryford		,,	11 56	12 20
Killagan		,,	11 59	12 23
				p.m.
Dunloy		,,	12 3	12 26
Ballymoney (Up Platform)		arr.	12 15	12 37
Ballymoney		dep.	12 30	12 52
Macfin		pass	12 35	12 57
Coleraine (Down Platform)		arr.	12 43	1 5
Coleraine		dep.	12 58	1 20
Castlerock		pass	1 8	1 31
Downhill Cliffs		arr.	—	1 37
Downhill Cliffs		dep.	—	2 15
Bellarena		arr.	1 20	
Bellarena		dep.	2 5	2 24P
Limavady Junction		pass	2 13	2 32
Eglinton		,,	2 25	2 44
Lisahally (No. 1 Crossing)		arr.	—	2 51
Lisahally (No. 1 Crossing)		dep.	2 30P	3 5
Londonderry (No. 2 Platform)		arr.	2 40	3 13

P—indicates passing time.

The Royal Party will join the train at Lisburn and alight at Lisahally, but some of those travelling on the train will join at Belfast (Gt. Victoria Street) and proceed to Londonderry.

---

honeymoon couple travelled and were served tea on the journey) and *Rosamund*, was hauled by Lord Nelson class 4-6-0 No 857 *Lord Howe* – an engine whose nautical class title was appropriate in the context of their early encounter in the shadows of the Royal Naval College.

The Queen and Prince Philip, Duke of Edinburgh, inherited the use of the former LMS royal train which they used for overnight and long distance journeys. The two principal 1941-built saloons, formerly used by the King and Queen, were now reserved for the exclusive use of the Queen and Duke of Edinburgh. Saloon No 799 now became the Queen's saloon, while the Duke of Edinburgh now used the former King's saloon, No 798. Their two young children, Prince Charles and Princess Anne often accompanied their parents on railway journeys of a more private nature. In 1954, as mentioned in chapter ten in relation to the East Coast royal train, the Duke of Edinburgh suggested that all royal train coaches should present a uniform appearance so far as their colour was concerned. As a result of what amounted to an edict from the Duke, the former LMS train now lost its private company identity, six years after nationalisation, to be repainted into a darker colour called 'royal claret', with vermilion red and black lining. In 1955 the two ex-GWR royal saloons, Nos 9006 and 9007, lost their chocolate and cream identity and were repainted in royal claret livery and, at the same time, internally refurnished. However, the Duke's edict did not eclipse the Great Western tradition of independence which was still very much alive on the Western Region. To operate with saloons 9006/7, two Hawksworth designed brake composites, Nos 7372 and 7377, were kept exclusively for royal train use and painted in chocolate and cream colours, but, no doubt, fear from higher places precluded adding the initials GWR! For day journeys, Queen Elizabeth, the Queen Mother, often made use of saloon 9006, plus one of the brake composites, and the two vehicles were not infrequently to be seen attached to the rear of an express from Paddington. One such occasion was in November, 1958, when the Queen Mother paid a visit to the sister towns of Leamington and Warwick and travelled in this way at the rear of the 9.10am Paddington to Birkenhead express to Leamington, hauled by engine No 6000 *King George V* displaying the normal two lamp express code, but carrying the special reporting number 002 on the smokebox door.

The year 1977 was the one in which Her Majesty celebrated 25 years as Queen, with Silver Jubilee celebrations taking place throughout the country. During the year the Queen and the Duke of Edinburgh made a series of Silver Jubilee tours to Scotland, Wales and provincial regions in England travelling by road, rail, air, and in the Royal Yacht *Britannia*. The journeys by rail gave opportunities for the Queen and Duke to relax and on several occasions, one or more nights were spent in the royal train. For the first of the Jubilee tours, to Scotland in May, the national press, unusually, spared a few inches of column space to report on the royal train which left Euston in the late evening of Monday, 16 May. The press interest surrounded a brief simple ceremony, on the platform before departure, when the then Chairman of British Railways, Mr (later Sir) Peter Parker, handed to Her Majesty the key of her new saloon and which she then ceremonially unlocked at the start of the overnight journey to Glasgow. The occasion was to celebrate what the press described as 'the Queen's new

high speed royal train'. The reality was that the former LMS royal saloons, Nos 799 and 798 had been replaced by two Mk III vehicles, No 2903 for the Queen and No 2904 for the Duke of Edinburgh.

To railway lovers and, not least to those who work in the railway industry, there is, quite understandably, great pleasure and pride derived whenever any member of the Royal Family travels by train or visits a railway installation. The Queen's love of horses and country life is no secret and also shared by other members of the Royal Family. It was, therefore, no surprise for your author to glimpse through the window of Her Majesty's saloon, during one of the Silver Jubilee tours, magazines and papers about horses and countryside topics lying on a table in her lounge, something with which to relax on rejoining the Royal Train, after a full day of people, smiles and handshakes. Not even the male members of the Royal Family could be considered to be dedicated railway lovers. Therefore, it is all the more significant that over the years, in addition to travelling by rail, railways have featured from time to time quite prominently in royal engagement diaries. This is particularly so in the current reign. The Queen, in addition to her visit as Princess Elizabeth to Swindon Works in 1950, has also paid visits to other major railway manufacturing centres, for example Wolverton Carriage Works in 1966 and 1976, the latter visit, a private one, to see work in progress on adapting the Mk III prototypes for royal use. In 1975 during a visit to Doncaster Locomotive Works accompanied by the Duke of Edinburgh, the Queen was presented with a brass and copper model of Stephenson's *Rocket*, made by apprentices in the Works' training school. In March, 1969, it was the Queen who performed the ceremonial opening of London Transport's Victoria Line and delighted those present by pressing a sixpenny coin into the ticket machine, which, at the first attempt, rejected it! Perhaps Her Majesty reflected when, as a girl, she and her younger sister, Princess Margaret, together with a governess, had a brief ride on the Northern Line. In October, 1968, the Queen

The Romney, Hythe & Dymchurch Railway was visited by the Queen, Prince Philip and their children, Prince Charles and Princess Anne on 30 March 1957 when they rode in a special train, with senior driver George Barlow at the controls of locomotive No 8 Hurricane, from New Romney to Hythe. Prince Charles is seen in the locomotive cab before leaving New Romney. (South Eastern Newspapers Ltd)

At Nine Elms locomotive depot in South London, a coloured headboard is placed on the front of the Southern Railway 4-6-0 locomotive No 861, Lord Anson, for the honeymoon train of Princess Elizabeth and Prince Philip from Waterloo to Winchester on 20 November, 1947. However, after this publicity photograph was taken it was felt that No 861 was not sufficiently run-in following overhaul and sister locomotive No 857, Lord Howe, carrying the same headboard, actually hauled the honeymoon special. (The Photo Source/Keystone)

(opposite) The operating notice for the running of the royal train over the Ulster Transport Authority and Great Northern Railway (Ireland) routes conveying the Queen and Prince Philip in 1953. (Courtesy Denis Grimshaw)

99

(top) *Liverpool Street Station, in the City of London, was rarely used for royal journeys to Sandringham because of the need for certain formalities to be enacted whenever the Monarch entered the City limits, so King's Cross was used instead. However, in more enlightened times and in the early years of the Queen's reign these formalities were relaxed on other than formal occasions as would have been the case on the afternoon of 22 December, 1960 when the Queen and her family left from No 9 platform of Liverpool Street Station, at 3.10pm in the ex-LNER royal train for Wolferton to spend Christmas at Sandringham. Hauling the royal train as far as King's Lynn was BR Standard Class 7 4-6-2 No 70009 Alfred The Great seen here in tip-top condition, with piles of Christmas luggage awaiting movement on the opposite platform.* (British Rail/OPC Collection)

(above) *The Queen visited Wolverhampton on 24 May 1962, arriving in the royal train at the town's now closed Low Level ex-GWR Station. Earlier, the Queen's train is seen passing Whitnash, on the approach to Leamington Spa, hauled by the Castle class locomotive carrying the name and numberplates 4082 Windsor Castle, but actually No 7013 Bristol Castle, which were exchanged in 1952 for King George VI's funeral train. Note the double indication of the royal train, four headlamps and the train's identification, X01. The leading vehicle is the LMS 1941 built combined brake/power/staff sleeping car, followed by three ex-LNWR saloons.* (Peter F. Chater)

Kenilworth Station on the ex-LNWR Leamington Spa – Coventry line received its first Royal passenger when Queen Victoria arrived there from Birmingham, on 15 June, 1858 on her way to nearby Stoneleigh Abbey. In subsequent years Queen Victoria passed through Kenilworth on many occasions during her journeys between Windsor and Balmoral. Though much less frequently, King George V and Queen Mary also passed this way, according to several elderly local residents who vividly recounted to the author an occasion in the early 1920s when Queen Mary waved from her saloon to a small group gathered at a crossing, south of the station, to watch the train's passing. Kenilworth was one of the many stations listed in Dr Beeching's report for closure. However, the establishment in nearby Stoneleigh Abbey Park of a permanent site for the Royal Agricultural Show in 1963 raised hopes that Kenilworth's station would be reprieved when it became known that the Queen and Duke of Edinburgh would arrive there on 4 July, en-route to the showground. Indeed Stationmaster Price hoped it would become an annual royal occasion and so it seemed, for on 9 July, 1964 Queen Elizabeth, The Queen Mother alighted there on her way to the Royal Show. The glory was not to last as closure took place in January 1965. A single line remains for Inter-City and freight trains but the main station building was demolished in 1983 to make way for housing development.

(top left) Kenilworth Station and the reception party on the up platform watch the royal train arrive, following an overnight journey from Scotland, hauled by English Electric Type 4 diesel locomotive No D308 on the occasion of the visit by the Queen and Duke of Edinburgh on 4 July, 1963. (Author)

(above left) The royal train in which the Queen Mother arrived at Kenilworth from Euston was hauled by an English Electric Type 4 diesel locomotive, but two days later on 11 July, 1964, the same train, composed of three ex-GWR vehicles (leading) and three from the former LMS royal train, was being hauled by a steam locomotive in the shape of ex-LMS Class 5 4-6-0 No 44919, taking the Queen Mother to Stratford-upon-Avon. The train is seen here on the line from Leamington and passing Claverdon. The normal express headlamp code is displayed, but the reporting No 1X03 indicates the train's true identity! (Gerald Batchelor)

(top right) The empty royal train leaves Kenilworth for servicing at Rugby with ex-LNWR converted brake first No 5155 bringing up the rear on 4 July, 1963. Note the two tail lamps.

(above right) A proud day for Stationmaster Price as he escorts the Queen Mother from Kenilworth Station to her car after she had arrived from Euston on her way to visit the Royal Show at Stoneleigh Abbey Park. 9 July, 1964. (Author)

officially opened the rebuilt Euston station and, in May 1974 on the northern part of the West Coast main line, unveiled a plaque at Preston station to commemorate the completion of the electrification throughout from Euston to Glasgow. The Queen Mother became the first member of the Royal Family to perform the official naming of a railway locomotive when she named a Class 47 diesel No 47541 *The Queen Mother* in October 1982 at Aberdeen. In fairly recent years other members of the Royal Family have performed railway orientated engagements. For example in May, 1961 the Duke of Edinburgh expressed great interest when he wandered amongst lines of steam and diesel locomotives at an exhibition in Marylebone Goods Yard, held to commemorate the Golden Jubilee of the Institution of Locomotive Engineers, and left to travel to Windsor by riding in the cab of Warship class diesel locomotive, No D829 *Magpie* which hauled the train in which he was supposed to have travelled instead! Preserved railways, too, have received visits by Royalty, the first being by the Duchess of Kent, to the North Yorkshire Moors Railway, in 1973. In 1982, the Prince and Princess of Wales travelled on the Talyllyn Railway during their Welsh visit – the Prince riding on the engine footplate.

Towards the end of 1984 a happy occasion which attracted, nationally, scant publicity occurred when The Queen Mother rode in a steam-hauled royal special to fulfill an official engagement in East London. In a less than affluent area of the nation's Capital, this very popular member of the Royal Family was assured of a warm reception, in particular by those old enough to remember the wartime visits when with the King she toured and spoke with the people who suffered the effects of enemy air-raids on their homes. Those people, who on first acquaintance may appear brusque, possess deep-rooted warmth of heart and loyalty, renowned beyond the confines of London's East End, and have never forgotten the expression of deep concern shown to them by the Queen during those uncertain dark days of war. The dictates of increased security, resulting from a near successful terrorist attempt to assassinate Prime Minister Margaret Thatcher and her Cabinet only weeks beforehand, resulted in few local people knowing about the Queen Mother's visit to open the North Woolwich Old Station Museum. Possible attempts to keep quiet the plan for Her Majesty to arrive at North Woolwich station by train were thwarted by the publication in one of the popular railway enthusiast steam monthlies, that the privately owned LNER locomotive No 4472 *Flying Scotsman* was being moved south from its home base at Steamtown, Carnforth, Lancashire, to haul a train of two Pullman coaches taking The Queen Mother from Stratford (Low Level) along the five mile branch and passing through the dockland stations of Canning Town, Custom House and Silvertown. However, the reported date, planned or otherwise, differed from the one on the official Clarence House engagement list for November. Security considerations apart, British Rail's Eastern Region officials were anxious to keep the whole affair as quiet as possible. As everyone knows, the simultaneous appearance of two well-known crowd pullers, the Queen Mother and Britain's most famous steam locomotive, *Flying Scotsman*, could be guaranteed to populate lineside roads, overbridges and, indeed, anywhere along the route offering the merest opportunity to see or photograph the rare combination of a steam train and royalty on a line whose staple custom is commuters

(facing page)

(top) The cavalry on parade as the royal train from Euston, conveying the Queen and other members of the Royal Family, approaches a temporary platform near Griffith's Crossing and where the Royal Party will alight for the short processional drive to Caernarvon Castle for the Investiture of the Prince of Wales on 1 July, 1969. Hauling the train are two class 40 diesel locomotives Nos 233 Empress of England and 216 Campania. (E. N. Kneale)

(centre left)
The concluding engagement of the Queen's Silver Jubilee tour to the West Midlands was an evening function on 27 July, 1977 for which the Royal Party detrained at Birmingham International Station. To avoid negotiating stairways and escalators, the Queen and Duke left the royal train at the end of the station's platform one and descended the red carpeted slope to their car. (Author)

(centre right) The Queen and Duke of Edinburgh bid farewell to two senior railway officials at the doorway of the Queen's saloon, before the royal train leaves Coventry Station on 27 July, 1977 during the Silver Jubilee tour of the West Midlands. (Author)

(bottom left)
During the Silver Jubilee Tour to the Bristol area, the Queen and Duke of Edinburgh arrive at Weston-Super-Mare on a special royal working of an Inter-City 125 High Speed Train on 8 August, 1977. Although the first such occasion Royalty had travelled by British Rail's flagship of their fleet, the significance of the event was a lost cause in the eyes of the press generally! (Author)

(bottom right)
The Queen opens the Victoria Line on London's Underground system by making a speech on the northbound platform at Green Park station before starting the royal train on the inaugural journey to Oxford Circus on 7 March 1969. (London Regional Transport)

The Queen Mother signs the visitors' book in the Pullman Car Diana, converted from a redundant BR coach, during a visit to the Kent & East Sussex Railway on 9 June, 1982 watched by KESR Deputy Chairman, Tim Stanger. (Kent & East Sussex Courier)

Queen Elizabeth The Queen Mother at the ceremony at Aberdeen Station on 20 October, 1982 when Her Majesty named Class 47/4 No 47541 The Queen Mother. (Author)

The Prince and Princess of Wales travelled on the Talyllyn Railway during a visit to Wales on 25 November, 1982. The Talyllyn's special royal train is seen at Ty Mawr, hauled by 0-4-0 well-tank No 2 Dolgoch, during the couple's brief ride on the 2ft 3in gauge line from Tywyn Pendre to Rhydyronen. (Geoffrey F. Bannister)

(opposite)
Writing desk in the LNWR King's saloon of 1902, seen in later years with a telephone. The notepaper is headed 'The Royal Train' and bears the Royal Arms. (Crown copyright, courtesy National Railway Museum)

and off-peak shoppers, travelling in two-car diesel trains.

Without doubt, it would have been a much simpler exercise for the entire journey from The Queen Mother's London home at Clarence House to have been by car instead of boarding a train more than half way to her destination. It is gratifying to know in a seemingly impersonal computer age, that someone originated the idea, to which Her Majesty graciously agreed, of a steam train arrival. Understandably there was concern about too many prying eyes and, in particular, the antics of those avid band of steam engine chasers who, even for such a short journey, might just attempt driving along the many lineside roads – a feature of this line – to take more than one photograph. Therefore, it was a somewhat private occasion to which only those, including the press, were privileged to observe at Stratford and North Woolwich stations. Shortly after 3pm, in fading light, on the afternoon of Tuesday, 20 November (by coincidence also the thirty-seventh wedding anniversary of the Queen and Prince Philip) the royal special steamed away from the curved narrow platform of Stratford Low Level station. *Flying Scotsman* displayed just the two lamp express passenger headcode instead of the four lamp code of a royal train conveying the Sovereign. Only the locomotive's white painted cab roof gave any real clue that the apple green engine was transporting royalty, for it was a tradition on former Great Eastern lines of the LNER, for locomotives chosen for royal train duty to have the cab roof painted white – a tradition continued after nationalisation until steam was replaced by diesel power. Her Majesty and her Lady-in-Waiting, together with other members of her party, travelled in the first of the two coaches, Car No 351, a second class Pullman parlour vehicle built in 1960 by Metropolitan-Cammell for service on the East Coast main line, now privately-owned and normally used in a

(facing page top)
The Queen, Queen Mother and Prince Philip seen arriving at Tattenham Corner station, from Victoria, to visit Epsom Races on Derby Day, 7 June, 1978. On this occasion the royal party travelled in Mk II open first-class coach No M3163 (seen in the background) marshalled in a special train formed otherwise of vehicles from the contemporary royal train fleet; in subsequent years the Queen and her party have occupied the royal dining saloon, 2902, on this visit. (Author)

(facing page bottom)
A special train, formed of royal train vehicles, arrives at Victoria Station, London, platform 2 from Gatwick Airport, conveying the President of Indonesia on a state visit on 13 November, 1979. The Queen and Duke of Edinburgh look on as electro-diesel, No 73142, draws to a stop. (Author)

The Prince of Wales rode on the footplate of Talyllyn Railway locomotive No 2, Dolgoch, from Tywyn Pendre to Rhydyronen in the company of senior driver Dai Jones and fireman Mike Green on 25 November, 1982. (Northpix [Kevin Reid] Ltd)

The Princess of Wales riding third class on the Talyllyn Railway on 25 November, 1982. Her Royal Highness is boarding the restored ex-Corris Railway carriage, No 17 of 1890 vintage, while her husband prefers a ride on the footplate. (Northpix [Keven Reid] Ltd)

(facing page top)
The royal train taking the Queen and Duke of Edinburgh round the International Garden Festival, Liverpool, on 2 May, 1984. Hauling the train on the 15in gauge 2½ mile railway, is one of the locomotives from the Romney, Hythe & Dymchurch Railway, 4-8-2, No 6 Samson. (Northpix [Kevin Reid] Ltd)

(facing page bottom)
The Duke of Gloucester is visible on the footplate of the 0-6-0 saddle-tank locomotive, G. B. Keeling, approaching Norchard platform, hauling two ex-GWR vehicles, an auto-trailer and an inspection saloon, during his visit to the Norchard Steam Centre of the Dean Forest Railway, Lydney, Gloucestershire on 8 November, 1983. (George Locker)

train of similar Pullmans for charter work all over the country. The rear vehicle, also in the traditional brown and cream Pullman colours, was a former BR Mk I brake first/second, in use as an escort coach. On arrival at the only remaining operational platform at North Woolwich, the Queen Mother met the train crew, driver Tony Gooding, fireman Reg Rowe and guard Louis Attoe. They presented her with an oil painting of *Flying Scotsman* to commemorate the journey, painted by Arthur Gills a Temple Mills goods guard. Then to the delight of those present, Her Majesty ascended a small temporary wooden stairway, conveniently placed at the entrance to *Flying Scotsman*'s cab, to see for herself the controls, which she no doubt thought looked like a mess of gauges, brass and copper pipes, if one can judge correctly the initial expression of her footplate experience!

It is likely, however, that while on the footplate the Queen Mother was reminded of an unpleasant experience of travelling on steam trains. Sometime in the early post-war years on a northbound journey from Euston, it became necessary for the royal train to make an unscheduled stop at Rugby, where a doctor from the local hospital was summoned to remove a piece of grit from one of Her Majesty's eyes. A Lady-in-Waiting confirmed to your author that Her Majesty still remembers the painful experience. Probably the exhibits of the Museum, which are mostly of Great Eastern Railway origin and housed in the former station building, did not seem quite so real to Her Majesty as the train that had brought her there. However, visitors to North Woolwich's Old Station Museum, which is supported by the Passmore Edwards Museum Trust, will catch sight of

The Queen Mother in the cab of Britain's most famous steam locomotive, Flying Scotsman, *on arrival at North Woolwich on 20 November, 1984. Looking on is Fireman Reg Rowe.* (Press Association)

Programme for the visit of

HER MAJESTY THE QUEEN
AND
HIS ROYAL HIGHNESS
THE DUKE OF EDINBURGH

to Isambard Kingdom Brunel's
Temple Meads Terminus in
Bristol on Friday, 26 July 1985,
to mark the 150th Anniversary
of the Great Western Railway

A smiling Queen immediately after naming diesel locomotive, 47508, S.S. Great Britain at Bristol Temple Meads on 26 July 1985 as part of the GWR 150 celebrations. The happiness of the occasion is reflected by Prince Philip's expression. Sharing the memorable event is Area Manager, Frank Markham, and (extreme right) Western Region General Manager, Sidney Newey. (Author)

the oval plaque recording the Royal opening and which, to local people, will remind them of that dreary November afternoon that brought a touch of the days when railway travel was more of a colourful experience.

As heir to the Throne, Prince Charles was acquainted with railways from a very early age when he and his younger sister, Princess Anne, accompanied their parents on holidays to Balmoral and Sandringham. A photograph widely published showed them in their nightclothes, standing by a window of the 'nursery coach' No 2900, at the end of a summer holiday to Balmoral. But, at the time of writing, little Prince William, who has already travelled to Australia, is believed never to have been on a train!

One of the happiest associations of Royalty's connection with railways occurred during the Queen's television broadcast on Christmas Day in 1971. On that occasion, Her Majesty was seated on a settee with her younger sons Andrew and Edward looking at photographs in a family album. After the Queen had turned several pages, a well-known photograph appeared and which she described to the young Princes by saying 'look there is Great Grandpa George V on a steam engine at Swindon'. That was the memorable and happy occasion which took place at Swindon in 1924. It is nice to think that the visit all those years ago should be recalled in this way. To any former Great Western employees at Swindon, it must surely have re-kindled, with pride, their memories of a red letter day.

But the Great Western was honoured again in 1985, when British Rail Western Region organised a programme of events to celebrate the 150th Anniversary of the Great Western Railway Act, 1835. Having been styled 'The Royal Road' by the Prince of Wales when the GWR celebrated its centenary, royalty honoured the railway's 150th anniversary with their presence at more than one event. The climax of the celebrations came on 26 July when the Queen and Duke of Edinburgh travelled in the royal train from Paddington to Cardiff and Bristol. At Paddington a diesel locomotive, No 47620, was named *Windsor Castle* by the Queen. In Cardiff the Queen and Prince Philip toured the GWR 150 Exhibition at the Welsh Industrial and Maritime Museum. Finally, on arrival at Temple Meads station in Bristol the Queen performed her second locomotive naming ceremony of the day on 47508 which she named S.S. *Great Britain* to honour Brunel's ship of the same name, now being restored in Bristol docks. The Royal couple concluded their visit by seeing Isambard Kingdom Brunel's partially restored original Temple Meads station.

8

SOME OVERSEAS OCCASIONS

For the concluding chapter on the royal journeys it is appropriate to mention some occasions when British Royalty have travelled to Commonwealth countries, once known as the British Empire, where the railway systems owed much to British influence. Generally, the Royal visitors rode in trains reserved for the exclusive use of each country's Governor-General or in India the equivalent being the Viceroy.

India was one of the first Empire countries where royal trains ran on a grand scale. Queen Victoria never visited the land of her passion. It was left to her Indian servants, whom she chose, to influence her thoughts on that distant land, to whom she was known as Queen Empress. It was not until King George V, accompanied by Queen Mary, went to India for his Imperial Durbar at Delhi in December 1911, that a reigning monarch of the British Dynasty had appeared as King-Emperor before his Indian people. Several railway companies were involved with journeys for the occasion, but it was the East Indian Railway which provided an Imperial Train of 10 carriages, with two separate saloons for the King and Queen. Not to be outshone, the Great Indian Peninsula Railway built an 11-coach train for a journey to Kotah. The GIPR also celebrated the event by painting about a dozen of its British-looking locomotives in a non-standard livery of blue with yellow and black lining which bore some resemblance to the Caledonian Railway of Scotland. Most were specially named after members of the Royal Family and included some who were deceased as, for example *Queen Victoria* and *Prince Albert*. The GIPR selected an Atlantic type locomotive for the King's train and gave it the name *Queen Empress* instead of what would have seemed more appropriate, *King Emperor*! However, *Queen Empress* was decorated with flags and carried on the

> SOUTHERN RAILWAY.
> SOUTHAMPTON DOCKS.
> _____
> Ticket of Admittance to Enclosure
> to witness arrival of Their Majesties
> **THE KING AND QUEEN**
> by
> R.M.S. "Empress of Britain,"
> on Thursday, 22nd June, 1939.
> No Car parking facilities available.
>
> CONDITIONS.—All persons are permitted to visit the Docks, and any vessel or plant, etc., entirely at their own risk, and subject to the special condition that they will keep harmless and indemnify the Railway Company and any other Company or persons owning, working, using, occupying or being upon the Railway Company's undertaking and/or any vessel, or plant, etc., therein or thereat harmless and indemnified from and against all claims, injury, loss, damage or liability, by whomsoever, or howsoever, preferred, caused or suffered, arising out of or in connection with such visit.
> R. P. BIDDLE, *Docks and Marine Manager*.

Southern Railway admission ticket to witness the return of King George VI and Queen Elizabeth from the Canadian and American tour of 1939 at Southampton Docks. (By kind permission of P. O. Reeves)

Sketch map of Canadian and USA 1939 tour by King George VI and Queen Elizabeth. (Courtesy The Railway Magazine)

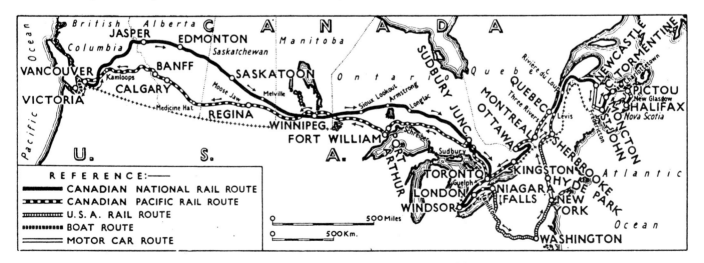

front the Royal Arms. Some 72 years later, in November 1983, George V's granddaughter, Queen Elizabeth II, visited India and went by train in another part of the country now known independently as Bangladesh. The Queen, with the Duke of Edinburgh, travelled from Dacca to Sripur aboard a blue and yellow striped train of the Bangladesh State Railway hauled by a diesel locomotive festooned with flowers, streamers and flags.

It was to Canada and America, when tension in Europe was mounting, that King George VI and Queen Elizabeth went in May 1939. The influence of the neighbouring United States is reflected in Canada's railways and journeys are long and distances great. Their Majesties' extensive travelling was mostly by rail for which a special train of 12 cars was provided jointly by the Canadian Pacific and Canadian National railways. All were painted in royal blue with silver panels between the windows and horizontal gold stripes above and below the window line. Included in the formation were the two private cars of Canada's Governor-General which had been redecorated for use by the King and Queen. There was also a private car for the Canadian Prime Minister (Mr Mackenzie King). The remainder of the train was made up of baggage, business, dining and sleeping cars. A pilot train, also of 12 cars, accommodated officials and pressmen, and contained the travelling royal post office. All the Canadian locomotives used for royal duty were finished in royal blue. The Canadian Pacific Railway chose one of its new Class H-1-d 4-6-4 locomotives, No 2850, for many of the journeys on its system. Decorated with the Royal Arms and a replica crown, these adornments, with the approval of the King, were later applied to all 45 of the CPR's H-1-c, H-1-d and H-1-e 4-6-4s built between 1937 and 1945 and so became known as the 'Royal Hudson' class. The Canadian National employed locomotives of the 4-8-4 and 4-6-2 types when the royal and pilot trains ran over its lines. From the time the royal train left Quebec travelling west over the CPR to Vancouver via Calgary and returning east-wards on the CNR via Edmonton to Toronto and then into America and over the New York Central, Pennsylvania and Boston & Maine railroads until the final arrival back in Canada at Halifax, it had covered a total distance of 8,377 miles. The declaration of war a few weeks after the King and Queen's return from Canada precluded any further marathon train journeys overseas until peace returned.

In the very early days of 1946, plans were made for the King and Queen, this time to be accompanied by Princess Elizabeth and Princess Margaret, to pay a visit to South Africa from mid-February to mid-April, 1947. It proved to be the King's last great State visit. The tour was planned to cover every province of the Union of South Africa, entailing nearly 10,000 miles of travel, of which 4,920 would be by train. For much of their two-month stay, home for the King and Queen and the two Princesses would be a train. However, no ordinary train then existing would be suitable without modification in meeting the needs of not only the Royal Family for such a lengthy tour, but also their entourage. In conjunction with South African Railways, it was decided that some vehicles of the Governor-General's 'White Train', together with several from the South African Blue Train should be prepared to supplement eight new carriages, still to be built. The decision resulted in an order being placed in England with the Birmingham firm of Metropolitan-Cammell towards the end of March, 1946, for eight

Princess Elizabeth and the Duke of Edinburgh on the observation platform of the Canadian National royal train at Niagara Falls, Ontario, during their 1951 Canadian tour. (Canadian National Railway)

(facing page top)
The royal train conveying the King and Queen westbound on the Canadian Pacific Railway near Leanchoil in the Rocky Mountains hauled by Hudson type 4-6-4 locomotive No 2850, during the 1939 tour of Canada and North America. (Canadian Pacific Corporate Archives)

(facing page bottom)
The royal train in which King George VI and Queen Elizabeth travelled during their tour of Canada in 1939 and shown here prepared for the eastbound journey headed by Canadian National Railway stream-lined 4-8-4 locomotive No 6400 at London, Ontario. On the left is the pilot train headed by sister locomotive No 6401. (Canadian National Railway)

carriages which, at the conclusion of the royal tour, would be transferred to the 'White Train' as replacements for older wooden bodied vehicles.

The new carriages, of steel construction with interior panelling of selected timbers, were designed for running on what is South Africa's standard 'Cape' gauge of 3ft 6in and included separate vehicles for the King and Queen and one for the joint use of the two Princesses. The remainder were for use by the Royal Household, railway catering and train staff, and one for South African ministerial use. As might be expected, such a prestigious order gave a boost to the morale of the designers and craftsmen to demonstrate what magnificent railway carriages incorporating every conceivable refinement of luxury and practical necessity, could be produced from the company's works in the Birmingham suburb of Washwood Heath. In these days when it is not unknown for one reason or another for manufacturers to miss agreed delivery dates, barely eight months were allowed before completion was required to allow sufficient time for shipment from England before the tour commenced. From drawing board to final coat of paint, the eight ivory-white gold-lined and lettered carriages, approximately 65ft long by 9ft 3in wide, stood ready for inspection in Metro-Cammell's paint shop on 19 November 1946, the day the King and Queen, with their daughters, went to look at the train they would soon be calling home. Such was the interest which the King and his family, personally showed in the train's construction, and in meeting many of those whose dedication and skill had achieved a near miracle at a time when industry and people, generally, were still in the throes of recovery from the nation's involvement with war.

Three months later, following a three week-voyage in the battleship HMS *Vanguard*, the King and Queen and their Princesses arrived in Cape Town. On 21 February, five days after their arrival, during which they visited townships in the Cape province, Their Majesties and Their Royal Highnesses stepped aboard the gleaming 'White Train' from a temporary

114

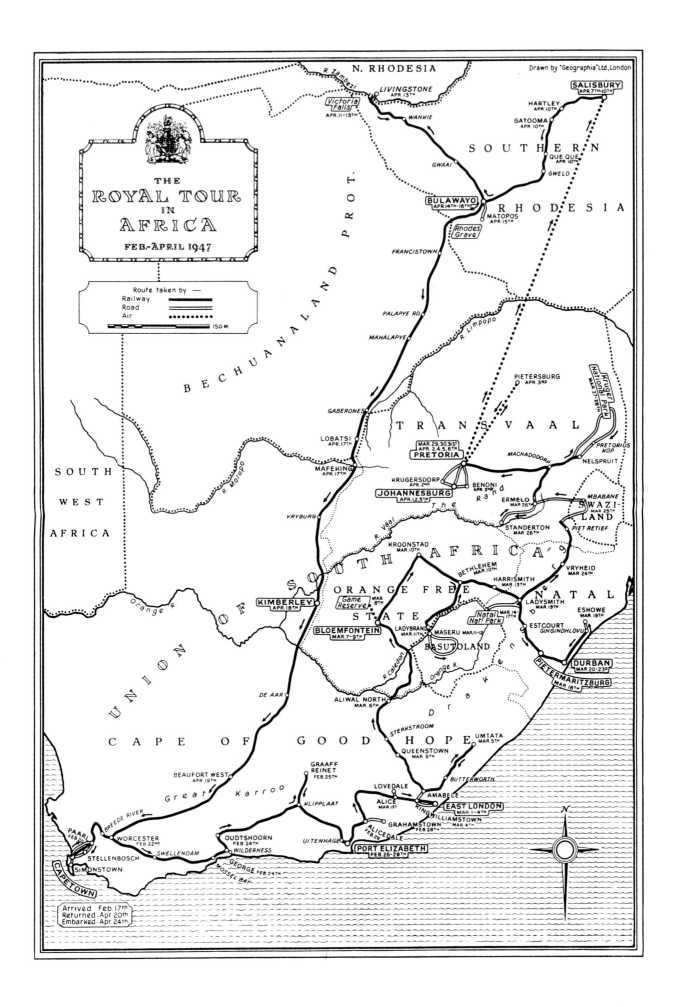

platform on the quayside at Cape Town. Preceding the royal 'White Train' was the older 'White Train', now repainted in standard SAR red/brown and cream with aluminium roof, which acted as pilot train conveying rank and file of the police and railway personnel, press representatives and also the King's barber. There was radio communication between both trains and they were each equipped with telephones which could be connected up to the national system when the train was stationary, and to countries overseas. The carriages of the 'White Train' used by the Royal Family were numbered R1 to R14 inclusive; those imported from England were Nos R1, R2, R5, R6, R7, R8, R9 and R13. Nos R7, R8 and R9 were occupied by the Princesses, Queen and King, respectively. In retrospect, the 'White Train' has become an indelible part of the 1947 royal tour of South Africa, and its 14 carriages formed at the time, the longest and heaviest passenger train ever to have traversed South African Railways.

Weatherwise, the sun did not always shine on the 'White Train', as on the morning of 29 March when it steamed into Pretoria station behind Class 15CA 4-8-2 locomotive No 2840. Approaching the station and looking out of his lounge window, His Majesty exclaimed 'ah this is the sort of weather I like'. Soft rain was falling from the leaden skies with but a trace of the sun's pale rays attempting to penetrate the morning mist. The train's air-conditioning system denied the feel, until the King alighted, of the cool air of that bracing Autumn morning. On 20 April, the Royal visitors bade farewell at Cape Town to their mobile 'white palace'. Subsequently, it proved to be the last time that a train was used for such a long period as a royal home during overseas tours. The development of air travel has seen to that! After the tour several vehicles were retained for use as the Governor-General's 'White Train'.

Other, perhaps less well known, occasions when British Royalty have used overseas railways have been by the Prince of Wales (later King Edward

The King, with Field-Marshal Smuts (Prime Minister) on arrival at Pretoria Station on 29 March, 1947, with class 15CA 4-8-2 locomotive, No 2840, following the 'White Train's' journey from Nelspruit and the Royal Family's visit to the Kruger National Park. (South African Transport Services)

The family photograph! Actually a large group of officials and staff from the White and Pilot Trains, with the Royal Family in the centre, taken towards the end of the 1947 Royal Tour of South Africa. The group are posing in front of Lounge Car No R10. (South African Transport Services)

VIII) when he visited Canada and Australia in 1919 and 1920, respectively. During his Canadian visit, the Prince tried his hand as driver at the controls of Canadian Pacific Railway 4-6-2 No 2231, and for a few miles drove his own royal train! In 1934 the Duke of Gloucester went to Australia and for the occasion, the Victorian Government Railways ran a royal train on its main South Western Line, using two Class A2 4-6-0 locomotives Nos 978 and 993. In the early part of 1935 the Duke, continuing his tour, arrived in New Zealand and in the North Island a train of 11 coaches, with rear observation platform, was placed at his disposal. Two locomotives were employed, both Class Ab 4-6-2s Nos 733 and 815. The leading engine was decorated with the Duke of Gloucester's coat of arms and the flags of England and New Zealand. The Duke showed great interest when the royal train was taking him up the famous Rimutaka spiral incline, requiring the combined power of five H class Fell type locomotives to reach the top.

It is reassuring to know that certain occasions still demand a more elegant way of travel and for which a train will, quite often, suffice along with some pleasantries too. Whilst touring Kenya and Uganda in February 1959, the Queen Mother found on St Valentine's Day, a card on her breakfast table, of the steam hauled royal train, from the engine crew and train staff. The verse on the card read: 'We railwaymen are deadly dull, Our lives run straighter than our line. Today our cup is more than full, For you provide our Valentine.'

In November, 1983, during a visit by the Queen and the Duke of Edinburgh to East Africa, the Queen was presented with a life-time season ticket from Kenya Railways, before leaving Nairobi station at 10.15am for Thika on a royal special drawn by two Class 72 diesel locomotives. Although a life-time travel concession for Her Majesty is of little practical value, the gesture is an indication of the pride and joy for the opportunity to provide transport for royalty.

117

9

THE VICTORIAN ROYAL SALOONS

As we have seen in Chapter 2 Queen Victoria's reign spanned the years from the railway pioneers of the 1830s, through the formative period of the next three decades and into latter part of the century when technical developments in all branches of railway engineering came thick and fast so that the railways of the new twentieth century were worlds away from the primitives of 70 years earlier. The railway carriage builders of the 1830s had little to guide them other than the contemporary road coaches and the first railway carriages were thus little more than a collection of road coach bodies mounted together as individual compartments on railway under-frames. Sometimes no more than two full bodies or compartments plus a coupé would form a single railway carriage, but some had three compartments and on the Great Western Railway, where the broad gauge allowed things to be much larger than elsewhere, four compartments were carried on a single underframe. Some carriages included a mail boot just as on their road coach predecessors, and lighting was by oil lamps suspended through the roof. Most railway carriages at that time were mounted on four wheels but again the Great Western was different and many of its broad gauge coaches were six wheelers.

The coaches just described were first class, equivalent to the inside seats of the road coaches. Usually seats and bodysides were padded and quilted to provide an element of luxury. The design evolved into what became the typical British compartment coach of later years which has survived into our own time although now fast becoming an endangered species. As for coaches for the middle and lower classes – second and third class – they have no relevance here since there was no link between such vehicles and royal coaches. They had wooden seats, bare wooden partitions, and were either open sided above the waist or totally enclosed with just the minimum of ventilation openings – windows were a luxury – if indeed they were covered at all since the early third class coaches were little more than open wagons with benches. Not until 1844 were third class travellers given the benefit of covered carriages and then only by Act of Parliament.

Thus by 1840 the most luxurious coaches on the railways of Britain were the first class compartment vehicles of varying sizes depending on the railway. An exception though were what were called Posting Saloons on the Great Western, four-wheeled coaches with a central doorway leading to a single saloon interior, with comfortable seats all round the sides and ends except at the doors. The body was a most peculiar shape since below the windows it was tucked in behind the wheels set to the broad gauge, but the windows themselves protruded over the wheels almost in oriel form. Between the seats was a table. These saloons included a clerestory roof, that is, following ecclesiastical architecture, the centre part of the roof was raised to a level higher than the remainder and the sides of the clerestory were usually glazed to give additional light. Although the clerestory was not widely used in the early years of the railways, and, indeed, quickly disappeared, it was revived in the 1870s and became a prominent feature on some railways from then until the first world war. But in these posting saloons were several elements which were to feature in later luxury and royal saloons. From the passengers' point of view they were in effect a super luxury first class, ideal for family parties or groups of friends travelling together.

However that luxury did not yet extend to the necessities of life, toilet facilities, refreshments or heating. They came later and such facilities were often pioneered in royal coaches although doubtless their royal occupants were not aware that they were being used as guinea-pigs for some new technical development. And yet it was so, for many of the improvements to passenger facilities were first seen on royal carriages and only came later into general service, as for example flexible gangways between coaches, used on Queen Victoria's London & North Western saloons of 1869, which were not used in public service for another 20 years and then only on a few special coaches with a more general introduction to corridor trains in the 1890s. Toilets and heating have just been mentioned, but in our own time air-conditioning, albeit a somewhat primitive type, was installed in the LMS royal saloons of 1941, but another 20 years passed before air-conditioning was used in some luxury diesel Pullman trains and a further decade until was used in ordinary everyday Inter-City coaches.

Queen Victoria did not venture on to a train until she had been on the throne for five years. However her suitor and eventual husband Prince Albert had used the railway to reach Windsor and so too had her aunt, the Dowager Queen Adelaide, consort of King William IV. Thus the railways had a few years to evolve carriage designs suited to the royal travellers, although again, without a precedent other than road carriages, the railway designers had to start from scratch, making use of the added dimension given by a railway carriage, that of space. Although the GWR's posting saloons were not well liked for ordinary travel, they were suited to special parties and clearly could be adapted for royal use. Thus the GWR's first royal saloon built in 1840 was of the posting saloon style although longer than initial examples. Similarly two years later when the London & Birmingham Railway was called on to provide a carriage for Queen Adelaide it adapted its standard 2½-compartment four-wheel first class carriage design.

As the Queen's reign progressed, so too did the desire on the part of the railway companies to reflect the latest comforts and improvements that designers and carriage builders could provide. It is known that Victorian designers were lavish when it came to decoration and railway carriages were no exception to this rule. In designing and building royal carriages in the knowledge that Queen Victoria was not a particularly easy passenger to please, there was always the reassuring thought that if a carriage could be made to look pleasing and comfortable, then it would be so. Alas, it was not always true as the Queen and her Household did, on occasions, point out! No fewer than 22 carriages were constructed for exclusive royal use. Fortunately, two principal royal carriages from the Victorian era still exist and can be seen in the National Railway Museum at York and the replica of a third carriage forms part of a Madame Tussaud's exhibition at Windsor. Two other what might be termed lesser saloons from this period have also survived to be preserved.

Few of the early royal saloons were numbered or if they were the numbers were not displayed. In less sophisticated times the railways presumably identified them simply as 'The Royal Carriage' for the needs of the accountants.

The descriptions of individual royal carriages built during Queen Victoria's reign include those built for her exclusive use, either new or adapted from older general purpose saloons. Also described are the saloons built for or used by her eldest son, the Prince of Wales, who succeeded her as King Edward VII, since Her Majesty was not overkeen on the Prince using her own vehicles. For one thing he smoked, but in any case the Prince would naturally prefer to use a carriage designed for a man in the fashion of and with the furnishings of a club rather than the frills and trimming of decor more suited to the tastes of Her Majesty his mother.

Most of the Victorian royal saloons were built piecemeal as single carriages and in no sense was a complete royal train built as an entity, except the train built for the Prince of Wales by the London, Brighton & South Coast Railway and, to an extent, the Diamond Jubilee train of the Great Western Railway. Some of the saloons built for the Prince of Wales were later formed into royal trains after his accession. They are described when built in this chapter but then subsequent use is traced as appropriate in the next chapter. Equally some saloons built in Victorian times were hardly used for royal journeys and were later made available for other uses.

London & Birmingham Railway
Four-wheel day and bed carriage No 2

Built: 1842
Length: 17ft 1in (headstocks) 16ft 6in (body)
Width: 5ft 6in (body)

The first royal carriage to be built by the London & Birmingham Railway was not for Queen Victoria but for her aunt the Dowager Queen Adelaide. It was built by the distinguished London coachbuilder of the day, Hooper, and mounted on an underframe built by the railway. In general appearance it was a typical first class coach of the period with two full compartments and a half compartment at one end. At the other end was a 'boot' where in normal carriages the mail was placed; in the case of Queen Adelaide's carriage there was no hinged lid to the top of the boot but instead there was an opening in to the boot by a hinged flap forming the seat back of the adjoining compartment. Because the compartments even of first class coaches of the early 1840s were very small, no more than 5ft – 5ft 6in between partitions, the use of a compartment for a bed would have been cramped. The bed was formed by placing stretchers across the gap between the seats and adding another seat cushion on top to form a continuous mattress on which the bed covers were laid. But to give adequate length for a passenger to stretch out fully the bed continued through the flap into the boot giving that extra length. One hesitates to say that the royal feet extended into the boot, but that is what happened. It was an arrangement used on a number of first class coaches of the time on night services of the L&BR.

Internally the coach was well padded with deep buttoned-in quilting on partition and side walls. Externally it had all the features of the transition period from road to rail with the turn-under body end (although at the end of the half compartment the end turned out, chariot style) and the curved three-cornered quarter-lights – the windows flanking the doors – and curved bottom and waist mouldings. The bed compartment had its own oil lamp but the other full compartment and the end half compartment had to share an oil lamp built above the partition. Although in royal use for only a short period – indeed the L&B built a saloon for Queen Victoria a year later – Queen Adelaide's bed carriage remarkably survived and can be seen today in the National Railway Museum.

It is difficult to imagine making a journey of a hundred or more miles in such a conveyance riding upon four wheels, but speed, the freedom from dusty roads and near total privacy were the attractions of railways that appealed to the early royal travellers.

Queen Adelaide's carriage of the London & Birmingham Railway, generally thought to have been built in 1842. However, the Dowager Queen is known to have made a rail journey in 1840, probably in an ordinary first-class carriage. It is probable that this is the same vehicle, used for the 1840 journey, with a new or altered body which is known to have been constructed by the firm of Hoopers of Gough Street, London. (London Midland Region, BR)

Great Western Railway
Four-wheel saloon broad gauge

The first royal saloon in Britain was built by the GWR in anticipation of patronage on visits between Windsor and London. Few details of it have survived other than contemporary reports which suggested that it was of posting saloon style with the body narrowing between the wheels. If that was so since the lower part of the body could not have been much more than 6ft wide to have fitted behind the wheels the upper sides and door

Built:	1840
Length:	21ft
Width:	

Built: 1843
Length: 13ft (approx)
Width: 7ft (approx)

The four-wheel saloon for Queen Victoria built by the London & Birmingham Railway in 1843.

areas must have projected quite prominently because descriptions at the time stated the interiors were 9ft wide. What is known is that the vehicle had a clerestory roof and was arranged with three compartments, two small ones 4ft 6in long at each end and the principal compartment 12ft long, and was built by David Davies of London. Internally it was furnished by Mr Webb, an upholsterer of New Bond Street. Louis XIV style hanging carved sofas were provided while the walls were panelled in crimson and white silk and paintings of the four elements by Parris. Each compartment also had a rosewood table and the floors had chequered India matting.

In this condition it was used by Queen Adelaide and Prince Albert. However it was not as steady as the Great Western's six-wheel carriages and early in 1842 Brunel suggested that it should be modified with a new frame carried on eight wheels, rigidly suspended from the side members but probably with some side play to allow movement on curves although with the short length not much would be needed. It was in its modified form that it was used by Queen Victoria for her first journey from Slough to Paddington on 13 June 1842, and continued in use though not by the Queen until the end of the following decade, after which it was altered internally to be used as an ordinary first class saloon until it was broken up in the late 1870s.

London & Birmingham Railway
Four-wheel royal saloon

In November 1843 Queen Victoria and Prince Albert made their first journey over the London & Birmingham Railway when they travelled from Watford to Tamworth to visit Sir Robert Peel. The Trent Valley line had not then been built and the train would have travelled via Hampton-in-Arden. For this occasion and in anticipation of continued royal patronage, the London & Birmingham Railway built a special carriage quite unlike anything else of the period. It was very short, no more than about 13ft long with narrow end compartments for attendants or the guard, which could have been no more than 2ft wide, access to which was gained through the end doors recessed into the sides, while the main royal compartment had a centre door on each side flanked by large windows. There was no communication between the small end compartments and the main saloon.

The roof was slightly domed and mounted on top in the centre was a large crown surrounding a ventilator. Wheels had wooden felloes with iron centres and tyres.

Externally the coach was ornately finished in dark lake with scarlet and gold lining and the heraldic devices of the royal family, but around the windows was liveried in French white. It was something like the carmine lake and off white of standard LNWR coaches of later years. Inside, the saloon was lined with blue satin, padded and deep buttoned and the window hangings were in white and blue satin. Furniture included an Ottoman and two chairs in Louis XIV style, with two console tables and two corner cabinets, and there was a wall-to-wall Axminster carpet. The most notable feature was the attempt at central heating with a closed circuit water pipe fed from a small cistern beneath the carriage and heated by being coiled through a lamp with four oil burners. The pipe was taken around the carriage between the flooring, the warm air entering the saloon through brass gratings in the floor. It was designed by Jacob Perkins, the inventor of an ineffective steam gun in 1824; perhaps he was more successful with heating the Queen's carriage! For the visit to Tamworth the Royal Party had gone by road from Windsor to Watford. Here the new royal carriage was marshalled between two of the company's ordinary first class carriages to which were added three carriage, trucks for the road vehicles, but not the horses. At this period in railway history, horses were not accustomed to the strange new railways, so another set would be waiting on arrival to complete the last lap of the journey.

London & South Western Railway
Four-wheel royal saloons

In 1844 the London & South Western Railway was called upon to provide a royal carriage for the visit to Windsor by King Louis Philippe of France, although the actual rail portion of the journey was from Gosport to Farnborough. The exact date of construction of the first saloon to be built is not now certain, but it was used for Louis Philippe in 1844 but might possibly have been used by the Queen when she travelled on the LSWR during the previous year. It was built as a four-wheeler and was based on the fairly standard three-compartment first class carriages of the LSWR but with two compartments joined as one to form the principal saloon, while the third compartment with an internal door to the main saloon was used by the equerries. Where the door and quarter-lights to the centre compartment would have been there was a single wide window of hexagonal shape while the quarterlights flanking the doors on each side were matching as half hexagons. There were windows in the coach ends and the body ends curved outwards chariot fashion. Like other royal saloons a noted upholsterer, this time Mr Herring of Fleet Street, was given a free hand; the interior was splendidly decorated with silk damasks trimmed in crimson and white lace. The ceiling was covered in white silk embroidered in crimson velvet and silver motifs.

Two more companion saloons were built to make up a royal train towards the end of the 1840s and one of the vehicles was exhibited at the Great Exhibition in 1851. This coach had a centre door with quarterlights

(facing page top)
Preserved LNER Class A3 4-6-2 No 4472 Flying Scotsman on royal train duty on 20 November 1984 when it headed a two-coach special conveying Queen Elizabeth the Queen Mother from Stratford to North Woolwich, where she performed the opening ceremony at a new railway museum at North Woolwich station. (Author)

(facing page bottom)
The royal train of Kenya Railways taking the Queen and Duke of Edinburgh from Nairobi to Thika, on 12 November, 1983, is greeted on arrival at Ruira. It is being hauled by two Class 72 diesel-electric locomotives, Nos 7103 and 7110; immediately behind the locomotives are two covered bogie vans. The train was preceded by a motor trolley manned by a patrol with a radio with similar arrangements in the rear of the special. During her journey the Queen drank morning coffee and waved to groups of well wishers, gathered in the hot sun, from the relative cool of the viewing platform in the centre of coach ICB 504. (Kenya Railways)

Built:	1844 and 1848/50
Length:	17ft 4½in (body panels)
Width:	7ft 3in

of conventional shape on each side and what appeared from the outside to be two half compartments at each end although internally the coach was arranged as two compartments. The 1844 saloon was rebuilt as a six-wheeler in the early 1850s but reverted to four wheels in the 1890s. The 1850 saloon assumed the role of the Queen's personal carriage until a new LSWR royal saloon was built in 1877.

The most interesting part of the history of these coaches is what happened to them in later life. They became ordinary first class saloons in the 1870s and in 1908 were sent by the LSWR to the Bere Alston and Callington branch in Cornwall. Col H. F. Stephens, the light railway entrepreneur was involved with this railway after its reopening in 1908 and acquired the former LSWR royal saloons. The 1844 saloon went to another of the Colonel's lines, the Shropshire & Montgomeryshire, while one of the 1848/50 saloons went to the Kent & East Sussex Railway where it was used as the Colonel's personal inspection saloon or for special party work. As such it was noted in 1928 as being in an excellent state retaining its walnut panelling. In 1936 it was sold to the Southern Railway for possible preservation but after a period in store its body was sold to a farmer as a shed where it lasted until the 1960s having fallen apart. The 1844 saloon fared no better. The army took over the Shropshire & Montgomeryshire Railway during the second world war, but the royal coach, like the other S&M stock which had suffered from neglect and then abandonment after the passenger service was withdrawn in 1933, was not in good condition. It was moved to the Longmoor Military Railway and although earmarked for preservation was so badly eaten away by woodworm or rotten timber there was little left by the 1950s when the remains were burnt.

Great Western Railway
Eight-wheel Queen's saloon, broad gauge

Built: 1848–50
Length: 30ft 8in
Width: 9ft 0¼in

Although this is one of the major Victorian royal saloons it is nevertheless the subject of a mystery over its exact date of building. It was always thought the coach dated from 1850 but a year earlier a 'new' royal saloon was listed in official records alongside the 1840 vehicle as already being in existence. C. Hamilton Ellis records in *Nineteenth Century Railway Carriages* that he unearthed a set of pre-1850s drawings for a new royal carriage with some highly unorthodox springs, and speculates whether it was ever built and quickly scrapped. Whatever the truth the royal saloon which was built around 1848–50 was arranged with the axles in two pairs but not in pivoting trucks. They were suspended in the usual way from the underframe but the springs bore down on compensating beams which rested on each pair of axleboxes, and limited side play allowed negotiation of curves. Mounted on the roof was a disc and crossbar signal so that the Queen's wishes for increasing or more likely decreasing speed could be transmitted to the officer supervising the engine crew by the lookout man sitting facing backwards on the tender. Internally the main saloon was flanked at one end by an attendant's compartment while at the other end was a small compartment fitted with that unmentionable necessity in Victorian social life, a lavatory, or more properly a closet, doubtless well covered to be inconspicuous when not in use.

126

The bodywork of the coach, like the 1840 saloon, was built by Davies on an underframe built at Swindon. The bodywork still featured the rounded bottom mouldings on the side panels. The sides of the main saloon bulged out to a width of 9ft from the 8ft 9½in of much of the coach.

The Queen used this saloon for all her Great Western journeys until 1874 when a new standard gauge Queen's carriage was built. By then in any case standard gauge existed from Paddington to Birmingham and to South Wales and within two years the standard gauge would have reached Exeter so that only journeys on from there to South Devon or into Cornwall would have needed the broad gauge saloon. Plymouth of course could be reached on the standard gauge by the London & South Western.

The 1848–50 saloon underwent a number of modifications over the years. Its single wide main saloon windows were replaced by a slightly

The GWR broad gauge carriage built in 1850 for Queen Victoria with a rigid wheelbase, the outer axles having lateral play to negotiate curves. Unusual is the miniature disc and crossbar signal on the roof, by which those attending the Queen could signal to a look-out man, positioned on the back of the locomotive tender, the desired speed of the train. Usually, for Queen Victoria, it was to slow down and rarely to go faster! (British Rail/OPC Collection)

Queen Victoria's GWR broad gauge saloon built in 1848/50 in its later years, much altered with the addition of a clerestory roof and after conversion to standard gauge in 1888. (Drawing Alan Prior)

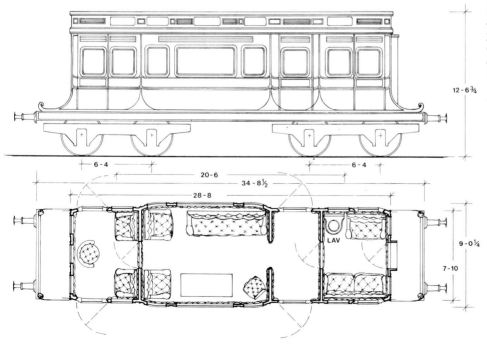

The GWR Queen's carriage of 1850 as rebuilt with a clerestory roof. In 1874 a new standard gauge saloon was built for the Queen; subsequently this carriage was converted to standard gauge to act as a standby, but, as another photograph illustrates, was frequently included in the Royal Train. (British Rail/OPC Collection)

Built: 1851
Length:
Width:

narrower central window flanked by two small windows, it was eventually mounted on a new longer underframe so that its end panels swept in a curve to the new headstocks, it was given a plain square ended clerestory roof, and in 1877 it was mounted on Dean four-point suspension broad gauge bogies; only two years later was converted for the standard gauge. After 1889 it was again usually included in the royal train but was not used by the Queen. It was scrapped in 1903.

South Eastern Railway
Six-wheel Queen's saloon

What has been described as the most elaborate royal carriage of the time for the standard gauge was built for the South Eastern Railway. It was a six-wheeler with the principal 12ft saloon compartment in the centre flanked at each end by a half compartment or coupé. The coach body at around 20ft in length was a little shorter than the underframe and the body end panels curved sharply at the bottom towards the headstocks of the underframe. Externally the coach was highly ornate with typical road coach style curved bottom mouldings to the panels, those surrounding the centre state compartment extending for its full length. Within the meeting point of the mouldings between the centre and end compartments were four carved gilt lions. Inside, the South Eastern's Carriage Superintendent, Richard Mansell, did not hold back on decoration, with side and end walls heavily padded and quilted in amber white and drab damask; there were similar coloured satin drapes, and the floor was covered with a velvet pile carpet. At one end of the principal saloon was a state chair with Maple carved fronts, spring stuffed and covered with silk damask, and in front of it a crimson silk velvet footstool. Alongside were two smaller chairs and at the opposite end two couches. In effect the saloon could be used as a travelling throne room for official audiences if the need arose. Like the GWR 1848–50 saloon the SER royal saloon was equipped with a toilet room in one of the end compartments and might have pre-dated the similar fittings in the GWR coach.

128

London & North Western Railway
Six-wheel Queen's saloon

By the mid 1850s, when the Queen and Prince Albert had acquired Balmoral Castle, journeys to and from Scotland were made in the small London & Birmingham four-wheel saloon dating from 1843 which had been inherited by the London & North Western Railway on the incorporation of that company in 1846. In 1861 the LNWR built at its Saltley Works, which were closed in 1865, a new saloon to replace the L&B vehicle, described in some sources as being a four-wheeler but which photographic evidence shows that at some time in its life in royal use was a six-wheeler. It was a fairly short, rather box-like coach, no more than 20ft long and possibly less, with two external doors on each side towards the centre. Internally the coach had two saloons, the principal saloon being the larger of the two, without any internal connection between them. Adjoining the royal compartment was a dressing room and toilet. The smaller compartment was used by the Queen's attendants. The principal compartment had chairs, a table and a sofa or bed, the latter alternatives being placed across the coach alongside the partition separating it from the smaller compartment.

The coach was painted in claret below the waist and white above, similar to the 1843 saloon and this livery became standard on the LNWR not only for the rest of its existence until 1923 but for another 16 years after that in the case of the LNWR 1903 royal train. Following the Great Western example on its 1848–50 saloon with a roof mounted signal, the LNWR provided a signal on the roof similar to the spectacle end of a semaphore signal but at that time showing only red or white lights. The 1861 royal saloon was first used to take the Queen and Prince Albert to Holyhead on their way to Ireland and was then used for the rest of the decade for the Queen's Scottish journeys until it was replaced by the pair of new saloons built in 1869.

Built:	1861
Length:	
Width:	

Great Eastern Railway
Six-wheel saloon for the Prince of Wales

With the purchase in 1862 of Sandringham for the Prince of Wales, clearly the Great Eastern Railway, which had been incorporated that year with an amalgamation of the various independent East Anglian railways, saw the possibility of regular royal patronage. The Queen had visited Cambridge in 1847 but the railways concerned had to borrow the L&B saloon for the journey. The Great Eastern thus put in hand the building of a saloon of its own, completed in 1864. It was a six-wheeler of about 26ft in length and was similar in layout to the existing GWR and SER saloons built a decade or so earlier, having a central principal compartment, flanked by a small compartment with toilet facilities at one end and a compartment for the royal attendants at the other. Among the embellishments were external door and grab handles in gilt and ivory. With the introduction of coaches with pivoting bogies in the 1870s the Great Eastern tried them out on a former four-wheel first class coach and this six-wheel royal saloon. Although it improved the riding, the Great Eastern stuck to non-bogie coaches until the end of the century.

Built:	1864
Length:	26ft
Width:	

London, Chatham & Dover Railway
Six-wheel Royal saloon No 1

Built: 1864
Length: 29ft
Width: 8ft 4in

The LCDR royal saloon is an example of a white elephant, for the Queen and other members of the Royal Family hardly patronised the line. The coach had one central principal compartment with its own central external door on each side while at each end were small compartments one for luggage and the other with toilet facilities. The Queen is believed to have travelled in it only once, in 1871, and the Prince of Wales in about 1893. It was also used to convey visiting royalty on occasions between Dover and London but by the mid 1890s had ceased to be a royal vehicle and was converted into a first class saloon seating 20.

London & North Western Railway
Twin six-wheel Queen's saloons

Built: 1869
Length: 30ft (each coach)
Width: 8ft

Without doubt the best known of the Victorian royal saloons is the pair of six-wheelers built in 1869 for the Queen's longer journeys, and particularly the twice-yearly visits to Balmoral, largely because they were used so often but primarily because in rebuilt form as a single coach it has survived to be preserved in the National Railway Museum.

These two saloons replaced the six-wheel vehicle that had been built in 1861 first used to take the Queen and Prince Albert to Holyhead at the start of a visit to Ireland. As some years had by then elapsed since Albert's death, the LNWR also felt that it would not now be considered disrespectful to replace the 1861 saloon with new saloons giving greater comfort for the long hauls between Gosport and Scotland.

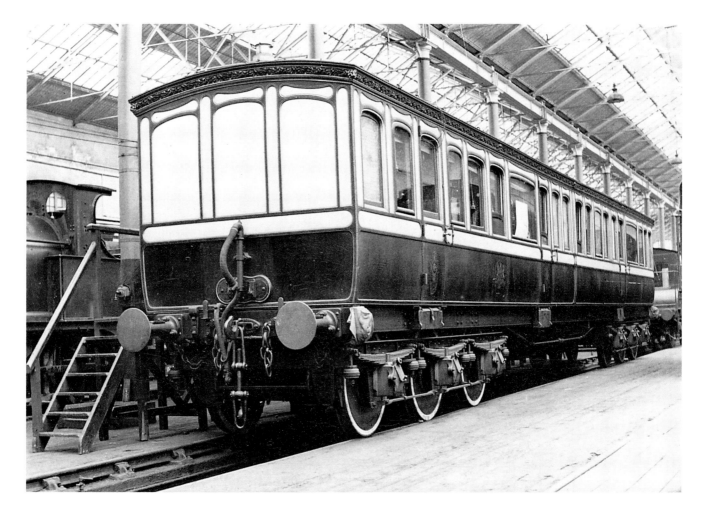

The LNWR twin saloons of 1869 were joined together in 1895 on a 12-wheel underframe as seen here in this photograph of the united Queen's saloon on display in the paintshop of Derby Locomotive Works in June, 1936. Now on permanent display, it is one of several royal carriages housed in the National Railway Museum, York. (L&GRP/David & Charles)

The twin saloons, for Queen Victoria, built by the LNWR in 1869. Note the bellows connection, through which the Queen would not pass while the train was in motion. (London Midland Region, BR)

A view of the GWR Royal Train, taken about 1890, showing the rebuilt 1850 Queen's saloon as the third vehicle from the locomotive. The fourth vehicle is the one built for the Queen in 1874 which, when the GWR wished to replace it in 1897, was, at Queen Victoria's insistence, rebuilt to incorporate, unaltered, the Queen's main saloon compartment. (British Rail/OPC Collection)

Here at last were the first royal saloons to break away from the cramped and very limited accommodation of the tiny four- six- and eight-wheeled saloons built until then. But this was a period in any case when British railway carriage design began to develop from the primitive and formative periods into a new generation of larger, longer coaches, some a little wider than hitherto and some with higher roofs, particularly the clerestory. The general improvements began to be seen during the 1870s and the Queen's new saloons thus anticipated some of these features.

One saloon was laid out for daytime use with a principal compartment 14ft 6in long containing a sofa, four armchairs and small tables. Adjoining the main saloon at the outer end was a footman's compartment, beyond which at the coach end was a small toilet compartment with wash basin and water closet. There was also a small table with a spirit lamp and kettle for making tea or coffee. At the opposite end of the main saloon was the principal toilet compartment which also formed a through passageway to the adjoining night saloon. Here was a new feature, a flexible corridor connection between the two permanently coupled coaches so that staff and the Queen could pass from one coach to the other while the train was on the move – the first corridor link between coaches in Britain. Alas the Queen did not like it, and refused to use it, insisting that the train should stop when she wished to move between the day saloon and the sleeping carriage. As for corridors on ordinary trains, it was almost 20 years before they made their first appearance.

The night carriage contained the Queen's bedroom with a door to a long compartment with longitudinal seats for the Queen's dressers; finally at the outer end of the night carriage was a toilet compartment corresponding to that of the footman at the far end of the day saloon.

If the 1869 saloons ushered in a new era of expanded design they continued the lavish decor and furnishings of previous carriages with heavily lined sides and ceilings in quilted silk in blue, white and red, with thick wall-to-wall carpet. There was no form of heating other than footwarmers, and lighting was by oil lamps and candles. Clearly the hot-water heater of the L&B 1843 coach had not been a success.

Queen Victoria was generally pleased, but in later years when, unasked, the LNWR replaced the original oil and candle lamps with gas lighting, Her Majesty tersely commanded the oil lamps and candles to be restored immediately. In later years electric lighting was also installed but the Queen never took advantage of the new illumination, preferring the softer glow of oil and candle lights which she insisted should be retained. Again, seemingly without Royal permission the LNWR rebuilt the two six-wheel saloons in 1895 to combine them as one long vehicle on a single

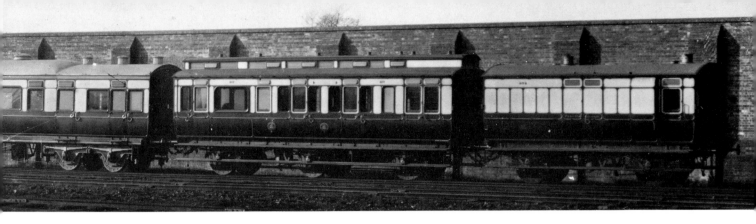

underframe carried on two six-wheel bogies and in which form it still survives in the National Railway Museum at York. By now, the Queen's stamina for continual remonstration with the progressive ideas of the LNWR was nearly exhausted and, in this particular instance, Her Majesty was relieved to discover that the interior, including the quilted decoration, remained unaltered. Elderly and rather frail, with failing sight, she quite probably welcomed the joining of the saloons for one very good practical reason, for no longer would she have to negotiate the concertina bellows gangway connecting the two saloons.

Great Western Railway
Eight-wheel standard gauge Queen's saloon

By the 1870s the broad gauge was reaching the beginning of the end even though it did not finally disappear until two decades later. Nevertheless all the Queen's journeys involving Windsor and London could be undertaken on the standard gauge and standard gauge had been de rigeur from Windsor to Balmoral for some years if a change of train was to be avoided. Thus the GWR with only a broad gauge principal saloon was at a disadvantage so that in 1874 a new standard gauge royal saloon was built. Like the 1848–50 saloon a feature was the central bulge, this time both in

Built: 1874
Length: 43ft
Width: 8ft 10¾in

Queen Victoria's GWR saloon of 1874 in its original condition. (Drawing Alan Prior)

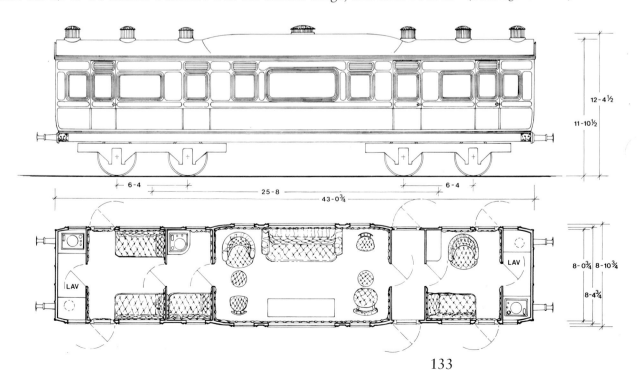

width and height to give the Queen's personal compartment in the centre more space. Externally the coach was almost arranged as a mirror image around the centre line; internally the principal saloon was flanked by a vestibule and toilet respectively on each side, beyond which were compartments and toilets for the footmen at one end and ladies in waiting at the other. The internal decor was still ornate with padded and buttoned in linings to the walls but without some of the drapes and hangings that characterised the LNWR twin saloons of 1869. Yet the toilet fittings were still carefully disguised in order not to look like toilet fittings, the wash basin being discreetly built into a table top and the closet completely covered by an upholstered seat.

Originally the coach was carried on eight wheels arranged in rigid pairs much as the old saloon had been, but it was soon modified to run on Dean Four-point suspension bogies. Oil lamps provided the main sources of lighting with massive surrounds to the tops of the lamps protruding from the top of the roof. On the headstock were carved lions heads in gilt, a decorative feature used on a number of royal saloons. The GWR royal train of this period was formed with the new saloon, the old saloon, once it had been converted for standard gauge in 1879, and a mixture of six wheel, and later bogie saloons and luggage vans, and lasted in this form for just over 20 years until a new royal train was built to mark the Queen's Diamond Jubilee. But that was not the end of the Queen's saloon as will be described later in this chapter.

OTHER LATE VICTORIAN SALOONS FOR THE QUEEN

Although the GWR 1874 saloon and the LNWR pair of six-wheel saloons of 1869 were undoubtedly the best known of the principal royal saloons and probably the most used, a number of other railways built or adapted saloons for the Queen and for the Prince of Wales during the latter part of the nineteenth century, the London & South Western and Great Eastern railways having two or three attempts to keep up with new developments.

London & South Western Railway
Six-wheel Queen's saloon

Even by the standards of the 1870s this vehicle was somewhat antiquated and could not be compared with the GWR's 1874 saloon which was so spacious, even though both were designed for daytime use only. The South Western coach would have been used only for short journeys between London or Windsor and Gosport. Externally it had a domed roof crowned by a short clerestory. As a royal saloon it had only a short life, lasting in this role for less than 10 years. Later it became an inspection saloon for railway officers and survived to be taken over by the Southern Railway.

Built:	1877
Length:	
Width:	

London & South Western Railway
Two bogie saloons

The 1887 six-wheel saloon just described was succeeded in its royal duties by a fine pair of bogie saloons much more imposing than the little six-wheeler and to a great extent setting a pattern for later LSWR ordinary stock in general appearance. Both had arc roofs following the style of the period but the coach designated as the Queen's saloon was given a massive square-ended clerestory, undoubtedly following Midland and Great Western practice on ordinary stock of the time, but certainly in this detail following nothing else on the LSWR. Indeed the LSWR was not what might be called a clerestory line, for the only other LSWR vehicles with clerestory roofs were a few dining cars early in the new century. Both of the coaches had two principal saloons internally separated by a lobby and a toilet compartment, with another lobby and toilet at one end. Surprisingly, gas lighting was fitted, but perhaps no-one asked the Queen whether she minded. By then the LSWR had standardised gas lighting so there was no question of reverting to oil. Both saloons were finished internally in the elaborate style of mid-Victorian years with deep buttoned-in quilting on partition and side walls, armchairs sofas, and padded and quilted ceilings. In 1897 the two saloons exchanged roles, the former secondary coach having a new roof of flattened elliptical shape, standard on the LSWR from

Built:	1885
Length:	47ft 6in
Width:	8ft 0¾in

135

then until the end of the first world war. Inside it retained the mid-Victorian style of decor and was fitted out with electric lighting. At one end the coach was given a flexible gangway so that it could be coupled to a Pullman or kitchen car to provide meal service to the Royal occupants. These two saloons were the last royal coaches built by the LSWR. The clerestory saloon was later converted for use as a party or picnic saloon, but what had become the royal saloon was used by the Prince of Wales after his accession as King Edward VII, with one of the compartments designated for use by the King and the other for Queen Alexandra. As such it survived in royal use until 1923, but both coaches were not withdrawn until the 1930s.

Great Northern Railway
Twelve-wheel royal saloon

Built: 1889
Length:
Width:

Not to be outdone by other railways the GNR decided to have its own royal saloon intended for the Queen's use. Most GNR stock of the eighties was relatively small, mostly six-wheelers of about 30 to 35ft in length, and 7ft 9in or 8ft wide. The royal saloon built by Cravens was a contrast indeed, a massive twelve-wheeler on six-wheel bogies, 60ft or so in length, with a large square ended clerestory roof. But it was a disappointment, for the Queen hardly used it and it was later adapted for use as an inspection saloon by railway officers. However its greatest claim to fame came right at the end of its life as a railway carriage, for in 1965 it was taken off its wheels and underframe to be grounded as a church at Gatehouse-of-Fleet in south west Scotland.

Continental
Twin six-wheel Queen's saloons

One more saloon – or to be exact a twin pair of six-wheelers used by the Queen – remains to be mentioned, although they did not run in Britain. For her journeys over the French railway system, the Queen used two six-wheeled saloons, one for day use, the other for sleeping, similar to those of the LNWR, which together with other saloons and sleeping cars combined to form a seven coach Continental royal train. The two six-wheeled saloons were the personal property of Queen Victoria and were kept mostly at Calais, although she nearly always preferred to travel from Cherbourg. Possibly, following the North Western's example of unifying its two six-wheel saloons, the Continental saloons were treated likewise by the time the Queen made her last visit to France in 1899. The Queen's Continental saloons were based largely on British design but were built in France.

Great Western Railway
1897 ROYAL TRAIN
Brake & luggage vans with toilets Nos 1069 and 1070

Built: 1897
Length: 56ft
Width: 8ft 6¾in

Built: 1897
Length: 58ft
Width: 8ft 6¾in

Attendants' and officers' saloons Nos 233 and 234

136

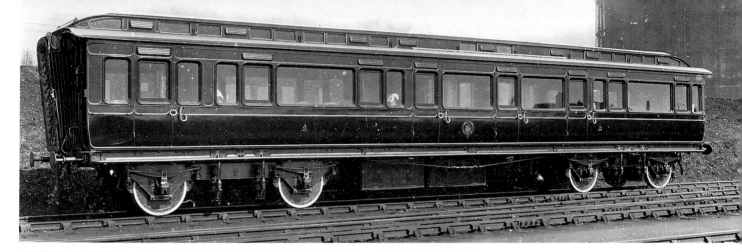

One of the 58ft saloons No 233 built in 1897 for the GWR royal train. It was renumbered 9002 in 1907, and is shown as running in 1928 in chocolate lake livery. (British Rail/ OPC Collection)

Interior of GWR saloon No 233 (later 9002), built in 1897 as part of the GWR royal train. (British Rail/ OPC Collection)

Corridor first No 283

Built:	1897
Length:	56ft
Width:	8ft 6¾in

Rebuilt Queen's saloon No 229

Built:	1897
Length:	54ft
Width:	8ft 10in

The Great Western's new royal train built for the celebration of Queen Victoria's Diamond Jubilee in June 1897 was a highlight in the twilight years of her long reign. However, when the Queen heard that the Great Western Railway was planning to build a new train including the replacement of her 1874 saloon, her displeasure at such a prospect was made clear. While the Queen appreciated the loyal intentions that the Great Western Railway wished to convey to Her Majesty and Suite from Windsor to Paddington for the Diamond Jubilee celebrations in London in the comfort of the finest carriages that Swindon craftsmen could build, her

The lounge of the GWR Queen's saloon which was left virtually unaltered during rebuilding in 1897. (British Rail/OPC Collection)

express wish, indeed command, was that the interior of her main saloon remained unaltered. 'Build a new train and as fine as you wish, but leave the private apartment in my carriage as it is', the Queen is reported to have said. So to the credit of the Great Western's Chief Mechanical Engineer, William Dean, and his staff a near miracle was performed. The centre portion of the Queen's saloon, forming her private apartment, was skillfully incorporated into a new lengthened carriage with the original bulge in the roof and bodyside of the 1874 saloon being retained. In this masterpiece of joining old and new, the opportunity was taken to provide a wide double door entrance vestibule through which Queen Victoria, who now mostly walked with the aid of a stick, could make a more regal entry than hitherto through the narrow single door of the original saloon.

To complement the royal saloon five new carriages were constructed to the very latest designs in carriage building. All were fitted with gangway connections which, for the first time, gave access throughout the train including the Queen's saloon. The outer ends of the two guard/brake vehicles did not have gangway connections, preventing access if coupled to ordinary coaches. A distinguishing feature of all five new carriages was the unique roof clerestory which sloped downwards at the ends in a similar manner to the American Pullman Cars that first appeared on the Midland Railway in 1874. When built, there were three different types of lighting – gas in the brake carriages, electricity in the rest of the train, with the sole exception of the Queen's own saloon, lavatory and vestibule where, as she had insisted in her London & North Western saloon, oil lighting was retained. Because of complaints that the main saloon became over warm in

138

hot weather the 1897 rebuild of No 229 included a double roof. The Queen's saloon served as hearse coach for the funerals of both Queen Victoria and King Edward VII and was scrapped in 1912. A section of the interior is preserved in the National Railway Museum, York, while a replica of it forms part of Madame Tussaud's Royalty & Empire exhibition at Windsor & Eton Central station. Similar in profile and appointments to the new coaches was the GWR director's saloon No 249, built in 1894 and occasionally used to supplement the royal coaches. No 249 has been preserved.

OTHER LATE VICTORIAN SALOONS FOR THE PRINCE OF WALES

As was mentioned briefly at the beginning of this chapter several railways built royal saloons primarily or specifically for the Prince of Wales and while some of the vehicles had little more than rare or occasional use for a few years, or were replaced by something more opulent, a few of the saloons took on a much more important role as King's or Queen's coaches after the accession of the Prince of Wales to the Throne in 1901. Indeed the London, Brighton & South Coast Railway produced a complete royal train for the Prince in 1897 which with the GWR Queen's saloon formed Queen Victoria's funeral train from Gosport to London Victoria, and then did duty as the King's train on the LBSCR from then on.

London, Brighton & South Coast Railway
Six-wheel royal saloon No 510

For the Prince of Wales' forays to the South Coast or to the racecourses south of London the LBSCR built a six-wheel saloon with two principal compartments plus a small smoking compartment and a single toilet compartment accessible from the rest of the coach. Like a number of LBSCR ordinary saloons of this period the royal coach was carried on Cleminson trucks, in which the centre axle was carried in a sliding assembly which allowed considerable lateral movement, this truck being attached by radial bars to the end trucks carrying the outer axles which were pivoted. Thus the whole axle assembly was always at a tangent to curved track unlike conventional rigid six wheelers where the outer axles were not at right angles to the track on a curve and the wheel flanges tried to dig-in to the rail. This saloon lasted for royal use until 1897 when it was replaced by a new royal train, but survived as a general saloon for private hire until 1925.

Built:	1877
Length:	32ft 3in
Width:	8ft

South Eastern Railway
Twelve-wheel Continental saloon No 1R

Although the Queen personally owned the twin six-wheel saloons normally kept at Calais for her use on mainland Europe she would not permit them to be used by other members of the family. Thus in the early 1880s a new royal saloon was ordered for Continental use to be owned by the South Eastern Railway but built surprisingly by the Manchester, Sheffield & Lincolnshire Railway at its Gorton Works from the design prepared by

Built:	1883
Length:	58ft 6in
Width:	8ft 6in

Built:
Length: 42ft
Width: 8ft 6in

Thomas Parker, the MSL Carriage & Wagon Superintendent. The link between the two companies was Edward Watkin, Chairman of both. The new coach primarily for the use of the Prince of Wales, was large, certainly the longest royal saloon at that time on a single underframe, and among the first of the new generation of long twelve-wheelers, first seen on the Midland Railway in the mid 1870s and developed for a few individual types, particularly first class restaurant cars on the MSL and Great Northern.

The saloon had three principal royal compartments, two for night use and one day saloon, two principal toilets and a small compartment with toilet for attendants, also a pantry. Decor was much less ornate than the Queen's British saloons of the time, with floral patterns on sofas and carpets, panelled walls, painted panelled ceilings and such fittings as ship's balanced swinging lamps. A corridor connection, at the attendants' end only, was soon provided for access to a dining car.

On 4 April, 1900 this saloon became the victim of a potential assassin's bullet when a youth aimed a revolver at the Prince of Wales who was seated with Princess Alexandra by one of the saloon windows just as their train was slowly drawing out of the Nord Station in Brussels, at 5.30pm for Denmark. Fortunately, neither the Prince nor Princess was hurt and after a few minutes they ordered the train to proceed. The Prince asked that the authorities should not punish the youth, who was only 15, too severely. He was placed under police supervision until he came of age. When not in use the saloon was kept alongside the Queen's twin six-wheelers in a shed at Calais. It was inherited by the Southern Railway, which numbered it 7931, but was sold in France in the late 1920s.

London & North Western Railway
Eight-wheel radial saloons Nos 5131 and 5153

In the 1880s the LNWR built two saloons classified for royal use, No 5131 designated for the Prince of Wales and No 5153 for equerries. They were eight-wheelers, but like other LNWR stock of the time were not arranged on bogies but in two groups of two axles, the centre ones attached rigidly to the underframes and the outer two in independent trucks pivoted radially. Later they were rebuilt on bogies. They were often included in the LNWR

140

royal train of the late 1880s and in the 1890s along with the Queen's twin six-wheelers, and an assortment of other six-wheel saloons and first class carriages, none of course with corridors except between the Queen's twin saloons. They were displaced from the royal train with the assembly of a new LNWR royal train in 1903 and did not last to be taken over by the LMS in 1923.

Great Eastern Railway
Six-wheel saloon

Built:	1894
Length:	31ft 6in
Width:	8ft

Bogie saloon No 31

Built:	1897
Length:	41ft
Width:	8ft 6in

Bogie saloon No 49

Built:	1898
Length:	48ft 3in
Width:	8ft 6in

Bogie saloon No 5

Built:	1901
Length:	50ft
Width:	8ft 6in

With Sandringham House on its system it was inevitable that royal journeys would be relatively frequent and the GER built a number of saloons largely for the Royal Family rather than the Queen, some exclusively allocated for royal use. Six wheel saloons were used by the Princess of Wales and for the Duke of York (later King George V). In 1897 the company built a new 41ft bogie saloon for the Prince of Wales, among the first proper bogie coaches to be built by the Great Eastern. Internally it comprised a principal saloon for day use, an ordinary first class compartment with a side corridor, a servants' compartment, ante room and two lavatories. Decor was by now much less ornate though still sumptuous, with royal blue buttoned-in Morocco leather and silk blinds, while panels and furniture were in walnut and satin wood. The ceiling was picked out in silver, cream and gold.

A year later the GER built another bogie saloon, No 5, for the Princess of Wales. It had small saloons no more than 12ft long at both ends, linked by a side corridor serving a smoking compartment, servants' compartment and toilet. Both Nos 31 and 5 were in varnished teak externally and they were gas lit.

Finally, although strictly belonging to saloons of the 20th century came saloon No 49 for King Edward VII and Queen Alexandra in 1901 and first used on 13 January 1902. At 50ft it was slightly longer than the 1898 coach but had a clerestory roof similar to some GER semi-corridor coaches of 1899. Inside, the coach had two saloons, one for the King and one for the Queen, a first class compartment, one for servants, and two toilets. Blue morocco leather upholstery was used for lining walls and for seats and couches. Frieze panels were of burr walnut inlaid with boxwood, and curtains in the saloons were in blue silk. Wilton wall-to-wall carpet had a pale blue fleur de lis on a dark blue background. Ceilings were finished in white lincrusta picked out in gold. Like the earlier saloons No 49 was gas lit, but all three bogie coaches were fitted with electric bell pushes indicated

(opposite)
The LNWR 1920-built Chairman's Saloon, No 45000, shown as running in lined LMS crimson in the royal train at Coventry on 30 June, 1970. (Author)

GWR saloon No 9007, built in 1945, seen here in use by the Queen Mother, whose personal insignia is shown on a detachable metal plate. On the left is the ex-LNWR brake first No 5155. They were photographed at Leamington Spa on 3 November, 1966. (Author)

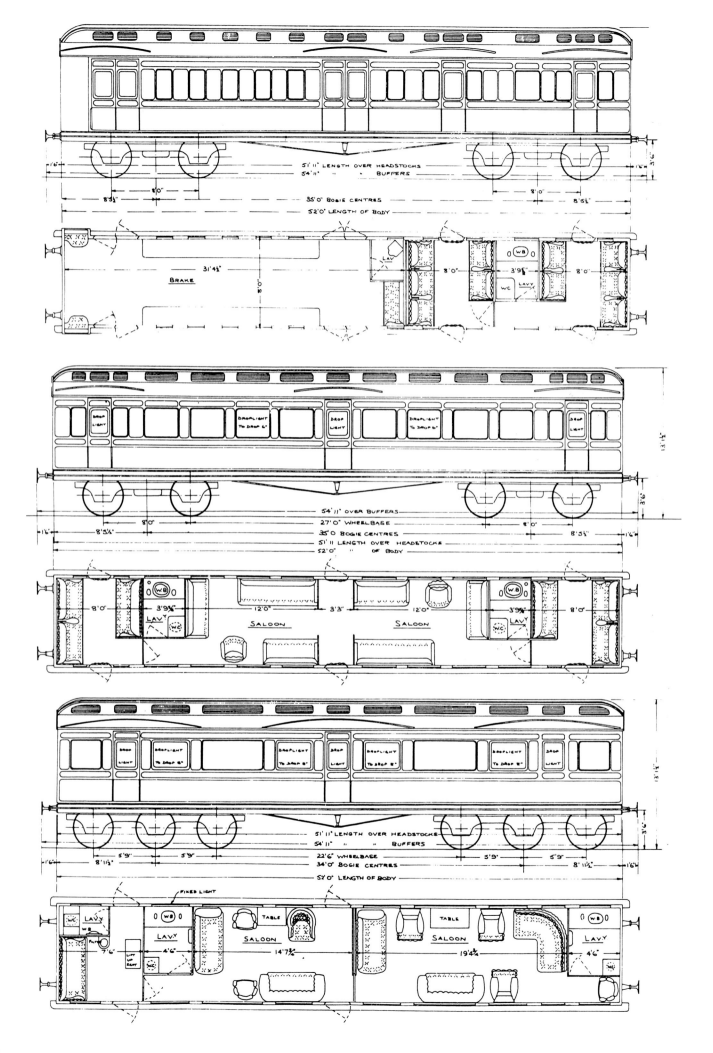

Top diagram (side elevation):

51' 11" LENGTH OVER HEADSTOCKS
54' 11" " " BUFFERS

35' 0" BOGIE CENTRES
52' 0" LENGTH OF BODY

1'6"
8'0"
8'5½"
3'6"

8'0"
8'5½"
1'6"

Top diagram (plan):

31' 4½"

BRAKE

15'0"

LAV.

8'0"
3'9½"
8'0"

WC LAVY

Middle diagram (side elevation):

DROP LIGHT
DROPLIGHT TO DROP 6"
DROP LIGHT
DROPLIGHT TO DROP 6"
DROP LIGHT

13'1½"

54' 11" OVER BUFFERS
27' 0" WHEELBASE
35' 0 BOGIE CENTRES
51' 11" LENGTH OVER HEADSTOCKS
52' 0" " " OF BODY

1'6"
8'5½"
8'0"
3'6"
8'0"
8'5½"
1'6"

Middle diagram (plan):

WB
WB
LAVY
WC
3'9½"
SALOON
12'0"
3'3"
SALOON
12'0"
3'9½"
WC
LAVY
8'0"
8'0"

Bottom diagram (side elevation):

DROP LIGHT
DROPLIGHT TO DROP 6"
DROP LIGHT
DROPLIGHT TO DROP 6"
DROP LIGHT
DROPLIGHT TO DROP 6"
DROP LIGHT

13'1½"

51' 11" LENGTH OVER HEADSTOCKS
54' 11" " " BUFFERS

3'6"

22' 6" WHEELBASE
34' 0" BOGIE CENTRES
52' 0" LENGTH OF BODY

1'6"
8'11½"
5'9"
5'9"
5'9"
5'9"
8'11½"
1'6"

Bottom diagram (plan):

FIXED LIGHT

WC
LAVY
WB
WB
LAVY
TABLE
SALOON
TABLE
SALOON
WB
LAVY
WB

7'6"
4'6"
14'7½"
19'4¼"
4'6"

LIFT UP SEAT

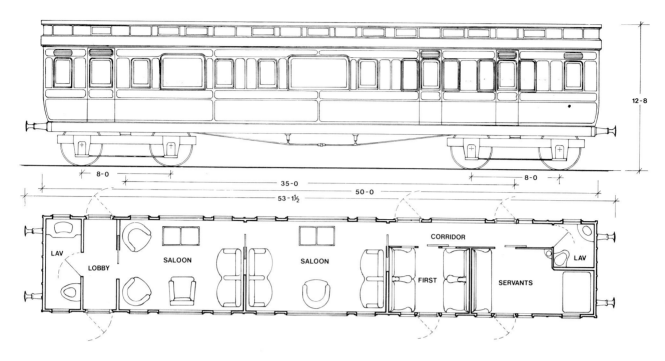

12-8

8-0   35-0   8-0
50-0
53-1½

LAV
LOBBY
SALOON
SALOON
CORRIDOR
FIRST
SERVANTS
LAV

in the servants' compartment. All three saloons had steam heating. After the Grouping in 1923 No 5 was transferred to departmental use as an inspection saloon; it underwent a number of internal alterations over the years and has since been preserved. Nos 31 and 49 were numbered 610 and 611 respectively and demoted to general saloons surviving at least to the late 1930s.

The Great Eastern Railway saloon built in 1901 for King Edward VII and Queen Alexandra.
(Drawing Alan Prior)

London, Brighton & South Coast Railway
1897 ROYAL TRAIN FOR THE PRINCE AND PRINCESS OF WALES
Brake first with toilet, Nos 565 and 566

Saloon for ladies and gentlemen in waiting, Nos 563 and 564

Royal saloon for Prince and Princess of Wales, No 562

Built:	1897
Length:	52ft
Width:	8ft
Built:	1897
Length:	52ft
Width:	8ft
Built:	1897
Length:	52ft
Width:	8ft 9in

Whatever the views of Queen Victoria might have been on the merits of Brighton and the railway that served it, the Prince of Wales had no inhibitions about the area and in 1897 the LBSCR built a complete train for him to replace the old six-wheel saloon which had served him until then. The new train was virtually uniform throughout in body style, the exception being the saloon of the Prince himself which was 9in wider than the other coaches. All had a massive clerestory roof sloping sharply down at the ends in the manner of American Pullmans, and the coaches were non-gangwayed at the express wish of the Prince so that he would not be disturbed on his journeys. The two brake firsts each had two conventional but larger than normal first class compartments linked by a short side corridor to a toilet compartment between them. One of the coaches had a

(opposite) Three vehicles of the LBSCR royal train of 1897, from top to bottom: Brake first; first class saloon; principal royal saloon.
(Drawings D. P. Eve)

145

The 12-wheel saloon built in 1897 for the Prince of Wales by the LB&SCR, which he subsequently used after becoming King Edward VII. It was No 562 and, by Royal Command, did not have corridor connections to other vehicles of the 'Brighton' royal train so eliminating disturbance during a journey by officials over-anxious to please their royal passenger! (The Railway Magazine)

dynamo to provide electric lighting through the train. The saloons, respectively for the ladies and gentlemen-in-waiting, each had four compartments and two toilets. Internally the walls and partitions were finished in sycamore panelling and mahogany mouldings while the lincrusta ceiling was finished in white but otherwise undecorated. Furniture upholstery was in silk plush, there were Axminster carpets, and a basically blue theme in the ladies' car and green for the gentlemen's saloon.

The saloon for the Prince had three compartments, one each for the Prince and Princess, and one for the servants. Compared with Queen Victoria's coaches the interior of this coach was a complete contrast being very much in the style of a London club, particularly the furniture with its deep buttoned dark green Morocco leather upholstery in the Prince's compartment. The Princess's furniture was much more gently upholstered in Utrecht velvet. Carpets too differed in colour with crimson for the Prince and grey-green for the Princess. Wall and partition panels were finished in satinwood inlaid with other woods to form floral patterns. Curtains were in green silk. Each compartment had access to toilet facilities, there was electric lighting throughout, and a new feature was the provision of electric heaters in the two royal compartments. Ceilings were in white lincrusta picked out in gold and some of the wall panels were also in lincrusta. Externally the coaches were finished in varnished mahogany with the royal arms on the doors and dummy doors along the sides, and etched into the frosted glass toilet windows.

The Brighton royal train continued to be used until the Grouping but then the royal saloons were reclassified as firsts and ran in an Eastbourne – London Bridge train, still with the royal furniture but later normal seats were substituted, and the saloons were used for private charter. The brake firsts ended their days on Oxted line workings and all were withdrawn in the 1930s.

At times the LBSCR basic five coach royal trains was strengthened with additional first class coaches, as for example Queen Victoria's funeral for which it was used between Gosport and Victoria, and on that occasion also included the GWR Queen's saloon as hearse coach.

10

SALOONS OF THE TWENTIETH CENTURY – THE FIRST 50 YEARS

As the new century dawned so the Victorian era came to a close and with it so far as the railways were concerned the opportunity to break away from the ultra conservative ideas of the old reign. That is not to criticise Queen Victoria, for Her Majesty had strong ideas on what she liked and disliked and she liked what she knew. She had grown up in the formative years of railways and much of what she liked stemmed from the early period. King Edward VII in contrast was enthusiastic for something more modern. Already we have seen how the saloons built for his use showed marked alterations in decor and furnishings, simpler and less fussy, but still in the grand style. Indeed the railway carriage builders' art undoubtedly reached its zenith in the 14 years from the beginning of the new century and the outbreak of the first world war, and the most opulent period had still to come, not only for royal saloons but in many other designs of coaches for principal express trains. But after the end of the first world war it was a different world, and things became much more utilitarian with accountants just beginning to look over the shoulders of railway engineering and operating departments, a trend which accelerated in the 1930s particularly on the LMS where Sir Josiah Stamp, an economist, as President, strengthened financial control of all activities on that railway. After the second world war the accountants took over. Thus the frills went out and everything was much plainer.

As far as royal trains were concerned the first decade of the new century saw a rapid increase in new royal vehicles with three new regular trains for the LNWR, the SECR and the East Coast companies. In Ireland too new trains were formed for a royal visit. One or two new saloons appeared after 1910, but then there was a lull. The existing trains served King Edward and his son King George V for nearly four decades. The only major change was in the GWR train when the old Queen's saloon was finally used for the funeral of King Edward VII in 1910 after which it was dismantled two years later. Its underframe was re-used for an inspection saloon, part of the interior was preserved but the rest was scrapped. The rest of the train survived until the mid 1930s by which time one or two other vehicles, including the directors' saloon, No 249, of 1894, which was similar in style to the attendants saloons, had joined the formation. No 249 survived as an inspection saloon and is today preserved on the Dart Valley Railway. The other saloons were sold as holiday homes in Wales, but one, as related earlier, has been retrieved and restored for the Royalty & Empire display at Windsor.

No new royal saloons were built from 1913 until 1941 when the LMS built three new vehicles, including two principal saloons for the King and Queen, by then George VI and Elizabeth, largely for security reasons, to

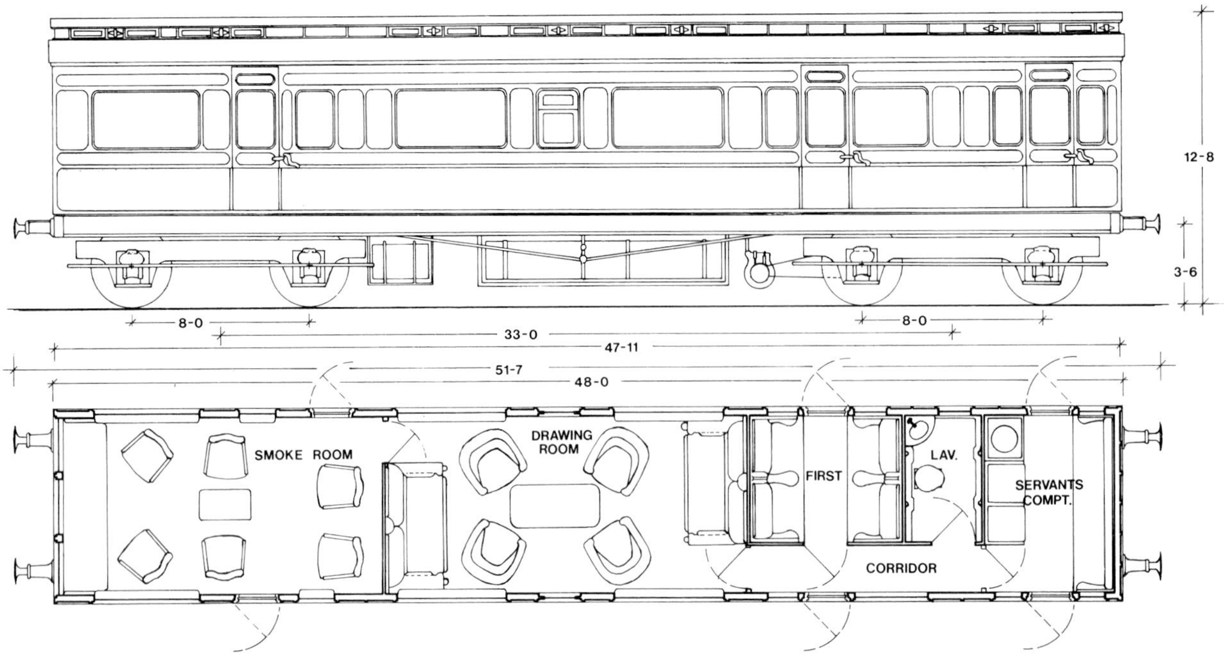
12-8
3-6
8-0
33-0
8-0
47-11
51-7
48-0
SMOKE ROOM
DRAWING ROOM
FIRST
LAV.
SERVANTS COMPT.
CORRIDOR

Great North of Scotland Railway saloon No 1 formed into the GNSR royal train and used by King Edward VII on several occasions, including journeys on the Great Northern main line. (Drawing Alan Prior)

replace those about to be described built in 1903. After the GWR royal train was disbanded in the mid 1930s the Great Western borrowed what by then was the LMS royal train which was basically the LNWR train of 1903. Meanwhile on the Southern the SECR royal train had become the principal train but was not used a great deal and then mainly for the royal trips to the Derby at Epsom racecourse, and to Portsmouth for Cowes week; it made its final royal journeys in 1939. The royal saloon is believed to have become a camping coach in Scotland but its fate is not known. After the second world war the Southern more often than not used Pullman cars for royal journeys, or on occasions borowed one of the East Coast royal saloons. After the accession of Queen Elizabeth II royal train provision became much more clear cut as will be described in the next chapter.

In the descriptions which follow, the coaches described are eight-wheel bogie coaches and are equipped with flexible end gangways unless stated otherwise.

Great North of Scotland Railway
First class saloon No 1, non-gangwayed

Built:	1898
Length:	48ft
Width:	8ft 6in

One of the first coaches to find use as a royal saloon at the start of King Edward VII's reign, not previously used as such, was the non-gangwayed bogie saloon No 1 of the GNoSR. It was built as a first class saloon available for charter. Originally it was internally arranged with two principal compartments one of which could be fitted out for night use, a first class compartment, toilet, and attendant's compartment and included a small pantry. Being owned by the GNoSR and based at Aberdeen it was readily available for royal journeys from Balmoral. The King and Queen used it on a number of occasions in Scotland; its most notable use though was when it was borrowed in 1903 by the Great Northern Railway for royal train duty taking King Edward from Kings Cross to Ollerton, and from Ollerton to Doncaster for the races.

After King Edward died in 1910 the saloon reverted to general purpose work and later when taken over by the LNER it became a departmental inspection saloon. Fortunately it was rescued upon withdrawal in the mid 1960s and is today preserved by the Scottish Railway Preservation Society, as the only royal saloon to be owned by a Scottish railway.

Duke of Sutherland
Private saloon, non-gangwayed, No 57A

This coach was not built for royal use but is included because it was effectively a prototype for what followed. Nevertheless it was used as principal royal saloon in 1902 when marshalled in the GNoSR royal train for it carried King Edward VII and Queen Alexandra from Invergordon to Ballater. The GNoSR saloon No 1 was used by the equerries. The London & North Western Railway had wanted to build a new royal train for Queen Victoria but received no royal encouragement. In 1899 the Duke of Sutherland, who not only had his own short private railway but virtually had the freedom to run his own private special train over much of the Scottish Highlands, since he had promoted the railway between Inverness and Wick, arranged with the London & North Western Railway to build him a new private saloon which was designed by C. A. Park the LNWR's Carriage Superintendent. It was magnificent.

The coach was arranged to be self contained for day and night use. Entrance was through enclosed end balconies rather than by doors along the side as in most Victorian coaches. Adjacent to one of the end balconies was a four-seat saloon with centre passageway, leading to a side corridor serving a toilet and two sleeping compartments, each with their own en-suite toilet compartments in between. The side corridor then led into an open dining saloon, beyond which was a further short side corridor to a small kitchen and an attendant's vestibule with its own access from the adjoining end balcony.

Built:	1899
Length:	57ft
Width:	8ft 6in

The bogie saloon built at Wolverton by the LNWR in 1899 for the Duke of Sutherland.
(Drawing Alan Prior)

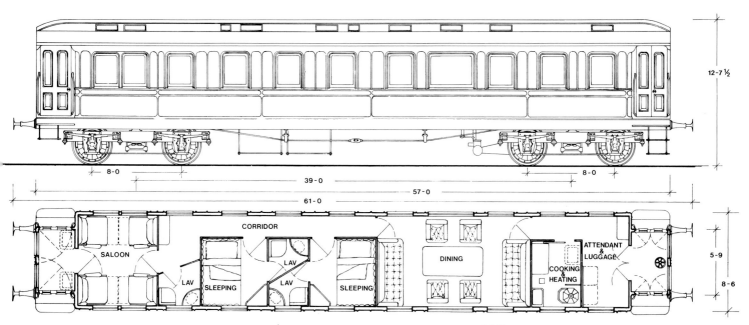

149

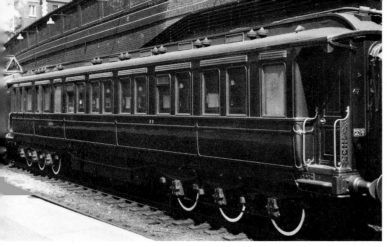

Internally the large dining saloon had a figured lincrusta ceiling in white and gold, with matching side panelling. The four easy chairs at the dining table and the two couches were upholstered in green figured tapestry, while friezes and curtains were in green silk. The coach had electric lighting, electric bell communication to the servants' area, electric ventilating fans, and a stove for the high pressure hot water heating system. A small oil cooking stove was fitted in the pantry for meal preparation. Externally the coach had an elegant clerestory roof, domed at the ends and the side panelling and mouldings were of the elaborate three layer style that characterised LNWR and West Coast Joint stock dining, sleeping, and special coaches then and during the next decade. Livery was very dark green below the waist and above the windows, also picking out the mouldings, and pale cream upper panels, with gold lining. The coach was eventually acquired for the National Collection and is today at the National Railway Museum.

London & North Western Railway
NEW ROYAL TRAIN FOR KING EDWARD VII AND QUEEN ALEXANDRA (the coach numbers are the final LMS numbers)

King's saloon No 800, twelve-wheel

Built:	1902
Length:	65ft 6in
Width:	9ft

Queen's saloon No 801, twelve-wheel

Built:	1902
Length:	65ft 6in
Width:	9ft

First class dining cars, twelve-wheel Nos 76 and 77

Built:	1900
Length:	65ft 6in
Width:	8ft 6in

Six semi-royal saloons, Nos 803–808

Built:	1903
Length:	57ft
Width:	9ft

Two Family saloons allocated to royal train, Nos 976 and 977

Built:	1899 approx
Length:	45ft
Width:	8ft

Two brake firsts, Nos 5154 and 5155

Built:	1906 (converted for royal train use in the early 1920s)
Length:	57ft
Width:	9ft

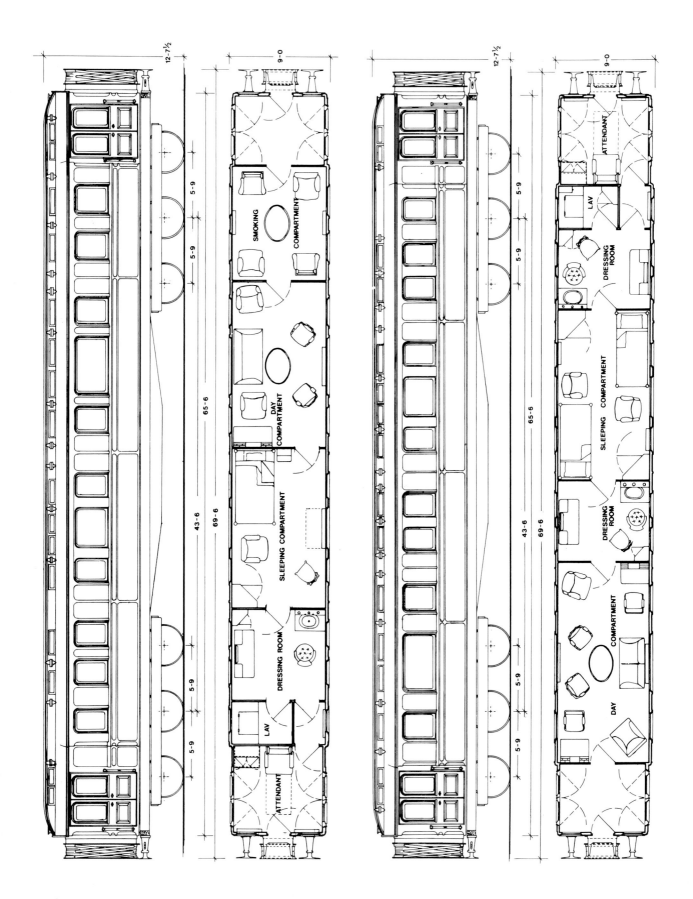

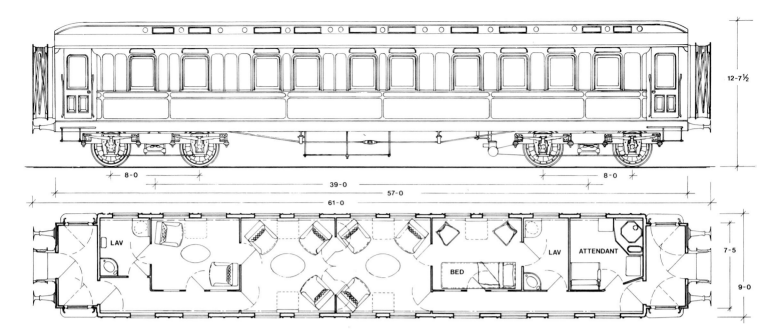

Dimensions shown on drawing:
12-7½, 8-0, 39-0, 57-0, 61-0, 8-0, 7-5, 9-0

LAV · BED · LAV · ATTENDANT

*One of the semi-royal saloons built
by the LNWR for the 1903 royal
train. The interiors could be altered
to provide varying accommodation.
(Drawing Alan Prior)*

At last with the new reign the London & North Western with royal blessing was allowed to indulge itself by building a new royal train, which not only marked the effective beginning of a new century, but parts of it lasted for well over half that new century in the role for which it was built. The new train is without doubt the best known of the British royal trains and much the most opulent. In following reigns it became by far the most important, especially for long distance journeys where overnight accommodation was wanted, and parts of it served through two world wars as a travelling palace on countrywide tours. Eventually it was used all over country as the royal trains of other companies reached the end of their useful lives. Although there is now no direct link with the royal train of today there is a thread of continuity since the LNWR 1903 royal train was never replaced in one fell swoop; as newer coaches replaced the old one or two at a time, there was always a link with the past. Some of the saloons of today's royal train, for example, ran corridor to corridor with some of the LNW saloons for some years and it is only in the last decade that final withdrawal came for the remaining coaches of LNWR origin which had spent the bulk of their working lives allocated exclusively to the royal train even though a few did not achieve royal train status at the start, while other vehicles included in the original 1903 formation were withdrawn from it before the Grouping. There is though, one exception since the LNWR 1920 Chairman's saloon at the time of writing is still allocated to today's royal train.

Without doubt the finest coaches of the new train were the saloons for King Edward and Queen Alexandra. They were massively and gracefully elegant, for at 65ft in length and carried on two six-wheel bogies they were the largest royal saloons yet built, but they did not have the pronounced ugliness of the Great Northern's 1889 coach nor the garishness of the massive American style domed clerestories of the Brighton train of 1897. Externally the six semi-royal saloons followed a similar graceful profile, and with the two principal coaches were panelled and liveried in a style which was adopted for the London & North Western's sleeping and dining

152

cars from the turn of the century until early LMS days, and was also seen on the coaches built specially for the American boat trains and the afternoon Anglo-Scottish service in 1908/9. The basic livery was the LNWR's carmine lake, often described as purple brown or claret, below the waist and above the windows, and off-white (often referred to as spilt milk) within the panels from the waist to the tops of the windows. The mouldings were picked out in purple brown and lined in gold. Door handles were in gilt, there were carved gilt lions heads on the ends of the headstocks, and on lower panels were the royal coats of arms.

Both the King's and Queen's saloons were similar in that they had enclosed end entrance balconies or vestibules with double doors, one of which in each coach was slightly longer than the other and included an attendant's seat which could extend into a couch for sleeping. In the King's coach, from the attendant's vestibule a short side corridor led past the principal toilet compartment to a dressing room, the full width of the car, and centre doors led through to the adjoining sleeping saloon, a day compartment, and finally a 10ft long smoking compartment with four chairs, adjacent to the other entrance balcony. In the Queen's saloon the attendant's compartment again led to a short side corridor past the one toilet compartment and into a small dressing room which gave access to the principal sleeping saloon. From the further end a door led to a second

LNWR 45ft family saloon of 1898, two of which were allocated to the 1903 royal train.
(Drawing Alan Prior)

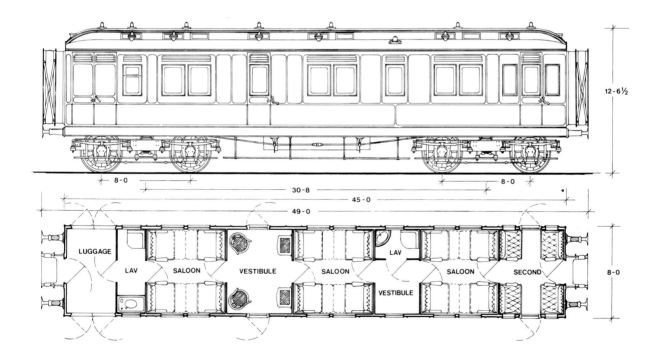

dressing room and then into the Queen's day compartment which was adjacent to the further balcony.

The decor of both saloons clearly owed nothing to Queen Victoria's ideas. Indeed the interiors of the King's and Queen's saloons reflected the King's nautical expression of wishing to feel afloat, for the majority of the wall finishes were a combination of white enamel gloss and eggshell. King Edward's saloon was fitted with electric cigar lighters and, quite separate

from the day and sleeping compartments, in the small mahogany-lined smoking room, were four green leather chairs in each corner with a carpet and curtains in similar tones of colour. While Queen Alexandra probably preferred to spend much of her time in her own day saloon, among furnishings in various shades of blue, the King's favourite spot was his smoking room where, when summoned, a footman would appear to light His Majesty's cigar. When use of the train passed to King George V and Queen Mary, this elegant, but cosy little room, became a favourite haunt during their journeys. The Queen's sleeping saloon was fitted with two beds, one for Princess Victoria, the second daughter of King Edward and Queen Alexandra who also used the second dressing room. The London furnishers, Waring, were entrusted with upholstery and furniture.

After the accession of King George V and Queen Mary in 1910 the LNWR royal train saw extensive use and with the outbreak of the first world war took on a new significance since it was used as a travelling home. Clearly more facilities were required among which was the installation of silver plated baths in the dressing rooms used by the King and Queen. The two 1902 saloons saw out another reign in 1936 but were hardly used by King Edward VIII during his short tenure on the Throne since he preferred to travel more simply, as described in an earlier chapter. In 1937 with King George VI and Queen Elizabeth on the Throne a new era opened, but so far as the LNWR royal saloons were concerned as we shall see, it was to last only a few more years.

The six semi-royal saloons for the Royal household were hardly less well appointed if but shorter and carried on two four-wheel bogies. Like the principal royal cars they had enclosed end balcony vestibules with single doors. From one end was a short side corridor past a toilet and a small

daytime compartment which had access from the corridor, into the first of two full width day compartments. From this compartment was a door to the smaller compartment. Double doors linked the two full width compartments from which one gave access to another side corridor leading to a toilet and an attendant's compartment before reaching the further entrance vestibule, while the other door from the large compartment led into a bedroom. Internal decor featured the white enamel walls, contrasting with the deep colour of the curtains and the lighter furnishings on sofas and armchairs. Unusually for coaches built specifically for royal train use these semi-royals could be hired for private travel — at a price — when not required for royal train duty. Over the years they underwent some internal alterations — baths were fitted as in the principal saloons for example — and one was adapted for use by Winston Churchill as wartime Prime Minister in the second world war.

Although the layouts were dissimilar, clearly some of the thinking behind the Duke of Sutherland's saloon was embodied in the 1903 royal train; indeed, externally apart from the subtle livery differences between the deep purple-brown of the LNWR semi-royal saloons, and the deep green of the Duke of Sutherland's coach, indistinguishable in certain lights, and the window arrangement there was little difference between them. Most of the LNWR semi-royals continued in royal train use for far longer than the King and Queen's saloons, lasting until 1968. One has been preserved privately.

Two LNWR family saloons were also designated for royal trains use. These were 45ft convertible sleeping coaches with a similar domed clerestory roof to the coaches built specially. They had end flexible gangways and a centre passageway right through, from an end second class compartment for eight with its own side doors, a four-seat compartment, a

Queen Alexandra's lounge in the LNWR 1902 saloon, subsequently used by Queen Mary, who altered the furnishings, and later Queen Elizabeth from 1937 until 1941. (Courtesy National Railway Museum)

vestibule and toilet compartment, another four-seat compartment, a vestibule with side doors and two loose chairs, a further four-seat compartment, a toilet, and finally a luggage compartment. A saloon of this type appears in photographs of the royal train during the reign of King Edward VII. The facing pairs of seats pulled forward to meet each other to form a bed. These coaches later gave way to conventional LNWR twelve-wheel first class sleeping cars in the make up of the royal train.

Although there were small electric stoves in the attendant's vestibules of the King's and Queen's 1902 royal saloons, clearly with longer journeys and tours proper facilities were required for meal preparation and service. Unlike Queen Victoria who to the end of her rail travelling days normally took meals at set station stops, eating while on the move became part of the normal royal travelling way of life. In 1900 the LNWR had built a first class dining car with kitchen for the West Coast Joint Stock and submitted it to the Paris Exhibition where it won a gold medal for craftsmanship. Apart from being a little narrower it was similar in outline to the royal coaches of 1902/3. Although it was electrically lit, gas was used for the cooking stoves. This coach, eventually No 76 in the final LMS numbering, and its companion No 77, became part of the LNWR royal train soon after it was formed. One car was used by the Royal Family and the other by the Household staff. Originally both cars had five bays of seats arranged two and four on each side of the off-centre passageway but No 76 later had some of the conventional seats removed and a longitudinal table and individual dining chairs substituted. During its life there were other modifications to such details as ventilators and it also had a new underframe. Both coaches lasted in royal service well after the second world war, No 76 being replaced by a new principal royal dining car in 1956 and No 77 lasting for a further decade. Both cars have been preserved.

Initially the LNWR's 1903 royal train was brought up at front and rear by full brake luggage vans, although sometimes only one van was attached. Both had the domed clerestory roof matching the passenger coaches but although panelled with mouldings it was not to the elaborate style of the saloons. Early in LMS days the full brakes were displaced by two corridor brake firsts Nos 5154 and 5155, each with two compartments and a toilet and a very large luggage and guard's compartment. They were originally built in 1906 with flattened semi-elliptical roof profiles turning sharply down at the sides, similar to the lower deck of the stock with clerestories. They were not converted for royal use until the early 1920s when they were given domed clerestory roofs to match the rest of the royal train. The compartments were adapted for sleeping accommodation for staff and a generator was provided in No 5154 to power the train when standing to avoid draining train batteries. The gangways at the outer end were removed and with the added equipment in the van part and new steel underframes the weight rose from 29 tons, when built, to 38/40 tons as altered. The full brakes displaced in the early 1920s were used from then on for ordinary parcels traffic, one at least to the mid 1950s, while the brake firsts survived in the royal train until 1978 and have since been preserved.

In its long life through the reigns of King Edward VII, King George V, King Edward VIII and into the first years of King George VI the basic LNWR 1903 royal train was joined by other coaches as occasion demanded. In King Edward's reign one or two of the 45ft family saloons were included together with the LNWR directors' saloon of 1897. Later, first class clerestory roof sleeping cars were included instead of the family saloons so that even in the late 1930s as King George VI and Queen Elizabeth came to the throne it was still very much the LNWR royal train, in LNWR livery, formed entirely of clerestory stock. But in that form time was running out and on the outbreak of the second world war the train was repainted in LMS crimson lake so that at a distance it would not stand out against any other ordinary LMS train. It was clear also that the King's and Queen's saloons would offer little protection in the event of air attack during the war. While little could have withstood a direct hit by a bomb or even blast damage from a very near miss, the wooden bodied coaches would have splintered to matchwood from nothing more than a machine gun attack. Thus two new principal saloons and a power car were built for the LNWR or now more properly the LMS royal train to provide more secure accommodation for the King and Queen on their tours. The two LNWR 1902 royal saloons were withdrawn and stored, were later preserved and are today at the National Railway Museum.

London Midland & Scottish Railway
King's saloon No 798, twelve-wheel

Queen's saloon No 799, twelve-wheel

Power brake car No 31209 (BR No 2910), twelve-wheel

Built:	1941
Length:	69ft
Width:	9ft

Built:	1941
Length:	69ft
Width:	9ft

Built:	1941
Length:	69ft
Width:	9ft

(facing page top)
HM The Queen's personal saloon No 2903, converted in 1977 from a proto-type Mk3 first class vehicle built in 1972. It is seen at Liverpool (Lime Street) on 25 October, 1978. (Author)

(facing page bottom)
HRH The Duke of Edinburgh's personal saloon No 2904, converted in 1977 from a prototype Mk3 second class vehicle constructed in 1972. It was photographed at Leicester (London Road) on 22 July, 1977. (Author)

The 1941 built LMS saloon for Queen Elizabeth, No 799 showing the protective armour plate shutters closed over the windows, fitted as a war-time precaution. (Courtesy National Railway Museum)

The new 12-wheel cars were of massive all-steel armour-plated construction, including for war-time use armour plated shutters to the windows. Their sleek smooth sides and elliptical roofs contrasted to the ornate panelling and clerestories of the original stock. Thus the LMS royal train lost its uniform appearance which with subsequent changes of stock it has never regained to this day. Unusually for LMS vehicles the new coaches had Pullman type gangways, buckeye couplers and hinged drophead buffers, but could still be attached by screw couplings to older coaches.

The basic design and layout of the King's and Queen's saloons was broadly similar to the 1902-built LNWR saloons although in fact the two LMS-built saloons were mirror images of each other. Both saloons had a double-door entrance vestibule at each end. Internally, there was self-contained day and night accommodation, plus small bed-sitting compartments for the King's valet and the Queen's principal dresser. Double-glazed windows were provided with dehydrators to prevent condensation. An innovation was the provision of a form of air-conditioning, using ice for cooling and steam and electricity for heating, with a choice of six temperatures controlled by thermostats, automatically maintaining the chosen temperature. The ice, carried in cabinets located under the floor between the bogies, had to be changed at frequent intervals and required more

Interior of HM The Queen's lounge in her personal saloon, No 2903. (British Railways Board)

The Prince and Princess of Wales have just arrived at the up side platform at Atherstone, Warwickshire, and are being escorted along the platform by Area Manager, John Brazier, before they leave the station to visit the Atherstone Festival '85 on 27 June 1985. Visible in the Royal Train formation are dining saloon No 2902 and part of the ex-LNWR 1920 Chairman's saloon (ex-45000) No 2911. (Author)

complex servicing than on any previous royal saloons. This equipment, and the sound deadening material and body insulation made them very heavy, weighing some 56 tons each – almost certainly the heaviest locomotive-hauled passenger carriages ever to run in Britain. The service car, usually referred to as the combined convertible sleeper, brake and power car, weighed slightly less at 52 tons. The main feature of this vehicle was the diesel generator supplying electric power throughout the train and it was normally marshalled at one end of the formation. One or other of the LNWR brake firsts was still used at the other end of the train.

The wartime window shutters could be partially opened as required when safe to do so. Not until the end of the war when the window shutters were removed were the aesthetic virtues of the saloon designs fully revealed. For those accustomed to the notion that royal carriages must be ornate with decorative handrails, embossed body panels, and fussily decorative furniture, there was disappointment. Designed for the practicalities of service at a critical austerity period in history their appearance reflected the mood of the time in providing only for the necessities required as shown in the accompanying photographs. However, their simplicity of appearance did not in any way make them less comfortable than the saloons they replaced. Their riding qualities, achieved by the combination of weight and heavy duty six-wheel bogies, were superb.

Interior of the LMS 1941 King's saloon showing the bedroom and doorway leading to the bathroom. In comparison to the LNWR saloons, the furnishing, though practical, is austere. (Courtesy National Railway Museum)

(overleaf)
The three new royal train vehicles built by the LMS at Wolverton in 1941. The drawings show from left to right, the King's saloon, the Queen's saloon and the brake/power/staff car. The photograph shows them as built, from left to right No 31209 combined brake/power/staff sleeping car, No 798 King's saloon and No 799 Queen's saloon. Protective armour plate shutters are partially opened on saloons 798/9. (Drawings Alan Prior; photograph courtesy National Railway Museum)

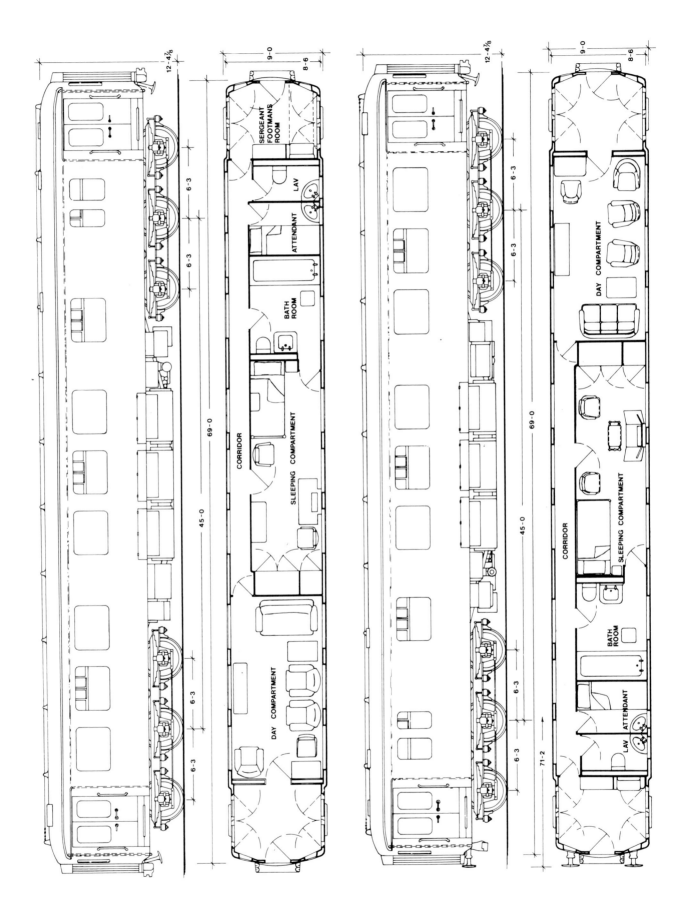

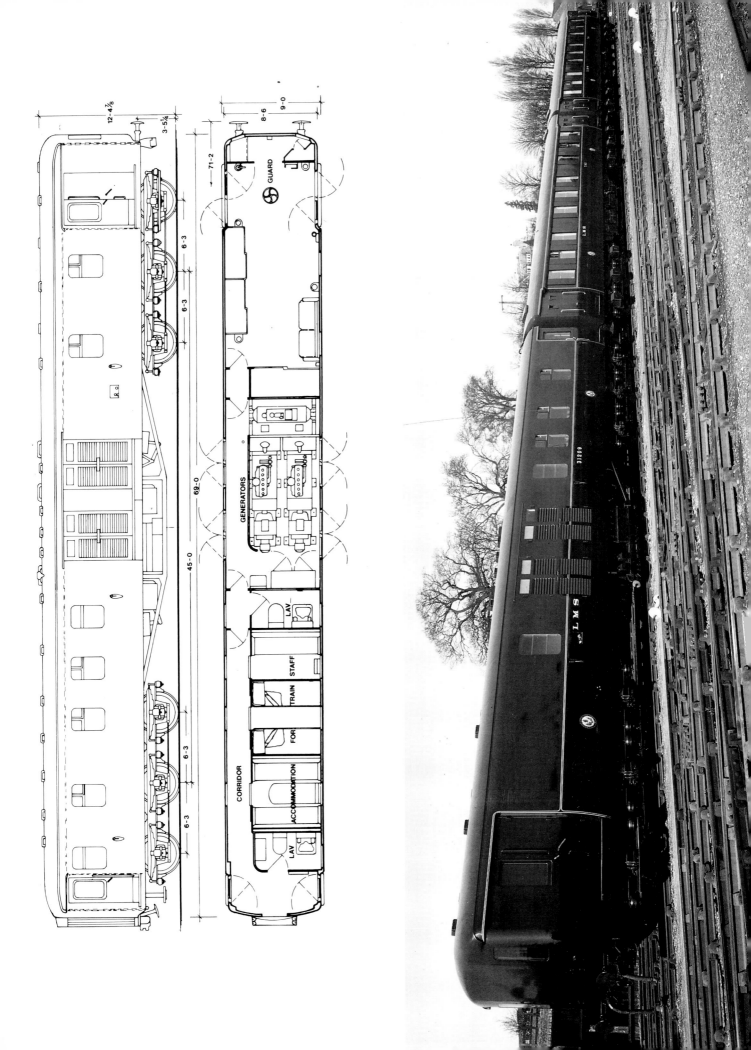

GUARD

71-2

8-6

9-0

GENERATORS

CORRIDOR

ACCOMMODATION

FOR

TRAIN

STAFF

LAV

LAV

12-4⅞

3-5¼

6-3

6-3

6-3

69-0

45-0

6-3

6-3

LMS

31209

LT8

From the entrance vestibule at one end a long side corridor led past a toilet compartment, the attendant's compartment, a bathroom, and main bedroom, before opening into the full width main lounge, the only part of the accommodation to extend right across the coach. Beyond the lounge was the other entrance vestibule. Pastel colours on wall finishes, curtains, carpets and furniture gave a light and spacious appearance and wall lights provided a homely touch so that when the curtains were drawn at night the lounge had all the intimacy of well furnished family homes up and down the country.

Both saloons remained in use although with roles exchanged as described later until May 1977 when they were retired from service, in favour of more modern vehicles and placed alongside their LNWR counterparts in the National Railway Museum at York. The power brake car remains in service as a stand-by for power supplies to the new royal saloons, if not available from the locomotive, but has been renumbered, from 31209 to 2910.

Other saloons allocated to the LNWR/LMS royal train

In its later years while still retaining much of its LNWR character a number of other coaches were allocated to it to replace or supplement some of the older coaches, particularly the 57ft semi-royal saloons which began to be withdrawn from the mid-1950s. While this aspect is really part of the story properly belonging the royal trains during the reign of our present Queen, the coaches concerned were built much earlier, and indeed had royal use during the reign of her father or uncle.

London & North Western Railway
Chairman's saloon No 45000 (BR 2911)

Built: 1920
Length: 57ft
Width: 9ft

Although built as the Chairman's saloon for the LNWR and subsequently inherited by the LMS and used by Sir Josiah Stamp, President of the LMS, this vehicle had royal use on and off during the first two decades of its life since it was made available when required to the Prince of Wales, later King Edward VIII. Thus it was not then part of the royal train but served the King's eldest son on his fact-finding tours round the country as when needed. After his accession King Edward VIII also used it as King, rather than the royal train. Thereafter it was another 20 years before it saw royal train use when from the mid 1950s it was included in the formation of the full royal train mainly for use by railway officers. It was fitted with a new underframe in 1967 and was upgraded for 100mph running, and in 1977 it was repainted in royal claret livery. It was renumbered as 2911 in 1982 and is currently the oldest coach allocated to royal train duties.

London Midland & Scottish Railway
Chairman's saloons Nos 45005 and 45006 (BR 2912)

Built: 1942
Length: 60ft
Width: 9ft

Originally built as saloons for the LMS Chairman and senior officers during the second world war, possibly as a mobile administration centre. As such they had a lounge at one end, an office, sleeping compartments, a bathroom and an attendant's compartment and galley. In 1948 they were converted for use by Princess Elizabeth and the Duke of Edinburgh. As altered No 45005 had a lounge, four bedrooms, two bathrooms, a toilet and an attendant's compartment. No 45006 had a dining saloon, three bedrooms, two bathrooms, a staff compartment and a kitchen. Both were later repainted in royal claret livery but No 45005 was then sold by BR for preservation privately; No 45006 is retained as a stand-by for the present royal train, renumbered as 2912.

South Eastern & Chatham Railway
NEW ROYAL TRAIN FOR KING EDWARD VII AND QUEEN ALEXANDRA

King's saloon No 1R (SR 7930) gangwayed at one end

Built:	1903
Length:	50ft 1in
Width:	8ft 0¾in

Saloon brake first Nos 2301 and 3493 (SR 7914 and 7915) non-gangwayed

Built:	1900/1
Length:	45ft
Width:	8ft 0¾in

Corridor first No 225 (SR 7254) gangwayed one end

Built:	1900
Length:	44ft
Width:	8ft 0¾in

Saloon firsts Nos 3514, 3785, 3786 (SR 7918, 7919, 7920)

Built:	1904/5
Length:	50ft 1in
Width:	8ft 0¾in

At one time equally as well known as the LNWR 1903 royal train, the South Eastern & Chatham royal train, also formed initially in 1903, is today perhaps forgotten in the mists of time, yet until the outbreak of the second world war, having served almost the whole of two reigns, and carried the crowned heads of Europe and other high personages of state from the Channel ports to London and back on official visits, it was the usual train for royal travel in Southern England. It was designed by Wainwright, Chief Mechanical Engineer of the SECR, renowned for his graceful locomotives and for continuing that quirk of South Eastern carriage design, the birdcage lookouts, that is the raised observatories above the general roof line over the guard's compartments. This was a necessity of space since because bridges and tunnels on the SER lines were not so generously proportioned partly by economies when first built and partly by repairs which left minimal side clearances there was no room for side ducket lookouts on SER coaches. So the normal roof profile remained fairly low and the guards could see forward from the elevated positions inside the roof observatory. It was a feature of many early lines but on the SECR it survived until the first world war for new construction and can still be seen today on preserved coaches. The birdcage was thus a feature of the end coaches of the SECR royal train.

The royal saloon though was distinctive among SECR stock for it had a graceful clerestory roof sloping at the ends. In many ways it resembled the Continental twelve-wheel saloon of 1883 kept at Calais, whose number curiously it duplicated, although the 1903 coach was shorter and on two four-wheel bogies. Like its Continental counterpart it had a gangway at one end only, but did not have night time accommodation nor did the train

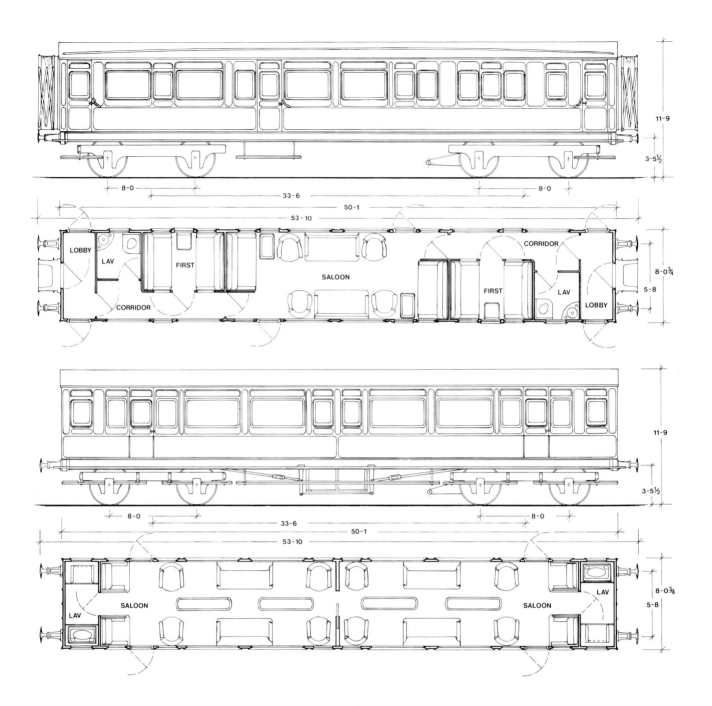

SECR corridor first class saloon No 3785 formed in the royal train used by King Edward VII and which survived until the late 1930s.

South Eastern & Chatham Railway saloon No 3514 used in the SECR royal train for the Household staff.
(Drawings Alan Prior)

have facilities for preparing meals. Internally it had a full width toilet at one end, two small saloons and a larger one between them, another toilet and a small attendant's compartment. A flexible gangway connection was provided at this end of the coach only. The interior had an elegant lightness, enhanced by the clerestory, with a dead white ceiling embellished with a light Adamesque pattern. While the smoking room was trimmed in leather, upholstery in the rest of the saloon was in a green silk material and, in contrast to the Great Eastern saloons, is known to have been much appreciated not only by the King, but by Queen Alexandra, who sometimes accompanied him on journeys between London and Dover.

The initial SECR royal train formed in 1903 consisted of four coaches. At the outer end were two 45ft first class saloon brakes with birdcage lookout at the guard's end. These two had been built in 1900 and 1901 respectively as common-or-garden brake thirds with three compartments, but in 1902 they were chosen for higher things being converted to saloons and fitted out with fairly opulent style first class furniture. The guard's and luggage compartments were retained. Toilet facilities were provided soon after if not right at the start. The fourth coach was also a conversion; it was originally built as a 44ft semi-corridor first and second class composite with toilets, but was not gangwayed at the ends. There were 3½ first class compartments linked by side corridor to one of the two parallel toilet compartments, while the other toilet served the two second class compartments by a short side corridor diagonally opposite that for the first class. On conversion the two second class compartments were upholstered in first class style though since there is no record of major structural alterations they must have retained their 6ft 5in distance between partitions against the 7ft 1in of the proper firsts, and a gangway was cut into one end, presumably at the original first class part so that there was through communication into the one gangwayed end of the royal saloon.

In 1905 three more coaches were added to the train to make a total of seven vehicles. One was a non-gangwayed saloon (No 3514) with two large identical saloon compartments linked by a central sliding door and full width toilets at both ends. Single fixed seats backed the partitions at the toilet ends but other furniture included loose single armchairs, sofas and tables down the centre of each saloon compartment. The other two saloons were gangwayed and were inserted between the King's saloon and the semi-corridor first class coach. There were some modern touches such as the end entrance doors and vestibules, not quite so elaborate as those of the LNWR royal train with their enclosed balconies, but more like the arrangements of ordinary corridor coaches three decades later. In No 3785 the layout was a mirror image around its centre line with a short side corridor past toilets and one side corridor compartment at each end leading to the one main saloon furnished with loose chairs, couches, tables and two fixed seats. The main saloon had external doors at diagonally opposite corners. No 3786 was different for it had two main saloon compartments and two toilets but was otherwise similar.

That this was a golden era there can be really no doubt for the SECR royal train was just one of several which appeared during the new reign. It was as though the railways had been waiting for the chance to show the sovereign what they could do, a chance which the late Queen had not given them. As originally finished in the rich maroon of the SE&CR with gold lining and, on the King's saloon, the royal monogram, the seven coach train, all carried on four-wheel bogies, hauled by one of Harry Wainwright's green 4-4-0 locomotives, with polished brass dome, beading, and copper-topped chimney, was one of the most handsome trains in the country and a striking spectacle dashing through the Kentish landscape of hop fields and oasthouses. In later years the royal engine was often No 516, a Class E 4-4-0 of handsome proportions with Belpaire firebox and extended smokebox, built at Ashford in 1908. Upon the formation of the Southern Railway in 1923, and the relegation of the Brighton royal train to ordinary service use, the SE&CR saloons were eventually repainted to olive-green livery and the King's saloon renumbered as 7930; as such the SEC royal train was used throughout the Southern system. It could be used on all routes which the LBSCR and old LSWR royal coaches could not. By the late 1930s, though, it became Southern policy to hire Pullman Cars for royal workings and from about this time the SECR's fine example of Edwardian beauty faded into quiet oblivion after its last royal journey in 1939. Indeed as far as is known the SECR royal train vehicles were not broken up after withdrawal; one or two at least became grounded bodies as holiday homes – the beach near Dungeness on Romney Marsh became a last resting place for several SECR saloons. As for the King's saloon – it was last reported to have been seen in the Scottish Highlands as a camping coach at Glenfinnan in the 1960s.

IRISH TRAINS FOR KING EDWARD VII

Midland Great Western Railway
State saloon, gangwayed one end

Built:	1903
Length:	54ft (headstocks)
	56ft (body)
Width:	9ft

Great Southern & Western Railway
Royal saloon non-gangwayed

Built:	1903
Length:	50ft
Width:	9ft

In July 1903, as recorded elsewhere, King Edward VII and Queen Alexandra toured Ireland and several railways formed up royal trains for their use. Two of the railways built new principal saloons for use by the King and Queen. Until 1903 a very early six-wheel saloon known as the Dargan saloon had served as a state coach on the Midland Great Western Railway but then the MGWR built a new bogie saloon at its Broadstone Works, primarily for the Lord Lieutenant but clearly with the royal visit very much in mind. Indeed the details were not finally approved until February 1903 but the coach was ready for the royal visit.

For the time it was a remarkable coach since it had a high elliptical roof, domed at the sides and ends but more striking were the curved panoramic windows wrapping round the coach ends. One end was fitted out as an observation compartment since the coach was intended to run at the back of the train. At the other end was a gangway connection. The coach was symmetrical externally around the double main entrance doors which gave access to an entrance lobby and toilet; towards the gangway end was one of the two main saloon compartments fitted out for dining, beyond which was a small pantry and kitchen. On the other side of the entrance was the main lounge nearly 19ft long, with sofas and armchairs, beyond which was the small observation lounge also doubling as a smoking compartment. The main decor was remarkable and included columns supporting the mahogany architrave, frieze and cornice. Originally the coach was on two four-wheel bogies but in 1915 it received six-wheel bogies. As built it was painted in blue and white but later received other liveries.

With the creation of an independent Irish State the coach remained as a principal state saloon and survived to be taken over by Coras Iompair Eireann, the Irish State transport system in the mid 1940s but, alas, was later broken up. As a royal coach in 1903 the MGWR assembled a very creditable train of other bogie coaches and brake vans all of broadly uniform appearance.

168

The Great Southern & Western saloon built in 1903 for the royal tour was constructed in the railway's workshops at Inchicore. It was though somewhat Victorian in external appearance with a square ended clerestory roof. It is possible that the coach might have had a flexible gangway at one end leading from an end entrance vestibule. The principal royal access was, though, through a single door about two thirds of the way along the side. From the entrance lobby in one direction lay a boudoir leading to a full width toilet, while in the other direction was the main 17ft long lounge, leading to a smaller smoking room and a further toilet and the end vestibule. Inside, the decor contrasted with the rather old fashioned appearance since it was described as 'art nouveau', with intertwined roses, shamrocks and thistles, painted figures of an Irish piper and harpist and the Royal Arms of Britain and Denmark featuring in the decorative detail. The general colour theme was green of varying complementary shades. The rest of the GSWR royal train for the 1903 tour was made up of a mixture of six-wheel and bogie first class and saloon coaches.

The Great Northern Railway (Ireland) formed up a train of first class and saloon coaches, including a 12-wheel dining car. All the coaches had the low elliptical roof that characterised both the Great Northern of Ireland and the Great Northern in England, but some of the GNRI coaches in the royal train also had domed end clerestories. The saloon used for the King and Queen already had a highly ornate floral pattern ceiling and had a richly patterned carpet. Armchairs and sofas in dark colours and patterned cushions and curtains provided all the ambience required for a royal saloon.

Special train on the Belfast & County Down Railway used by King Edward VII and Queen Alexandra in July 1903 with Beyer-Peacock 2-4-0 locomotive No 6. (L&GRP/David & Charles)

King Edward VII and Queen Alexandra travelled in this splendid royal train during their tour of Ireland, provided by the Great Northern Railway from Dublin to Newtownards. On the way, there were stops for water at Dundalk and Portadown where the Royal couple received local dignitaries. But the townspeople of Lisburn were disappointed that the train was not stopping there and to counter the railway's decision to close the station to the public they placed ladders against a wall and stood in coal wagons to gain a view! No doubt this was a posed photograph before the journey which took place on 25 July 1903. (Watson Collection, courtesy C. P. Friel)

East Coast (Great Northern and North Eastern railways)
NEW ROYAL TRAIN FOR KING EDWARD VII AND QUEEN ALEXANDRA
King's saloon No 395, twelve-wheel

Built:	1908
Length:	65ft 6in (headstocks)
	67ft (body)
Width:	9ft

Queen's saloon No 396, twelve-wheel

Built:	1909
Length:	65ft 6in (headstocks)
	67ft (body)
Width:	9ft

First class saloons Nos (4)1280 and (4)1281

Built:	1906
Length:	57ft (headstocks)
	58ft 6in (body)
Width:	9ft

First class saloons Nos (4)3099 and (4)3100

Built:	1908
Length:	57ft (headstocks)
	58ft 6in (body)
Width:	9ft

Full brake and luggage van No 109 (originally numbered ECJS 82)

Built:	1908
Length:	55ft (headstocks)
	56ft 6in (body)
Width:	8ft

(facing page left)
The East Coast King's saloon No 395 built by the Great Northern Railway in 1908. In 1925 this carriage was extensively altered to become Queen Mary's personal saloon, and was later used by Queen Elizabeth the Queen Mother after 1952.
(Drawing Alan Prior)

(facing page right)
The East Coast Queen's saloon No 396 built by the North Eastern Railway in 1909 depicted in its original condition. It was modified in 1925 for use by the King and Queen for daytime journeys.
(Drawing Alan Prior)

The third new British royal train to be built for King Edward VII and Queen Alexandra was by two of the East Coast partners although the North Eastern Railway was involved only with the Queen's saloon No 396. A complete train was formed using two ancillary saloons built in 1906 and altered for royal train use and two others also built in 1908.

The two principal saloons, almost identical in external appearance, were massive looking 12-wheelers. Like the LNWR saloons they had double door entrance vestibules at each end, but there the similarity ends. The general appearance followed closely the by then Gresley's standard East Coast route coaching design of the period, but the two royal saloons looked so much bigger partly by the high elliptical roof profile, and below accentuated by the inverted bowstring girder, between the pair of six-wheel bogies, forming the frame. The body panels were of solid Burma teak, highly varnished, enhancing the appearance of this beautiful wood in natural form. King Edward's saloon was built at Doncaster in 1908 and numbered 395. Early in 1909, the second saloon, for Queen Alexandra, emerged from York Works carrying the number 396. The interiors of both saloons provided accommodation for day and night use. In the King's saloon, his bedroom could, if required, be converted to a dining room with seating for six at a transverse table. There were also day and smoking rooms. The Queen's saloon contained a second bedroom for her second daughter, the Princess Victoria, by then a mature lady of 40. The dayrooms of both saloons were decorated in Louis XVI style by Waring & Gillow. Reports of the time stated that the coaches would each cost £3,500. Parts of both coaches were finished in white enamel like the saloons of the LNWR, but the East Coast saloons were very much more modern in appearance because of the clean internal lines and spaciousness of the high elliptical roof unbroken by a clerestory and with a suggestion of

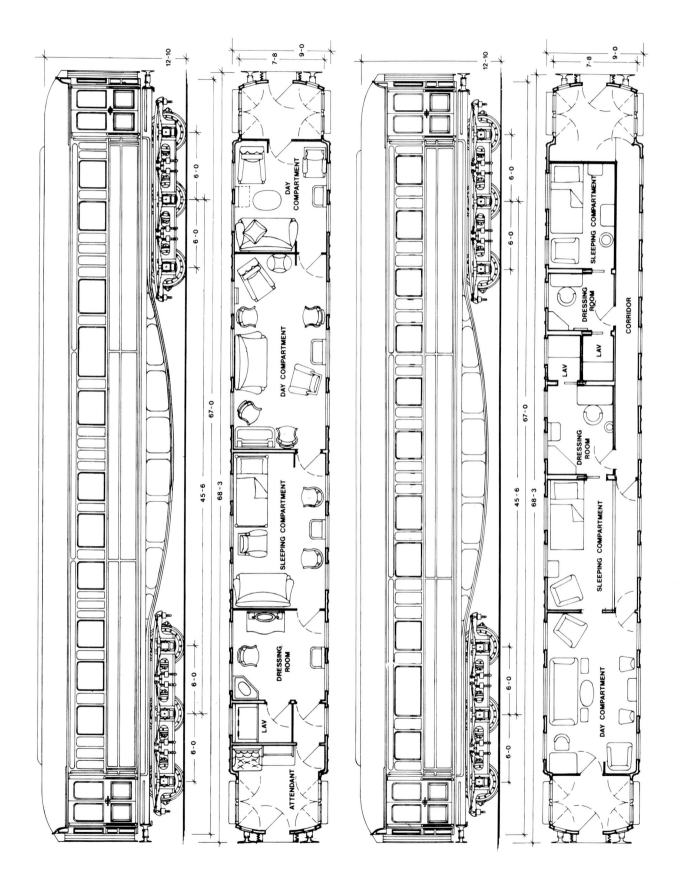

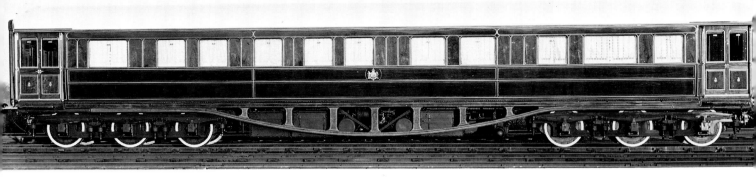

*East Coast saloon No 396, built by
the North Eastern Railway at York in
1909 for Queen Alexandra and
similar to the one built the previous
year by the GNR at Doncaster for
King Edward VII. In 1925 the LNER
altered the interior, enabling it to be
used jointly by King George V and
Queen Mary, and fitted the elaborate
door handles from the former King's
saloon, No 395. It is shown when
new and in varnished teak livery.
(Courtesy National Railway
Museum)*

ornamental decoration. In the King's saloon the balcony vestibules were panelled in polished sycamore while His Majesty's smoking compartment was decorated in Jacobean style with walls panelled in oak inlaid with boxwood and dark pollard oak. Although the furnishings in the rest of the saloon were much lighter in style the two armchairs and settee in the smoking saloon were in reindeer plugh hide. Among the special features of both saloons were the concealed tubular lights hidden behind the cornices – first seen in the first class dining saloons of the Kings Cross – Sheffield trains two years earlier – and pressure ventilation.

The formation of the train was completed by the addition of the four first class saloons which virtually became semi-royals like their eight-wheel saloons of the LNWR train, plus two full brake and luggage vans one of which, No 109, was permanently allocated to the train. All four of the saloons had a different internal layout although there were similarities between Nos 3099 and 3100, which were broadly of side corridor pattern serving individual compartments with either fixed first class seating or loose armchairs, or convertible compartments for night use. Both had central full width compartments of differing size to which the side corridors led, laid out with chairs and a table or casual armchairs and a sofa. The other pair, Nos 1280 and 1281 had a mixture of accommodation part side corridor to two compartments which could be arranged for day or night use, and two open bays with a centre passageway each with four single seats or two longitudinal sleeping berths. Beyond was another side corridor compartment or an office, and all four saloons included toilets and the latter two included a bath. There was, though, some flexibility in the way the saloons were arranged internally.

The East Coast royal train never quite achieved the popularity of use that was attached to the LNWR train which became the firm favourite, as was its predecessor when Queen Victoria reigned. In 1925, extensive alterations were made to the two East Coast royal saloons as they were no longer required for overnight journeys and it appears that by this time the LNWR train was well established for this purpose and used on any part of the railway system. The King's saloon, No 395 became Queen Mary's personal carriage and later still, after the death of King George VI, that of Queen Elizabeth the Queen Mother in succession to Queen Mary. The bedroom area was altered to become a private saloon. Interior furnishings were replaced to reflect, first, Queen Mary's tastes and later still those of Queen Elizabeth. The more elaborate exterior door handles were replaced by those from saloon No 396, as originally it was only the King's carriage that displayed the more decorative examples denoting his seniority as King. The original Queen's saloon, No 396, now became the more important of the two, with the fitting of the exterior door handles from 395, and refurbished for the joint use of the King and Queen making day journeys together. It was referred to as 'Their Majesties' Saloon' and frequently used by them when travelling between London and Sandringham. The complete formation of the East Coast royal train survived until the early 1960s, but the last recorded occasion on which it was used as such, was in June, 1961, when HM The Queen and other members of the Royal Family travelled from King's Cross to York and back for the wedding in York Minster of the Duke and Duchess of Kent. Thereafter, saloons 395 and 396 were used as required individually, sometimes being attached to ordinary service trains for journeys of a private nature. For several years No 396 was also used as the principal saloon in otherwise Pullman Car royal specials on the Southern Region. It was a particular favourite of HM The Queen when, with her guests, she travelled from Victoria to Tattenham Corner each year to see the Epsom Derby. Very regrettably in the 1950s, at the Duke of Edinburgh's suggestion, Nos 395 and 396 were repainted into the dark Royal Claret livery of all other royal coaches. There were reported to be many sad expressions among those in the Doncaster paintshop when news of the change and firm instructions to implement it were first given. Happily, on withdrawal in 1977, they were at first stored at Wolverton and later No 395 was sent to the National Railway Museum, York, for immediate public display. However, space limitations at York provided an opportunity for 396 to return to East Anglia and not far from Sandringham, in which area it was frequently seen, to be given a temporary home at the Bressingham Steam Museum, near Diss, Norfolk. The brake van No 109, specially built for the East Coast train in 1908, has now been restored to its former teak livery and placed in the National Railway Museum.

Interior of East Coast saloon No 395, built by the GNR in 1908. The view shows the day saloon as altered in 1925 by the LNER for use by Queen Mary and subsequently HM Queen Elizabeth, the Queen Mother. Last used in 1972, it is now part of the National Railway Museum's collection of royal vehicles. (Courtesy National Railway Museum)

Midland Railway
Royal saloon for King George V and Queen Mary, No 1910 (LMS No 809)

Built: 1912
Length: 59ft
Width: 8ft 10½in

(above)
Midland Railway royal saloon No 1910, completed at Derby Carriage & Wagon Works in 1912, and now preserved by the Midland Railway Trust, Butterley, Derbyshire. (By kind permission of J. B. Radford)

Midland Railway royal saloon built in 1910. (Courtesy J. B. Radford)

In July 1912, yet another royal train was provided for King George V and Queen Mary, this time by the Midland Railway. Embarrassed, no doubt, by having to borrow the LNWR royal train for journeys to Midland line destinations, the directors of the Midland Company had sanctioned the construction of a new royal saloon in April 1910. Although the completed saloon did not emerge from Derby Carriage & Wagon Works until 1912, it was given the running number 1910 to mark the accession to the throne of King George V. The saloon was 59ft long with a clerestory roof and carried on two four-wheel bogies. Built to the designs of David Bain, the Midland's Carriage & Wagon Superintendent, the accommodation comprised a saloon compartment, boudoir, and smoke room together with two separate toilets and an attendants' compartment with facilities for providing light refreshments. In addition to the royal saloon, five other coaches were set aside for form a six-coach train which included a dining carriage and first class family saloon, both of which were refurbished for royal use.

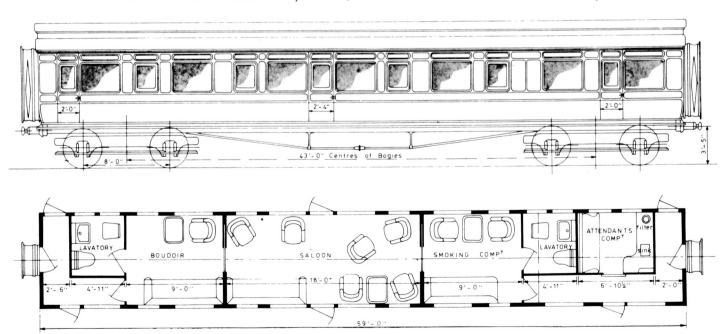

The Midland Railway royal train was used for the first time in July 1912, when the King and Queen chose the Midland route by travelling to St Pancras upon their return to London at the conclusion of a visit to Yorkshire. However, the Midland train was not a particular favourite of the King and his family, due, probably, to the lack of sleeping accommodation, and the feeling of overcrowding when several members of the Royal Family and their entourage were travelling. In 1923, when the Midland became part of the London, Midland & Scottish Railway, the Midland train was disbanded, but the royal saloon proper, No 1910, was retained and saw occasional royal use until the mid 1930s. By 1935, it had been renumbered as 809, in the LMS saloon carriage series, when its very last royal journey occurred on 6 November, that year, to convey the Duke and Duchess of Gloucester, after their wedding in the Chapel of Buckingham Palace, from St Pancras to Kettering to spend their honeymoon at nearby Boughton House. Happily, this coach has survived – in the 1950s it was in the North Wales Land Cruise train – and is now preserved by the Midland Railway Trust at Butterley in Derbyshire.

London, Tilbury & Southend Railway
Royal saloon, No 2799, non-gangwayed

In 1913, a special saloon for royal and VIP use, ordered by the London, Tilbury & Southend Railway, was delivered after the Tilbury company had been absorbed by the Midland Railway. It is believed that the coach did in fact have royal use when King George V's eldest son, the Prince of Wales used it to visit Southend in 1920. The Tilbury saloon, which was not gangwayed, had an elliptical roof with a 47ft 8in bow-ended body mounted on two four-wheel bogies. Unusual features were two fireplaces (with electric fires) and overmantels in the outer ends of the smoking and lounge

Built: 1913
Length: 47ft 8in
Width: 9ft

The London, Tilbury & Southend Railway saloon delivered in 1913 after the company had been absorbed by the Midland Railway. (Drawing Alan Prior)

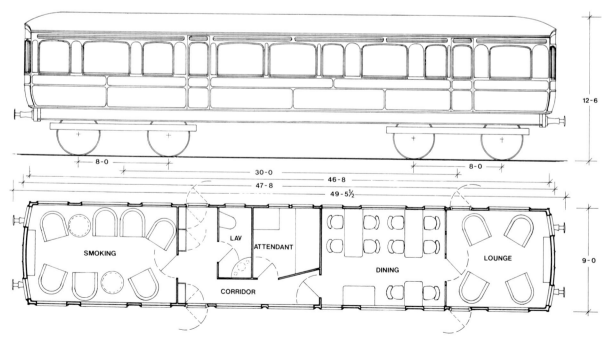

175

compartments. One of the fireplaces housed a writing desk and cabinet.

Between the end lounges was the entrance lobby giving direct access to the smoking compartment and in the opposite direction a short side corridor past a toilet compartment, attendant's compartment equipped with electric kettles, urn and grills, to a full width dining compartment seating 10, with a door to the end lounge. The partition between the dining saloon and lounge could be dismantled to make one large dining area. Although the ceilings were white, the general finish to walls and partitions was in dark woods, the dining and adjoining lounge in dark Spanish mahogany and the smoking saloon in wainscot oak. Wicker chairs furnished the smoking saloon while the dining chairs were in mahogany upholstered in brown pigskin. The toilet compartment was lined in Italian marble with the washbasin and fitments in nickel silver. The external livery was polished teak, but the underframe and bogies were painted in royal blue, lined in white.

After 1913 no new rolling stock specifically for royal use was to be built until 1941 – five years after King George V had died – when two saloons and a power brake car were completed by the LMS for his second son King George VI, described on page 158.

Great Western Railway
Special saloons Nos 9001 and 9002

Built: 1940
Length: 60ft 11¼in
Width: 8ft 11in

Ordered in 1938 and designated as special saloons these two coaches were delivered in July 1940. Mounted on six-wheel bogies, they were designed without sleeping accommodation to provide day-time luxury facilities for VIPs and also for members of the Royal Family when the type of journey and persons to be accommodated did not require the use of the ex-LNWR or LNER royal trains. They were frequently used by Queen Mary while she was living at the Duke of Beaufort's home at Badminton during the second world war. However, the dictates of war necessitated another use for these saloons when they were selected to be used for government VIPs including Prime Minister (later Sir) Winston Churchill and Allied commander General Eisenhower. When the war ended in 1945 Nos 9001 and 9002 were joined by two more special saloons, Nos 9006 and 9007, to form a post-war GWR royal train. Of almost identical design, the interiors consist of a coupe, lounge, dining room, kitchen and toilet.

Many members of the Royal Family are known to have travelled in them including the Queen and Queen Mother, particularly when travelling to Cheltenham for the races. No 9001, purchased privately in 1968, is now at The Birmingham Railway Museum at Tyseley. Fully restored, it was re-commisioned by the Duke of Gloucester in a ceremony at the Museum in June 1985 when His Royal Highness subsequently rode in it to Moor Street station, Birmingham. Saloon No 9002 was also purchased for preservation and is kept at Didcot Railway Centre where restoration work is still taking place. Both coaches always retained their chocolate and cream livery, but were given a 'W' prefix to their numbers upon nationalisation in 1948.

Great Western Railway
Special saloons Nos 9006 and 9007

Ordered in 1943 and designated as special saloons these two coaches were delivered in December 1945. The bodies were mounted on two salvaged underframes whose original coach bodies were damaged by enemy action during the second world war. No 9006 was a fully self-contained saloon having day, night, kitchen and bathroom facilities. No 9007 was similarly arranged except that it had no catering facilities. Originally designed for VIP use they were internally refurbished in 1948 and provided with air conditioning, and formed the nucleus of a new Great Western royal train completed with a pair of new post-war brake composite coaches. As such the train was intended for short distance daytime journeys with only the immediate royal attendants, which would not justify the full LMS royal train and avoid the need to borrow saloons from the LMS or LNER.

In 1955 both saloons were re-equipped internally and joined the other permanent royal coaches in the LMS and LNER trains by being painted in royal claret livery. The brake composite coaches were later withdrawn while the saloons were last used for a royal journey in 1978 having run at times with other GWR saloons 9001/2 or stock from the LMS royal train. The two former GWR saloons were finally withdrawn in 1983 and moved to the National Railway Museum.

Built:	1945
Length:	60ft 11¼in
Width:	8ft 11in

(above)
GWR Special Saloon No 9001 at The Birmingham Railway Museum, Tyseley, on 5 June 1985 – the day it was re-commissioned by the Duke of Gloucester. Note the two tail lamps denoting a royal train working.
(Author)

11

THE ELIZABETHAN ROYAL SALOONS

When Princess Elizabeth acceded to the Throne as Queen Elizabeth II in 1952 she inherited the use of three royal trains. Most important, since it was used for major tours and overnight journeys, particularly the annual holiday journey to Balmoral, was the LMS train (described on page 158 onwards), which was still very much the LNWR train since the semi-royal saloons, the dining cars and both the clerestory brakes all of LNWR origin were regularly used. Only the two principal royal saloons and the power brake sleeper of 1941 had replaced the equivalent LNWR vehicles and even then both the LNWR brake coaches were still available although only one was used if the LMS power brake was in the formation at the opposite end. In the 1920s and 1930s one or two ordinary LNWR first class sleeping cars with elliptical roof were in the formation of the royal train and during the new reign these had been superseded by LMS Stanier pattern cars. With the train painted in LMS colours, even though the railways had been nationalised in 1948, there was for a year or two little problem in finding coaches in matching colours.

By the mid 1950s further new saloons were built, basically for Prince Charles and Princess Anne, together with a new principal royal dining car.

Typical royal train formation on BR in the late 1950s and early 1960s. (Drawing Alan Prior)

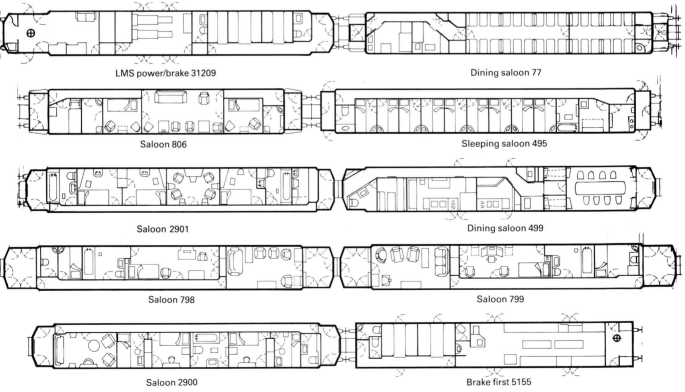

LMS power/brake 31209

Dining saloon 77

Saloon 806

Sleeping saloon 495

Saloon 2901

Dining saloon 499

Saloon 798

Saloon 799

Saloon 2900

Brake first 5155

By then also the two saloons built as LMS Chairman's saloons in 1942, and converted in 1948 for the use of Princess Elizabeth and the Duke of Edinburgh were included as required in the LMS train. Gradually the LNWR semi-royal coaches were withdrawn, the last going in 1968, the second LNWR diner was replaced by a BR Mk I restaurant car and by 1978 when the sleeping brake coaches were withdrawn the last vestiges of the LNWR train had gone. From now on it was to be very much the British Railways royal train.

In 1977, to mark the Queen's Silver Jubilee on the Throne, came new principal royal saloons for the Queen and the Duke of Edinburgh, and at the end of the 1970s and into the 1980s there were numerous other vehicle changes, almost entirely by adapting or rebuilding existing coaches from ordinary service. Indeed the two 'new' principal Silver Jubilee saloons were adaptations although the royal carriage builders had started with completely empty steel body shells.

The second royal train of the 1950s was the East Coast train (described on page 170), by then used only for daytime journeys with as many or as few coaches as was required for a fair number of Household staff or simply a lady-in-waiting. And it was the Royal ladies who were well to the fore in carrying out royal duties. Gradually the role of the East Coast train declined, its last duty as a full royal train formation being in 1961. Saloon No 396 became effectively the day trip coach, perhaps accompanied by another saloon or brake first for attendants and a senior railway officer. The East Coast saloon was often used in other parts of the country since it was not confined to former LNER territory. It was often used on the Southern Region, for the Southern no longer had a royal train. Occasionally the Southern formed up a Pullman train for royal use; the Queen for example travelled in the first class Pullman *Orion* to the Medway towns in 1953. On other occasions the East Coast saloon was used accompanied by Pullmans for the Royal attendants. This was often the formation used for visiting royalty or heads of state arriving at London Victoria from the Channel ports, or in more recent years from Gatwick Airport, having flown in. Yet the Queen has also used ordinary first class coaches on occasions, travelling at least once in a first class compartment of an SR electric multiple-unit from Windsor to Portsmouth, and on another occasion in a first class open section of an Inter-City 125 train to Weston-super-Mare.

The President of Brazil on a State Visit travels from Gatwick Airport to Victoria in a special train of five coaches, of which all but the fourth from the locomotive are from the royal train, hauled by Class 31 diesel locomotive No 31230 and passing Streatham on 4 May, 1976. The Presidential Party are travelling in East Coast Saloon No 396, the second vehicle from the locomotive. (John Scrace)

The honeymoon special conveying the Prince and Princess of Wales from Waterloo to Romsey after their wedding, on 29 July 1981, speeds through Hook watched by local well-wishers who had earlier followed the wedding ceremony on television. The locomotive, appropriately bearing the headcode of the initials of the bridegroom and bride, is No 73142, Broadlands – the name of the home of the late Earl Mountbatten of Burma, where the Royal couple spent the first few days of their honeymoon. (Basingstoke Gazette)

179

Finally the third royal train was the short formation put together by the Great Western just as the railways were nationalised (described on page 176). Again it was used for the shorter day time journeys and often by other members of the Royal Family. Sometimes, too, a saloon and one of the GW 'royal' brake composites would be attached to an ordinary train to save an independent working.

In the early 1960s, the ex-*GWR* saloons Nos 9006/7, together with the two remaining East Coast saloons, Nos 395/6, under a BR Workshops re-organisation were moved to Wolverton Carriage Works to join the other vehicles of what was then principally, the former LMS royal train. Wolverton Works has a long tradition of building and maintaining royal carriages and no doubt felt that the few remaining saloons on the Eastern and Western Regions could be more economically looked after by experienced Wolverton staff. There is a very real sense of pride enjoyed by many of the Wolverton workers that *their* Works is responsible for the maintenance and turn-out of the most prestigious train in the British Rail fleet. However, only a small team of men, about a dozen in number, are usually employed on the maintenance of the royal vehicles. Chosen not only for their trade skills but also for their temperament it is this team of tradesmen – electricians, plumbers, carpenters, metalworkers and uphol-sterers – led by a foreman, who accompany the royal train taking the Queen, Duke of Edinburgh and other members of the Royal Family on their journeys. These men regard the honour to travel with the train as a privilege and it is, perhaps, some reward for their labours in maintaining it. It is also very practical common sense, for should any technical defect arise, they can usually effect a remedy, which to the uninitiated, might be something of a catastrophe. Typical examples of known situations have been lack of heating in the Queen's saloon and a saloon door that cannot be opened, except by force, when one royal passenger was ready to alight! No, the door had not been overlooked in preparations, but with old wooden-bodied coaches infrequently used, slight movement of the bodywork during the journey after weeks of standing still could cause a door to stick.

Now by the mid 1980s there is but one royal train which occasionally although more rarely runs as a full formation, while individual saloons or combinations of a principal saloon and other coaches as required will run on their own, depending entirely on the nature and duration of the journey. Nevertheless as often happened in the past when dealing with royal trains the Southern went its own way in providing a train as the honeymoon special from Waterloo to Romsey for the newly married Prince and Princess of Wales on 29 July 1981 by using its own resources instead of calling on coaches from the formal BR royal train. A three-coach train was formed up of an ordinary BR Mk II first class coach, a Mk I brake composite, and the Southern General Manager's saloon at the back, used as the royal carriage. This vehicle is fitted out with a lounge, toilet and small pantry, and is noticeable for its narrow flat sided body since it is suitable for running on the Tunbridge Wells – Hastings line which has always been restricted to coaches no more than 8ft 2½in wide, although this restriction will shortly be lifted following track alterations and electrification.

British Railways
ROYAL TRAIN FOR QUEEN ELIZABETH II AND THE DUKE OF EDINBURGH

Saloon No 2900 (For Prince Charles and Princess Anne; used by Royal Household)

Built: 1955
Length: 63ft 5in (headstocks)
Width: 8ft 7½in

Saloon No 2901 (Queen's private secretary, Royal Household or Prince Charles)

Built: 1957
Length: 63ft 5in (headstocks)
Width: 8ft 7½in

Dining saloon for Royal Family No 2902 (originally 499)

Built: 1956
Length: 63ft 5in (headstocks)
Width: 8ft 7½in

HM The Queen's saloon No 2903 (Formerly Mk III prototype open first No 11001)

Built: 1972 (converted 1977)
Length: 22.150m (headstocks)
Width: 2.740m

HRH The Duke of Edinburgh's saloon No 2904 (Formerly Mk III prototype open second No 12001)

Built: 1972 (converted 1977)
Length: 22.150m (headstocks)
Width: 2.740m

Power car/staff sleeper/brake coach No 2905 (Formerly Mk IIB brake first No 14105)

Built: 1969 (converted 1977)
Length: 63ft 5in (headstocks)
Width: 9ft

Escort coach/staff sleeper/kitchen brake No 2906 (Formerly Mk IIB brake first No 14112)

Built: 1969 (converted 1977)
Length: 63ft 5in (headstocks)
Width: 9ft

First class Restaurant car (Royal Household) No 2907 (Formerly No 325)

Built: 1961
Length: 63ft 5in (headstocks)
Width: 9ft

Sleeping cars Nos 2908 and 2909 (Formerly Nos 2500 and 2013)

Built: 1957/8
Length: 63ft 5in (headstocks)
Width: 9ft

Sleeping cars Nos 2914 and 2915, Mk IIIA type

Built: 1983
Length: 22.150m (headstocks)
Width: 2.740m

Royal saloon, No 2900, built in 1955 for use by Prince Charles and Princess Anne, but later used by other members of the Royal Family and the Royal Household. (Author)

The BR Mk IIb brake first converted as escort/staff car No 2906 for royal train use. (G. M. Kichenside)

Remaining vehicles are the LMS 1941 Power brake No 2910 as stand-by, the LMS Chairman's saloon of 1942 No 2912; and the LNWR chairman's saloon of 1920 No 2911.

In each of the years, 1955, 1956 and 1957, three new royal saloons, the first to be built since the two principal 12-wheel saloons, Nos 798 and 799 were completed in 1941, appeared from Wolverton Carriage Works. Designed to complement saloons 798/9, in the former LMS train and to the same bodyline, all three externally were similar. However, unlike 798/9 with their double door entrance vestibules and six-wheel bogies, the new saloons had inward opening single door entrance vestibules and were carried on four-wheel bogies. The first of the three saloons, No 2900, was intended for use mainly by Prince Charles and Princess Anne, but when not required by them, it could be used by members of the Royal Household in attendance upon the Queen. It was inspected by the Queen and Duke of Edinburgh, at St Pancras station when they arrived there in the royal train from Nottingham, on 6 July 1955. Carrying the original number, but with the Royal children's nursery furniture long since removed to storage for possible future use, the 'nursery coach', as it is sometimes referred to by railway staff, is now used by various members of the Royal Family, and,

The former LNWR chairman's saloon of 1920 seen in the early 1980s in royal train use, retaining its LMS number 45000.
(G. M. Kichenside)

when marshalled in a formation in which the Queen is travelling, by her Ladies-in-Waiting. The second saloon, which appeared in 1956, was a combined kitchen/dining car and was curiously numbered 499. It replaced the elderly ex-LNWR 12-wheel dining car, No 76 dating from 1900, but used for royal train duty from the early years of King Edward VII's reign. The dining area of the new saloon had an internal layout similar to that of the vehicle it replaced, of an oblong centre table with three individual armchairs on each side. In 1977 it was renumbered 2902 and in recent years the Queen and her party have travelled in it from Victoria to Tattenham Corner to watch one of the horse racing spectacles of the year – the Epsom Derby. The third saloon, completed in 1957, was No 2901 and provided office and living accommodation for the Queen's Private Secretary and other Royal Household staff. It is still used for that purpose, and also, on some occasions, by Prince Charles and Princess Anne.

As mentioned in chapter 7, the Queen's Silver Jubilee was marked by the presentation to Her Majesty of the keys of her new saloon, one of two new royal saloons to replace the former LMS twelve-wheel saloons built for her mother and father in 1941. They were not, though, newly built, having been built originally in 1972 as part of the prototype High Speed Train for ordinary service. As far back as 1974, consideration had been given to replacing the two ex-LMS saloons with vehicles of more modern design and, in particular, a more sophisticated method of air conditioning. Although the two 1941 saloons were not really life expired, their braking and steam heating systems would have needed replacing. So the decision was taken to replace them with vehicles which when required would permit a maximum speed of 100mph rather than the then permitted maximum of 75mph. The two prototype Mk III vehicles were very considerably rebuilt at Wolverton Works, while the preferences of the Queen and Duke of Edinburgh were sought regarding interior decoration and furnishing. Externally, the most noticeable alteration to the original bodyline concerns the Queen's saloon, No 2903. To assist Her Majesty in making a dignified exit and entry, an inward opening double-door entrance vestibule has been provided at one end of the saloon. The windows in each of the doors are vertically hinged for inward opening to permit conversation by the Queen on taking leave of her hosts after closure of the doors before departure. When accompanying the Queen, the Duke of Edinburgh uses the double vestibule of the Queen's saloon for formal arrivals and departures. Each saloon has lounge, bedroom and bathroom facilities. The Queen's saloon has a second bedroom and bathroom for her dresser. Similar bedroom and bathroom facilities are also provided in the Duke's saloon together with a separate bedroom and bathroom for his valet; the inclusion of a kitchen usually eliminates the need to include the dining saloon No 2902 in the royal train formation when the Duke of Edinburgh is travelling alone. A small silver-coloured circular plaque, affixed to the wall in the double-door entrance vestibule of the Queen's saloon, records that it entered service in the Silver Jubilee Year of the Queen's reign, 1977.

Also in 1977, the two ex-LNWR service vehicles 5154 and 5155, converted for royal train use in the early 1920s with added clerestories to harmonise with other royal vehicles of the period, were replaced. Along with LNWR dining car No 76, Nos 5154/5 have been preserved in working order, in LNWR livery and LMS insignia, housed at the National Railway Museum, York. The replacements for the ex-LNWR service vehicles were obtained by adapting two BR Mk IIB brake first side-corridor coaches, built in 1969. No 2905 has been equipped with a diesel generator to supply electric power throughout the train, together with staff sleeping accommodation, and compartments for the guard and luggage. The successor to 5155, as escort car, is No 2906 which has seating and sleeping accommodation for staff, and a small kitchen area. The remaining vehicles, that is those built in 1955/6/7, were fitted with new bogies and equipped for electric heating.

Over the years the ex-LNWR clerestory roofed semi-royal saloons had gradually been replaced. By 1970 two BR standard Mk I vehicles were in use: one was a sleeping car and the other a combined kitchen/restaurant car, both for the use of railway staff. However, one elliptical roofed ex-LNWR vehicle remained; this was saloon No 45000, built in 1920 as the chairman's saloon and in LMS days used by the President of the LMS, Sir Josiah Stamp. As mentioned in chapter five, it was also used by King Edward VIII. The wooden panelled body of No 45000 had already been mounted on a BR Mk I underframe in 1967 and equipped with bogies to permit 100mph running.

The Royal Train vehicles currently used, at the time of writing, include two Mk III sleeping cars (both in claret livery), used for the first time when the Queen and Duke of Edinburgh arrived at Newark (Northgate), en-route to Southwell Minster for the Maundy Thursday service there, on 19 April 1984. They were fitted out for royal train duty from new and include showers.

While the manuscript of this book was in the final stages of preparation in March, 1985, a surprise announcement by the Parliamentary Under Secretary of State for Transport, David Mitchell, revealed Government approval to British Rail's plan to refurbish the Royal Train fleet. The total cost, based on 1984 prices, of £7½ million is to be spread over four years

The BR royal train, seen at Totnes in March 1981 when the Queen and the Duke of Edinburgh toured the South Hams area of South Devon.
(G. M. Kichenside)

Caught quite by chance by the author (see text of chapter 11) were these Mk III bodyshells forming a special southbound freight, hauled by an unidentified Class 31 diesel, passing Nuneaton Station on 19 July, 1984. They were new carriages for the royal train en-route from Derby to Wolverton Works for fitting-out, as part of the re-equipped royal train announced by the Government in March 1985. (Author)

and grant-aided by the Department of Transport. The plan is to replace many of the older vehicles in the fleet which are between 29 and 44 years old and do not comply with current operational and security requirements. Several also contain asbestos. Asbestos problems would arise if alterations are to be made involving the disturbance if the insulating layers on the inside of the bodyshell. Asbestos linings were generally used in railway carriage construction during the 1950s and 1960s before the health hazards of handling asbestos became known. Complete replacement of stock built in the 1950s would be more straightforward than trying to modernise and refurbish existing stock if asbestos removal is required. The announcement, given in answer to a Parliamentary Question, stated that eight vehicles will be converted from new or surplus rolling stock. Two will be built from scratch. Four vehicles of the existing fleet will remain in service. No official information, so far, has been given on the identity of the vehicles to remain in service and those to be replaced. However, by a process of elimination the plan appears to be as follows:

Saloons Nos 2900, 2901, 2902, 2907, 2910, 2911 and 2912 will be withdrawn. Saloons Nos 2903 and 2904, used by HM The Queen and HRH The Duke of Edinburgh, respectively, will be retained and improved.

It is understood that vehicles Nos 2905 and 2906 will also be retained. However, it would also appear that the two Mk III staff sleeping cars Nos 2914 and 2915, which first appeared in the formation in 1984, will continue to form part of the fleet, but are included among those described as being converted.

APPENDICES

SOME NOTABLE OCCASIONS OF ROYALTY'S ASSOCIATION WITH RAILWAYS

Year	Occasion	Year	Occasion
1842	13 June, Queen Victoria's first railway journey – Slough to Paddington, Great Western Railway.		railway to view Birmingham Corporation's waterworks scheme in the Elan Valley, Wales.
1848	28 September, at short notice, Queen Victoria began her first journey by rail from Scotland to England	1906	10 July, King Edward VII opened the King Edward railway bridge, Newcastle-on-Tyne, North Eastern Railway.
1850	29 August, Queen Victoria declared open the Royal Border Bridge at Berwick-upon-Tweed.	1910	20 May, Funeral train conveyed King Edward VII's coffin from Paddington to Windsor, GWR.
1863	28 March, Wolferton station, Norfolk, received its first royal passengers when the Prince and Princess of Wales arrived for their extended honeymoon at Sandringham.	1913	21 April, King George V and Queen visited Crewe Locomotive Works.
1867	23 August, Queen Victoria arrived at Ballater station for the first time, on her way to Balmoral.	1915	Silver plated baths installed in the saloons of the King and Queen on the LNWR royal train to facilitate overnight wartime journeys.
1890	4 March, The Prince of Wales (later King Edward VII) opened the Forth Bridge.	1924	28 April, King George V and Queen Mary visited Swindon Railway Works; afterwards, the King, accompanied by the Queen, drove locomotive No 4082 *Windsor Castle* from the Works to Swindon Junction station.
1890	4 November, London's first deep level underground electric railway, the City & South London, conveyed the Prince of Wales from Clapham Common to Oval.	1925	1 and 2 July, the Duke and Duchess of York (later King George VI and Queen Elizabeth) attended the centenary celebrations of the opening of the Stockton & Darlington Railway.
1897	21 June, Queen Victoria travelled from Windsor to Paddington in the new GWR royal train for the London celebrations of her Diamond Jubilee.	1926	6 August, the Duke of York drove the first passenger train on the 15in gauge Romney, Hythe & Dymchurch Railway, Kent.
1900	27 June, Prince of Wales rode the underground Central London Railway from Bank station, in the City, to Shepherd's Bush.	1926	20 October, the Duke and Duchess of York visited the Southern Railway works at Ashford, Kent, and subsequently rode on the footplate from the works to the station of locomotive No E850 *Lord Nelson*.
1900	6 November, Queen Victoria's last journey from Scotland to England (Ballater to Windsor).	1936	23 January, Funeral train conveyed King George V's body from Wolferton to King's Cross, LNER.
1901	2 February, Funeral trains conveyed Queen Victoria's coffin from Gosport to Victoria (LSWR and LBSCR) and Paddington to Windsor (GWR).	1936	28 January, Funeral train conveyed remains of King George V from Paddington to Windsor, GWR.
1902	7 March, King Edward VII and Queen Alexandra travelled in GWR royal train, Paddington to Kingswear – 228½ miles non-stop in 4 hours 20 minutes and the first non-stop journey on that route.	1936	18/19 November, King Edward VIII visited mining and industrial areas of South Wales travelling in a special GWR train of VIP saloon coaches. Thought to have been the King's last railway journey before his abdication the following month.
1902	10 March, GWR royal train ran non-stop Plymouth to Paddington – 246½ miles in 4 hours 44 minutes.	1941	LMS completes new personal saloons for King George VI and Queen Elizabeth, fitted with protective armour plate window shutters as a precaution against enemy attack.
1903	14 July, Royal special, conveying Prince and Princess of Wales (later King George V and Queen Mary), from Paddington to Plymouth reached a maximum speed of 87mph, then the fastest recorded speed for a royal train on the GWR or any other British railway.	1947	February – April, King George VI, Queen Elizabeth, with Princess Elizabeth and Princess Margaret toured South Africa in the 'White Train', mostly built by Metro-Cammell of Birmingham.
1903	July, in the last week of the month King Edward VII and Queen Alexandra visited Ireland travelling in four separate royal trains.	1947	20 November, wedding of Princess Elizabeth and Prince Philip who travelled by special train to
1904	21 July, King Edward VII and Queen Alexandra made a nine-mile return trip on a temporary		

Year	Occasion	Year	Occasion
	begin their honeymoon from Waterloo to Winchester on the Southern Railway.		of the Merseyrail underground when the Queen rode in a special train from Liverpool Moorfields station to Kirkby, formed of a class 507 electric multiple-unit.
1950	15 November, Princess Elizabeth visited Swindon Railway Works, names the last Castle class 4-6-0, No 7037 *Swindon* and rides on footplate of Star class 4-6-0 No 4057 *Princess Elizabeth*.	1979	5 September, special combined royal and funeral train, in which the Queen and other members of the Royal Family travelled, conveying the body of Earl Mountbatten of Burma from Waterloo to Romsey.
1952	11 February, Funeral train conveyed King George VI's body from Wolferton to King's Cross, British Railways (Eastern Region).	1979	1 November, Queen Elizabeth II, accompanied by the Duke of Edinburgh, re-opened the Glasgow Underground Railway and later British Rail's new Argyle Line to Hamilton (Central).
1952	15 February, Funeral train conveyed King George VI's body from Paddington to Windsor, British Railways (Western Region).	1982	14 May, Milton Keynes Central station opened by The Prince of Wales after arriving in the Royal Train hauled by Class 86 electric locomotive No 86211 *City of Milton Keynes*.
1953	3 July, Queen Elizabeth II and the Duke of Edinburgh travelled in special train, during tour of Northern Ireland, from Lisburn to Lisahally, near Londonderry, provided by Ulster Transport Authority.	1982	20 October, Queen Elizabeth the Queen Mother named Class 47/4 diesel-electric locomotive No 47541 *The Queen Mother*, in a ceremony at Aberdeen station.
1968	14 October, the rebuilt Euston station opened by Queen Elizabeth II.	1984	2 May, The Queen and Duke of Edinburgh travelled on the 15in gauge miniature railway at the International Garden Festival, Liverpool, in a train hauled by Romney, Hythe & Dymchurch Railway 4-8-2 No 6 *Samson*.
1969	7 March, London Transport Victoria Line opened by Queen Elizabeth II who rode on the new underground line from Green Park to Oxford Circus. The Queen later returned to Victoria station to unveil a commemorative plaque.	1984	30 May, The Queen and Duke of Edinburgh rode on the Maglev magnetic hover train from Birmingham Airport to Birmingham International railway station.
1972	2 August, Isle of Man Steam Railway conveyed the Queen, Prince Philip, Princess Anne, and Princes Andrew and Edward from Castletown to Douglas in saloon No F36, hauled by 2-4-0 tank locomotive No 13 *Kissack*.	1984	20 November, Queen Elizabeth, The Queen Mother, opened the North Woolwich Old Station Museum after arrival in a special train, hauled by preserved LNER 4-6-2 No 4472 *Flying Scotsman*.
1973	1 May, The Duchess of Kent re-opened the North Yorkshire Moors Railway and travelled with other guests in a special train from Grosmont to Pickering. During her visit the Duchess accepted a painting from artist John Wigston of the LMS Princess class 4-6-2 No 6212 *Duchess of Kent*.	1984	29 November, Princess Anne, after arrival in the royal train at Lime Street station, Liverpool, opened the British Rail Liverpool Lime Street redevelopment.
1974	7 May, Queen Elizabeth II unveils plaque at Preston station to inaugurate the completion of the West Coast Main Line electrification scheme.	1985	No fewer than six BR locomotives/power cars were named by the Royal Family – three by the Queen Mother, two by the Queen and one by the Duke of Edinburgh.
1975	27 September, The National Railway Museum, at York, opened by Prince Philip, Duke of Edinburgh.		
1978	25 October, official opening by Queen Elizabeth II		

Appendix 2

SUMMARY OF 1983 RAIL JOURNEYS AND OCCASIONS MENTIONED IN THE COURT CIRCULAR

Date	Journey/Occasion	Date	Journey/Occasion
25 February	Visit by the Prince of Wales to Gwent and South Glamorgan. The Prince, following an evening engagement, left Cardiff in the Royal Train.		83,' the Festival of Castles, at Caerphilly Castle and later left Queen Street Station, Cardiff, in the Royal Train.
28 February	The Prince and Princess of Wales attended an evening launch of 'Castyll	1 March	The Prince of Wales, Colonel Welsh Guards, arrived at Brookwood Station in the Royal Train to visit the Regiment at Pirbright, Surrey.

Date	Journey/Occasion	Date	Journey/Occasion
9 March	The Prince and Princess of Wales arrived at Heathfield Station, in the Royal Train, to visit Bovey Tracey.		at the Palace of Holyrood house.
30 March	The Queen and the Duke of Edinburgh left Paddington Station for an overnight journey to Exeter.	7 July	The Prince of Wales, in the evening, left Cambridge Station in the Royal Train for an overnight journey to North Wales. (The Court Circular for the following day, July 8, did not disclose the station at which the Prince alighted from the Royal Train.)
31 March	The Queen and the Duke of Edinburgh arrived at St David's Station, Exeter, in the Royal Train and subsequently drove to Exeter Cathedral to attend the Maundy Thursday Service where The Queen distributed the Royal Maundy.	15 July	The Duke of Edinburgh travelled in the Royal Train to Salford Station for his visit, as Chancellor, to the University of Salford where he presided at the Degree Congregations.
9 May	The Duke of Edinburgh arrived at Llantrisant in the Royal Train and later drove to the Mwyndy Works of Maxiheat Anthracite Briquettes Ltd.	20 July	The Queen and Duke of Edinburgh, in the evening, left Euston Station to travel overnight to Central Wales.
9 May	The Princess Anne, Mrs Mark Phillips, who travelled by road, toured the factory of Metropolitan-Cammell Ltd (where carriages for the South African 'White Train' were built.	21 July	The Queen and Duke of Edinburgh arrived at Builth Road Station, in the morning, to visit the Royal Welsh Show at Builth Wells. Later there were separate engagements for the Queen, at Brecon, and for the Duke of Edinburgh, who flew back to London. The Queen subsequently rejoined the Royal Train at Abergavenny Station where also, in the late evening, the Duke of Edinburgh boarded the Royal Train following a flight from London in an aircraft of The Queen's Flight.
12 May	The Prince of Wales, travelling in the Royal Train, attended the formal Dedication Ceremony of the Maureen Production Platform at Kishorn, Wester Ross, Scotland.		
27 May	The Prince and Princess of Wales arrived at Bodmin Road Station in the Royal Train to visit areas on the Prince's Duchy of Cornwall Western District.	22 July	Following an overnight journey in the Royal Train from Abergavenney, the Queen and the Duke of Edinburgh, in the morning, arrived at North Road Station, Plymouth, to visit the Royal Naval Engineering College, Manadon, for the Graduation Ceremony.
1 June	The Queen, Duke of Edinburgh, Queen Elizabeth The Queen Mother, Princess Anne and the Duke and Duchess of Gloucester arrived at Tattenham Corner Station, in the Royal Train, to attend the 204th Epsom 'Derby'.	4 August	The Queen travelled from Waterloo Station, in the Royal Train, to Southampton Docks where she embarked in the Royal Yacht, *Britannia*, to sail to the Western Isles of Scotland and, ultimately, to begin her annual holiday at Balmoral.
27 June	The Queen and the Duke of Edinburgh left Oxford Station, in the early evening, for an overnight journey in the Royal Train to Edinburgh. (Oxford's local paper *The Oxford Times* reported that 'the Royal train was allowed to travel northwards up the southbound track.' Translated it meant that the Royal Train departed from the up platform, normally used for Paddington departures, which eliminated the inconvenience of the Royal Party having to negotiate narrow flights of stairs and a claustrophobic subway, adorned with a modern mural, to reach the down northbound platform.)	5 September	The Princess Anne, Mrs Mark Phillips, travelled in the Royal Train to York where she opened the XXII Annual Congress of the British Equine Veterinary Association.
		8 September	The Duke of Gloucester, travelling by air, visited the Scottish Railway Preservation Society at Bo'ness.
		19 September	The Princess Anne, Mrs Mark Phillips, at Glasgow Central Station, named Class 47/4 diesel locomotive No 47562 *Sir William Burrell*.
28 June	The Queen and the Duke of Edinburgh arrived in the morning at Waverley Station, Edinburgh, in the Royal Train and began their customary annual stay	8 November	The Duke of Gloucester visited the Norchard Steam Centre of the Dean Forest Railway, Lydney, Glos.

Date	Journey/Occasion
15/16 November	The Prince of Wales, as Duke of Cornwall, visited districts of the Duchy in Devon and Cornwall using the Royal Train for his two-day tour.
23 November	The Prince of Wales, following an overnight Royal Train journey, visited the IBM Factory at Greenock, Renfrewshire.
7 December	The Prince of Wales, in the morning, arrived in the Royal Train at Newcastle-upon-Tyne Central Station and subsequently visited the Wildfowl Trust, Washington and the Coast-guard's Maritime Rescue Sub-Centre at Tynemouth.
14 December	The Duke of Edinburgh left Euston Station in the late evening to travel overnight to Cumbria.
15 December	The Duke of Edinburgh arrived, in the morning, at Wigton Station to under-

take various engagements there and, later, in Carlisle.

This is fairly typical of a full year's rail travel when British Rail was not affected by any major industrial action of its workforce. Such action or threat of disruption results in the Royal Household opting for alternative transport. Frequently, the use of rail is in one direction only resulting in an aircraft of The Queen's Flight providing the return leg. All royal train movements are subjected to the strictest security and it is therefore impossible to detail journey by journey the locomotives used. In the course of one journey, particularly where the route traversed may not be electrified throughout or if reversal is necessary, it is not unusual for at least two locomotives to be used. Some locomotives on 1983 royal train duties were Nos 47500 *Great Western*, 47513 *Severn* and 47555 *The Commonwealth Spirit* on the Western and London Midland regions. The Southern Region's favourite was Class 73 electro-diesel No 73142 *Broadlands* for journeys on 1 June and 4 August.

Appendix 3
PRESERVED ROYAL TRAIN CARRIAGES

Date Built	Railway	Type	Where Preserved
1842	L&B	Queen Adelaide's bed carriage	National Railway Museum
1869	LNWR	Queen Victoria's saloon	National Railway Museum
1874	GWR	Queen Victoria's saloon (small part only preserved)	National Railway Museum
1889	GNR	Saloon (in existence as grounded body as a church)	Gatehouse of Fleet
1894	GWR	Director's saloon No 249	Dart Valley Railway
1898	GER	Royal Saloon No 5	Carnforth, Steamtown Museum
1898	GNoSR	Royal saloon No 1	Scottish RPS, Falkirk
1899	Duke of Sutherland	Personal saloon No 57A	National Railway Museum
1900	LNWR	Royal dining car No 76	National Railway Museum
1901	LNWR	Royal dining car No 77	Quainton Railway Centre
1902	LNWR	King's saloon No 800	National Railway Museum
1902	LNWR	Queen's saloon No 801	National Railway Museum
1903	LNWR	Semi-royal saloon No 806	
1906	LNWR	Brake power and staff car No 5154	National Railway Museum
1906	LNWR	Brake and staff car No 5155	National Railway Museum
1908	ECJS	King's saloon No 395	National Railway Museum
1908	ECJS	Full brake and luggage van No 109	National Railway Museum
1909	ECJS	Queen's saloon No 396 (later King & Queen's saloon)	Bressingham Gardens Steam Museum (National Collection)
1912	MR	Royal saloon No 1910	MR Trust, Butterley
1940	GWR	Special saloon No 9001	Birmingham Railway Museum
1940	GWR	Special saloon No 9002	Didcot Railway Centre
1941	LMS	King's saloon No 798	National Railway Museum
1941	LMS	Queen's saloon No 799	National Railway Museum
1942	LMS	Chairman's saloon No 45005	Carnforth, Steamtown Museum
1945	GWR	Special saloon No 9006	National Railway Museum
1945	GWR	Special saloon No 9007	National Railway Museum

ACKNOWLEDGEMENTS AND BIBLIOGRAPHY

To accomplish all but the simplest of tasks usually requires to a greater or lesser extent the assistance and co-operation of others according to the magnitude of the task in hand. In writing, collecting and assembling material for a book, one discovers, very early in the process and however strong the will, that assistance and co-operation quickly become indispensible ingredients, effectively lubricating the author's will to pursue an objective – the finished manuscript. Therefore, I sincerely wish to thank the many people who have so readily given assistance in a variety of ways although, for reasons of space, I am unable to mention each and every one of them by name. If by chance anyone, turning the following pages recalls some specific request, then please accept this collective apology and take pride in the knowledge that it would not have been possible without you. Photographers, past and present, are credited where their pictures appear, but to those who have specially made their work available, I record my gratitude to them by quoting the saying 'a picture speaks a thousand words'.

However, I specially wish to record the sincerest of thanks to the following and without their contribution my task would have proved impossible: the gracious permission of Her Majesty The Queen for the use made of material from the Royal Archives, the Buckingham Palace Press Office, in particular Mrs A. C. Neal, Ronald Allison, formerly HM The Queen's Press Secretary, and Mrs Anne Wall, formerly Assistant Press Secretary to HM The Queen, Major John Griffin, Press Secretary to HM Queen Elizabeth, The Queen Mother; the staff of various British Rail regional Public Affairs offices, but in particular John Hughes of Southern Region Headquarters at Waterloo Station; John Edgington, of the National Railway Museum, York, for his unfailing help in making photographs from the Museum's collection available for use; R. B. Beggs, Ulster Folk and Transport Museum; Denis Grimshaw, Northern Ireland Railways; George R. Barbour, Scottish Record Office; Messrs. C. C. Green and Ifor Higgon for details of some Welsh journeys; the Director General of South African Transport Services; Nathan Berelowitz of the Railway Society of Southern Africa; Peter J. Allender of Metro-Cammell Ltd; L. A. Cook, Manager, Commercial Travel Services Department, Thomas Cook Ltd; H. R. Stones for his early recollections on the 1911 Investiture ceremony arrangements at Caernarvon; Charles P. Friel for notes on an Irish journey; George Barlow; Hugh Ballantyne; W. A. Camwell; J. A. G. H. Coltas; L. Colin Jacks; Brian Stephenson; and E. Talbot. To many of my friends and particularly Beryl Ball, Janice Warwick-Smith, Malcolm Allinson, Walter Capers, Stan Butler and John B. Gosling, all of whom have given me practical and encouraging support. A very special mention to another friend, John Ford, whose assistance with clarifying dates and some of the locomotives used on several journeys proved invaluable. As for the detail of the coaches built for and used in the royal trains over the years I must acknowledge the assistance of Geoffrey Kichenside, an author well-versed in railway carriage history with five books to his credit on the subject, who prepared much of the material forming chapters 9, 10, and 11. For assistance with typing the manuscript, my thanks go to Norma Verney. Last and by no means least a very special note of thanks to my Mother who helped with checking the final manuscript and, at other times, provided a home atmosphere which gave me the continued inspiration and will to accomplish my original objective.

The following publications, consulted during research, provided significant and helpful sources of information for which sincere thanks are expressed to the authors and publishers concerned. Your author acknowledges that without their existence, the contents of this book would have been the poorer and, possibly, might never have been published at all.

An Illustrated History of LNWR Coaches (including West Coast Joint Stock), David Jenkinson, 1978, Oxford Publishing Company

British Railways Coaches, abc, Geoffrey Kichenside, 1962, Ian Allan

British Rail Coaching Stock, 1980, Railway Correspondence & Travel Society

Carriage Stock of the LB&SCR, P. J. Newbury, 1976, The Oakwood Press

Carriage Stock of the SE&CR, David Gould, 1976, The Oakwood Press

Crown, College and Railways, Raymond South, 1978, Barracuda Books

Elizabeth of Glamis, David Duff, 1977, Methuen Paperbacks Ltd.

Fifty Years of Western Express Running, O. S. Nock, 1954, Edward Everard Ltd.

Forgotten Railways – East Anglia, R. S. Joby, 1977, David & Charles

Great Central, Vols. 2 & 3, George Dow, 1962 and 1965, Ian Allan

Great Western Coaches, Parts 1 & 2, J. H. Russell, 1972 and 1973, Oxford Publishing Company

Great Western Coaches from 1890, Michael Harris, 1985, David & Charles

Gresley's Coaches, Michael Harris, 1973, David & Charles

History of the Great Western Railway, E. T. MacDermot, 1927, Great Western Railway

Irish Railways Since 1916, Michael H. C. Baker, 1972, Ian Allan

King Edward The Seventh, Philip Magnus, 1964, John Murray

Edward VIII The Road to Abdication, Frances Donaldson, 1974, Weidenfeld & Nicolson

King George the Fifth, Harold Nicolson, 1952, Constable & Co. Ltd.

King George VI – His Life and Reign, John W. Wheeler-Bennett, 1958 Macmillan & Co. Ltd.

LMS Coaches, An Illustrated History, David Jenkinson and Bob Essery, 1977, Oxford Publishing Company

Majesty, Robery Lacey, 1977, Hutchinson & Co. Ltd.

Midland Carriages, An Illustrated Review, David Jenkinson and Bob Essery, 1984, Oxford Publishing Company

Nineteenth Century Railway History through the Illustrated London News, Anthony J. Lambert, 1984, David & Charles

150 Years of Railway Carriages, Geoffrey Kichenside, 1981, David & Charles

Once Upon a Line, Vol. 2, Andrew Britton, 1984, Oxford Publishing Company

Palaces on Wheels, David Jenkinson and Gwen Townend, 1981, Her Majesty's Stationery Office

Preserved Railway Carriages, Michael Harris, 1976, Ian Allan

Queen Mary, James Pope-Hennessy, 1959, George Allen & Unwin Ltd.

Queen Victoria, Elizabeth Longford, 1964, Harper & Row

Railway Carriage Album, Geoffrey Kichenside, 1966, Ian Allan

Railway Carriages in the British Isles, C. Hamilton Ellis, 1965, George Allen & Unwin Ltd.

Railways in the Cinema, John Huntley, 1969, Ian Allan

Recollections of Three Reigns, Sir Frederick Ponsonby, prepared for publication by Colin Welch, 1951, Odhams Press Ltd.

Royal Journeys, C. Hamilton Ellis, 1953, British Transport Commission

Steam Railways in Retrospect, O. S. Nock, 1966, Adam & Charles Black

The Great Eastern Railway, Cecil J. Allen, 1955, Ian Allan

The Great Western at Swindon Works, Alan S. Peck, 1983, Oxford Publishing Company

The Northern Counties Railway, Vol. 2: 1903–1972, J. R. L. Currie, 1974, David & Charles

The Royal Deeside Line, A. D. Farr, 1968, David & Charles

The Royal Family in Africa, Dermot Morrah, 1947, Hutchinson & Co. Ltd.

The South Western Railway, C. Hamilton Ellis, 1956, George Allen & Unwin Ltd.

The Royal Trains, C. Hamilton Ellis, 1975, Routledge & Kegan Paul

Veteran & Vintage Railway Carriages, Geoffrey Kichenside, 1964, Ian Allan

'Carriage Stock of the MGWR', P. O. Cuimin, *Journal of the Irish Railway Record Society*, June/October, 1971

'Great North of Scotland Royal Trains', Neil T. Sinclair, *Railway World*, November, 1966

'King George V – The Railway Progress of an Eventful Reign', "Voyageur", *The Railway Magazine*, March, 1936

'Queen Victoria's Funeral Journey', W. A. Willox and Charles E. Lee, *The Railway Magazine*, March, 1940

'Royal Tram Rides', J. H. Price, *Modern Tramway*, April, 1964

'The Last Journey of King George V', Charles E. Lee, *The Railway Magazine*, March, 1936

'The Royal Wedding: GWR Honeymoon Train', *GWR Magazine*, December, 1934

Great Western Railway Magazine, various years, particularly 1907, 1914 & 1936

Modern Railways, The Locomotive Magazine, The Railway Magazine, invaluable sources of reference, especially for the years from 1901 to 1953.

Railways, Railway World and, finally, *Trains Illustrated* 'Motive Power Miscellany' columns for detailed reports of royal train workings.

INDEX